The Silver Teacup

Tales of Cadiz

LOUIS VILLALBA

D1403376

Publisher: www.louisvillalba.com

Except for one true story, "Victoria Beach," the tales narrated here were created by the author's imagination and should not be considered as real. Any resemblance to events or persons, living or dead, is purely coincidental.

ISBN: 1468196588
ISBN 13: 9781468196580

To my parents

Your hands guide mine,
As I trace the outline of life
With our fingers intertwined.

I am here, far away,
In an embrace of man and land,
Witness of the sap
Pulsing in your ashes and sand,
Of words spoken
By the rocks sprinkled with life,
Of secrets whispered
In my ears at the ebbing tide—

CONTENTS

INTRODUCTION

Me llamo Francisco, *he said, interrupting* what he was doing to offer his hand. A moment before, I'd reached the top of a tight spiral staircase and entered the bell tower of a small church. He was seated on a stool, wearing a green cardigan, and a beret. His fingers were a blur, braiding what looked to be strands of wicker. I'd been on the road a week, traveling on my own: first Cordoba, then Seville, and now north of Cadiz in Arcos de la Frontera: the white-washed village a friend in Madrid insisted I see on my first trip south—in the summer of 1988.

In addition to hand-weaving baskets and hats, *Don* Francisco, a stocky and sturdy man in his seventies, was a weaver of tales: soccer feats, saints, local bullfighters, Lorca, the Spanish Civil War... My new friend, in fact, had been coerced to fight both *for* and *against* the Spanish Republic. But throughout the afternoon I spent with him, he betrayed no strong political allegiance or ideology, except to express how much he loved his native city, Cadiz—which brings me to the matter at hand.

Louis Villalba has achieved in *Silver Teacup* what I'll call generous and sprawling "love poems" to *Don* Francisco's hometown. In the best of these I find myself transported—not only to the narrow streets, plazas, and seaside promenades I wandered with pleasure before boarding my bus to Arcos, but also shuttled back *in* time... For history, both contemporary and ancient, feels like the bedrock underlying these pages, pages that sing this port city in Andalusia.

Emblematic of this is "The Poppy Flower." On one level, we're treated to a ghost story; on another, a singular tale of love. But it's also a lesson or reminder of how the Spanish inquisition played out in Cadiz, persecuting *conversos*—Jews who converted to Catholicism to avoid expulsion in 1492. The vivid fragments presented here of dubious church history are as compelling as the focal narrative thread.

In another example, "The Man in the Blue Tunic," we're introduced to "Plinio," time traveler who refers to Cadiz by its Roman name, Gades, and describes its ancient splendor to such a degree that he inflames the imagination of "Pepe," contemporary inhabitant who has befriended him: "The bustle of the ancient forum came alive: the men wearing togas plain or with purple stripes, the slaves with their short tunic helping them through, the women with their long dresses and their veils—married with stoles and single without—some of their attendants holding parasols to protect them from the oppressiveness of the sweltering sun ..."

And one gathers that Villalba, himself a native of Cadiz, may have a primary source for a third example, "The Ruby Ring," which is the story of a ring passed down from uncle to nephew. But it is also a parable about deep family ties, and how those ties can evolve, fade, or even fray over the passage of time.

Although comparisons can be a double-edged sword, I couldn't help but think of *Tales from the Alhambra* as I navigated these "Tales from Cadiz." Both use history to accentuate their stories, but neither is meant to be read *as* history. Like Irving, Villalba deploys good old-fashioned storytelling. And I use that term ("old fashioned") in a good sense: writing that relishes and delights in painting pictures with words—with contagious engagement, narrative skill. The author's attention and dedication to his craft is evident.

But I can't close these remarks without speaking to the ethos that informs the publication of this book. Small press publications, whose objectives aren't dictated by economic incentives, but rather artistic ones, are the trenches of American literature. Small press publishing is a labor of love. What guides Louis Villalba to publish these stories on his terms are his goal and desire to build community, not only among English readers of his acquaintance, but readers of Spanish, as well. In the Spanish-language version of this book, he writes (and this is my loose translation): "Initially, I wrote this book in English to share with my English-reading friends the hidden marvels beneath the ever blue skies of my city. Now, with affection, I have translated this book into Spanish—to share these stories with my people."

The Silver Teacup: Tales of Cadiz is indeed, a gift.

—Francisco Aragón
Institute for Latino Studies
University of Notre Dame

PREFACE

Cadiz, Spain, is a small Atlantic island located a few miles from
the Gibraltar Strait. In the course of time, a narrowed isthmus
moored it to the European continent. Yet, the land has never lost
its uniqueness. As a child, I was wonderstruck by the underwater
seascape. In the days with the lowest tides, when large expanses
of seashores were left in the open, I could make out wide roads,
streets, and alleys hemmed by rocks of many sizes and shapes.
Over the years, the waters had smoothed out their edges and
dead and live layers of small crustaceans had carpeted their surfaces. My imagination revived a sunken metropolis that harbored
histories and legends spanning over 3000 years. The ancient city,
the oldest in the western hemisphere, had served as the far fron-
tier of ancient civilizations.

The surviving Cadiz went on to play an important role in
shaping our contemporary world: major outpost in the discovery of America, most important center of commerce between the
old and the new continent, cradle of democracy of the modern
Spanish nations. I could have written this book in Spanish. But
being here in the U.S. for so long, I have decided to tell my neighbors in their own language about the marvels hiding under the
ever-blue skies of my hometown.

THE MAN IN A BLUE TUNIC

I overhear an officer on the phone informing his superior of the corpse that has been found on the seashore this morning.

"Captain, it's kind of weird. The man was lying face up, his eyes red and his body pale like a fish thrown out by the waters." His mandible tightens as he listens. "No, Sir, no documentation on him and no tattoos ... he's wearing a deep blue tunic." He presses the phone against his ear as if he had a bad connection. "No, not Moor ... he's blond, looks Swedish."

Then I see the body lying on a stretcher, as a couple of paramedics are about to place a blanket over his face.

"It's him!" I say to myself.

I stand still watching. There is no point in identifying or explaining to the police. They would not believe me. A tear slips down my cheek as my mind goes back to one day earlier when I met the victim for the first time. It was May 29, 2000. I thought it was going to be a day like any other day. In Cadiz, my hometown, nothing usually happens. Its almost 130,000 inhabitants, many retirees, lead a tranquil life amid beautiful plazas full of palm trees and flowers.

Yesterday as soon as I woke up I went to my terrace, which looked out on Santa Maria Beach. It was a beautiful morning. The silvery reflections of the nascent sun tinged intensely blue waters with a peaceful hue. The cries of the seagulls soaring overhead and the mint fragrance of the sea did away with my lingering drowsiness. Nothing seemed unusual. Perhaps the only remarkable observation was that the tide had ebbed lower than I had seen in a while. I could distinguish the remnants of the Via Augusta, a stony thoroughfare that connected Cadiz with ancient Rome 1500 miles away. Part of the ancient city still lay under waters on account of several earthquakes and tsunamis over the years. For an instant, the ragged edges of the road brought to my mind images of the old Roman carts and men dressed in tunics treading back and forth from the capital of the Empire.

I put on my tee shirt, my shorts, and my running shoes and jogged down the seashore. A cool breeze kept the place almost deserted. I felt invigorated and reached Cortadura, an old fortress that indented the 10-mile-long beach which extended up to Sancti Petri channel, a navigable narrow arm of the Atlantic Ocean that isolated Cadiz from the rest of Spain. It turned Cadiz into an island. At the level of this military landmark, the high-rises flanking the coastline gave way to low sand dunes topped with dry brushes, which grew alongside the waters as far as the eye could see. This was a no-man's land except for occasional nudists who had found their haven away from crowds and regulations.

I kept running and, as I stumbled on the wet sand, saw a man lying down alone between two dunes. In the past I had come across quite a few loving couples making their courting dance. But a man alone was unusual. When he stood up, my eye caught sight of his intense azure-blue tunic that reached the middle of his legs. I had seen my share of weird people around this area, German hippies, British homeless, and other poor souls who had descended from the cold areas of the continent looking for a warmer subsistence. I had even espied more than one exhausted illegal immigrant from Morocco, whose rickety boats had capsized on the high seas crossing the Gibraltar Strait. Few of those made it. Mangled-up corpses of men, women, and children were washed up on the seashore.

This man that I just saw was strong and healthy-looking, about my age, twenty-eight or twenty nine, a little taller than me, 5' 7" or 5' 8", boasted shoulders as broad as a boxer's, and wore leather sandals. As I came closer, a gesture of nervousness became evident. The palm of his right hand wiped away drops of perspiration as his fingers raked back the short bangs of curly blond hair, which rested upon the pearly white skin of his forehead. Clean-shaven, his square-shaped face bore blue eyes, which gazed at me with a mixture of wonder and apprehension, but not fear. His bluish lips were tensed up like a bow by an arrow. I did not know whether he was about to cry or smile. The expression set off his prominent straight nose and cleft chin, which rendered him an air of manliness and distinction. There was no aggressiveness in his facial appearance, but rather hesitant friendliness.

For a moment, I had an eerie feeling, a weird foreboding, but I disregarded it. I concluded he was another crazy Swedish hippy. He approached and raised his right arm and the short sleeves of his tunic clung to his bulky bicep muscles. At first it upset me, for he did it with his forearm and hand extended, the way fascists used to salute. Then I noticed his left hand over his heart, which reassured me that it was some kind of free-spirited greeting. Seen close, his tunic showed whitish wavy lines of dry salt, revealing that it had been sopped with ocean water and had dried out. He wore a shiny golden ring on his right hand and a soft fragrance surrounded him as if he had spent the night sleeping under pine trees.

"*Salve,*" he said, greeting me in Latin.

"*Salve,*" I said, almost smirking.

"*Nomen Lucius Plinius Flavus est mihi,*" he said his name in Latin, smiling. "But you may call me Plinio."

"*Habla español o inglés?* Are you a priest? How do you know I studied Latin?"

He shook his head and raised his eyebrows unable to understand what I had said.

I stood there astonished. I studied his expression and there was nothing that made me believe that he was pulling my leg. I smiled back.

Don't tell me you are going to make me go back to the time I conversed in Latin with my friends before I quit the seminary, I thought. This guy must be an erudite, maybe a professor of Latin in some northern European country.

"Jose Lopez Martinez *nomen meum*," I said. "But you can call me Pepe."

He assented with his head. I made use of a universal sign language for food—I put my right fingers together as if forming the beak of a bird and lifted them up, pointing to my puckered lips.

He nodded and raised his eyebrows. For a minute I thought about my mother's warning,

"You and your caring heart! Why do you have to help every single homeless you come across? Feeding them and finding shelter for them? Just give them a few coins and keep going ... one of these days you are going to get in trouble!"

As we walked toward my condo, I observed him. His legs were strong like those of a soccer player, and his poise straight and lofty. He was less surprised to see topless young women than I was. No one paid any attention to his attire. I guessed it was because Cadiz enjoyed a diversity of immigrants from Morocco and sub-Saharan countries who wore tunics too. He kept looking ahead at the nearby view of downtown Cadiz. I saw his eyes settling on the intense yellow glitter of the cathedral cupola that overlooked restful waters. He seemed to study it. Next his eyes wandered towards a line of small houses painted in different colors, which flanked a road that ran along a stone wall and reached the entrance of a long jetty. He gazed upon the long narrow strip of land all the way up to a fortress penetrating deep into the sea.

"Nice colorful houses—" he said.

At the western end of the fortress was a lighthouse that rotated its perennial rays now dimmed by the morning sun. He admired it.

"*Speciosa* Gades—beautiful. Splendorous lighthouse."

"I am surprised you know the Roman name of my hometown. Where are you from?"

"Gades," he said.

"What do you mean by Gades? You didn't understand me. Where have you come from?"

He pointed toward the ocean.

"Oh, American. I thought you were Swedish."

He shrugged and looked at me surprised as if he did not understand what I had said. He kept on watching a group of boys playing with a ball. Once we arrived at my home he went to my terrace and stood there spellbound by the view. The beach looked like a giant seashell. On the southeast side, the beach was embraced by the long jetty and on the northwest side by a section of the stone wall encircling the old town.

I prepared a couple of ham sandwiches and while I toasted them I reached for my Latin dictionary, which had lain idle for quite a while. I heard him make a comment,

"I see that the citizens of Cadiz have nostalgia for their Roman past. I can see two broken columns in the small square next to the beach."

"Those are replicas," I cried out from my bedroom as I walked back to the terrace. "Youngsters have smeared them up with graffiti. Some people have no respect for city property."

"I know. It saddened me to see ancient stones scattered on the beach like worthless ballast rocks. Are you aware that those are remnants of the Roman aqueduct that brought drinking water to the city from the mountains forty miles away?" A sigh broke loose from his throat as he added, "Now the ancient city is gone."

"What do you do, teach history?"

"The splendor of Gades was such that it could not be overshadowed by any other metropolis in the world but Rome."

"What can you expect? So many years have gone by. Natural disasters have wiped out this area. Even the ruins have disappeared. But not everything is gone. A few years ago we dug out the Roman Theater ... well, part of it. You probably read that also."

"I do not behold it."

"You can't see it from here. It's located at a lower level than the rest of the city," I added smiling, "except for the underground parking garages."

He did not seem to catch my joke.

"I notice that all the ancient buildings have disappeared," he said.

"C'mon, Plinio! Are you trying to tell me that you saw those buildings? Stop pulling my leg, would you?"

"Never mind. Would you fetch the victuals?" he said as hunger staunched his loquacity. "Would these suffice?" He pulled out two coins.

"It'll be my treat. But what kind of coins are these? Let me see."

Two silver denarii—the ancient Roman currency—lay on my palm. They glittered as if they had been in circulation only for a few years. I examined them. The first denarius had the head of Caesar Augustus and an inscription:

'CAESAR AVGVSTVS DIVI F PATER PATRIAE' which meant Cesar Augustus, Son of God, Father of his Country.

"What are you trying to do? You can get this on EBay."

But then I looked at the second coin. Its obverse was carved with a club and a bust of Hercules wearing the head of a lion as a hood and its reverse featured two tuna fish encircled by an inscription:

'PONT BALBUS' which stood for Pontifex Balbo.

I was familiar with this coin. I had studied it at the Archeological Museum where I worked. The olden City of Gades minted it around 14 BC.

"This is a rare coin ... hard to come by," I said. "Balbo was born in my hometown and built Roman Gades. His uncle was Caesar's banker and through his lobbying, *Gaditanos*—as people from Cadiz are called—were granted Roman citizenship in 49 BC."

"The Balbo family was kind and generous, but he was a cruel man," Plinius said.

"Yes, so I read."

"These are the only coins I have."

"Keep them. You might need them to go back to wherever you came from."

I handed the coins back to him before I rushed to the kitchen to fetch the food. For a moment I had been tempted to phone my girlfriend and my mother and tell them about my new weird acquaintance. I decided against it. I thought they would probably be alarmed I had invited him home.

We ate in silence for a few minutes. I noted his pensive face; something must have been bothering him. There was also sadness in his eyes. He stared at everything around him and, after looking at the emptiness for a while, he smiled at me.

"Pepe, would you join me for a stroll?"

"Where are we going?"

"I will let you know when we get there."

We walked about half a mile and found ourselves in front of the Puertas de Tierra, the main gate of the fortified wall that separated the old town from modern Cadiz. Past this entrance, he kept describing the now extinct Roman metropolis of Gades. He was the best storyteller I ever met. Every word, every remark fueled my imagination. Buildings, statues, and scenes of the past sprang back to life. I could picture the two big reservoirs where the aqueduct ended, the amphitheater shaped like the Roman Coliseum, the forum full of columns and temples and the hot springs with their flowery fragrance.

"We built a society where man could prosper, where anyone born anywhere in the Roman Empire could claim the highest office."

I disregarded the "we," which I considered part of his acting, but I was not going to let him twist the truth of what went on back in those days.

"If you had power and money and were born into a noble family," I added.

"Excepting Rome, Gades was the richest municipality in the Empire. We had over fifty wealthy families."

As he talked, my mind wandered. The bustle of the ancient forum came alive: the men wearing togas plain or with purple stripes, the slaves with their short tunic helping them through, the women with their long dresses and their veils—married with stoles and single without—some of their attendants holding parasols to protect them from the oppressiveness of the sweltering sun, the citizenry going in and out of the temples to offer sacrifices to their gods.

After walking down a steep slope, we entered into the Plaza San Juan de Dios, about 300 yards from the waters of the bay. He stamped his foot on the center of the square.

"Here was the harbor," he said. "It was always full of merchant ships, navy vessels, and fishing boats. Vessels kept on docking and sailing out of the port one after another. In our shipyard we constructed the biggest ships in the entire Roman Empire. The harbor was so busy that we had to build another port on the other side of the bay."

"Oh! You heard about it, didn't you?" I said, expressing my dissatisfaction. "You read that Cadiz just lost the shipyard to globalization."

"Globalization?"

"C'mon Plinio, I don't know the Latin translation."

He smiled and shrugged.

"The temple of the goddess Minerva stood over there for a while," he said pointing toward a corner. "The main columns tilted and the whole building caved in. Balbo condemned the architect to be buried in mud and burned alive."

I did not know what to say. Corruption in construction raged all over the world, but if such a draconian handling of architects were implemented nowadays, it would chill their bones and put an end to all projects. As he talked, my doubts about his mental sanity intensified. Was I before a crazy man, one with a weird type of delirium, someone who was so clever and knowledgeable that he could describe fiction as convincing as if it were real? His face showed such a persuasive expression. He loved my hometown, though; I had no doubt. Otherwise how could he know so much about its history? Besides, I observed him raising his eyes to heaven and saying in admiration,

"Its waters and its sky have not changed. They embrace Gades like a bracelet on a delicate woman's wrist."

There was passion in his voice. Again the word Gades came out of his mouth with a soft sound as if he were kissing each one of the letters.

We strolled toward the unearthed theater. Its grounds, less than a fourth of the original building, lay in the midst of a sepulchral silence. It was the mummy of a building. Plain ruins. No sparkle anywhere, everything was somber. Rough. With his voice breaking with emotion, Plinio kept on talking while my mind recreated the magnificent venue. I could see the oyster-stones glittering under the sun, full of life, and even heard the excitement of the audience waiting for a new play to start. Their voices sounded far and dim.

After walking through the Campo del Sur Road next to the ocean, we soon passed by the entrance to the jetty where a long narrow road led to the lighthouse. A breeze combed the waving sea as if scooping the sparkling reflections of the evening sun. He described other extinct temples and buildings. The details given were such that had I been an artist, I would have been able to draw them out to perfection. As the sun set over the horizon, we reached La Caleta Beach, where Plinio stood enthralled by the view. Charming and shaped like a heart, the cozy spot shone with placid waters and golden sands, which blushed with the sunset like a shy maiden. Two large fortresses stood imposingly at either end of the beach.

My imagination kept me engrossed so much that I did not realize Plinio had crossed to the other side of the promenade and sat on a huge root. I thought he was admiring this millenary dragon tree of fleshy leaves and wide branches as thick as big whales. He was not. He was crying, caressing the ground with his right hand.

"Here was my home, right where this tree stands," he said. "I remember my kindhearted father and my mother, her eyes full of love for me, and my brother and my sisters. Happiness filled this house until I left on my fateful trip. My father might have had a foreboding because he said,

'My son, must you go to Rome? We have already established our commercial attaché there.'

'I need to see to it that our facilities at Pozzuoli have the necessary guaranties for our salty fish and fish sauce, the precious *garum*,' I said. 'We are increasing our exports and our fortune might suffer a major setback if we fail to be cautious. As knights of the Empire we should heed any danger that could lower our ranks. Besides I heard that there are beautiful wedding dresses in Rome. I want to surprise my betrothed Claudia.'"

I noticed that he was fighting back the tears. His face bore a painful expression and his eyes took on a deep honey color. He looked away from me and stared at the calm waters, seeking relief for his discomfort. I had heard of Pozzuoli before. Located about one hundred miles from Rome, this little town had been the most important harbor in the Roman Empire.

"Are you okay?" I asked.

He assented with a nod and resumed his narration.

"Claudia was to become my second wife. My first wife and son had passed away in childbirth. My father arranged my first marriage, but the second was my own choice as I had fallen in love with her. My father asked,

'Why do you not go by land? It is safer.'

'I want to be sure that our boats are properly manned,' I said. 'The Mediterranean is a calm sea at this time of the year and Pompeyo cleaned the sea of all pirates. Do not fret about my safety.'"

Plinio paused for a moment again. His eyebrows arched and his mouth revealed a grimace of annoyance. I thought that he regretted his disregard for his father's warning, for his face showed an expression of concern as if he were afraid of the upcoming words.

"The trip to Pozzuoli was calm," he said. "I contracted with other businessmen for the safe storage and distribution of our products. No amount of fish could satiate Romans' appetite for our mackerels and tunas. I stayed in the house that belonged to one of Balbo's relatives. The imperial city was familiar to me. After I had come of age at 16, my father had sent me to Rome to study at a private school. I studied Latin, Greek, and literature. I also improved my martial arts in preparation for my military service under Nero Claudius Drusus, serving as *praefectus cohortis*—auxiliary officer—with honors until the end of the Germanic campaign in 745 *ad urbi condita.*"

I was listening spellbound to his description, which now seemed to have become more and more real by the minute. Fiction and reality flooded my mind. At times I could have sworn that he was telling a true story. I was confused—as if I had been flown to the past on a time machine.

"Seven hundred and forty-seven *ad urbi condita* … you mean 9 BC, don't you?" I asked.

"Yes, it was then that I got acquainted with patricians and knights in the capital of the Empire. Gades was at the pinnacle of its influence. I witnessed the triumphal celebration of Balbo's war campaign in Africa on March 27, 19 BC. He was received in Rome like a god and became one of the most powerful men in the Empire. The Balbo Theater, which he began to build in Rome the same year, would surpass the beauty and magnificence of all its predecessors. Its large columns of onyx and marble floors mesmerized the people. The importance of Gades was so great that we Gaditanians sat in the Coliseum at a box next to the Emperor."

"I read that. Now we barely have representation in the Spanish Senate."

"I stayed in Rome for four weeks, enough time to buy Claudia's wedding tunic and successfully make the proper contacts to enlarge our operation, for I had learned from my father the art of communicating with businessmen. Our return to Gades promised to be pleasant. After crossing Hercules' columns—or the Strait of Gibraltar as you call it today—we found high winds and rough waters. I lost many of my men since the fury of god

Neptune had no pity on us. No sooner had the tempest ended than I espied a group of vessels heading toward us at full rowing strokes. Aboard were Berber's pirates who intended to destroy what little had been spared by the wind. During the fight, I heard the clash of swords and the outcry from the wounded. Then I felt a terrible blow on my back and fell headlong overboard. Unconscious, I sank into the depth of the waters but revived as I was entering right into what seemed to be an open giant clam. The shell closed behind me. I found myself in paradise, or so I thought. I had survived the fall, and now lay before a land of beautiful mountains, placid rivers, exuberant flowers, lush vegetation, and colorfully feathered birds. A sweet fragrance and a celestial music enwrapped me and soothed my pain."

I listened to Plinio attentively. But he looked at me unsure whether I believed him or his words had gone over my head. I already had so many surprises that a new one was not going to change my constant expression of astonishment.

"When did this happen?"

"At the start of the last month of the year 748 *ad urbi condita,* 6 BC. Anyway, soon I found myself among a group of people who introduced themselves. The words of their priest explained what had happened to me: I had fallen precisely on the only door to their land at the precise moment when Saturn and Jupiter had come together in the sky forming a big confluent star over the horizon in the position of the constellation Pisces. It was precisely at the time of this conjunction in Pisces or Taurus that any of the inhabitants of this underwater paradise could rescind the offer from the gods and return to a mortal life on earth. What they did not expect, and the gods had failed to mention, was that the same window of opportunity could work for someone else coming from the outside. It happened to me. I was too weak to leave and had no choice but to remain beyond its closing time."

It intrigued me his mentioning of those two constellations. I had always been a believer of the effect of the stars on humans. The personality of people born under the same zodiac sign seemed to share some common traits. But what he was talking about was quite farfetched.   Plinio went on to describe what happened afterwards:

"I never regretted staying. Everything that I saw and experienced in this underwater paradise enthralled me. But, there was a painful sacrifice to endure, a terrible price to pay. I watched from afar as my parents, siblings, and fiancée grieved my loss and I suffered along with them in their daily torment, for in this land one is able to witness everything that occurs upon earth. The realization that I would not be present at their deathbeds saddened me greatly. It frustrated me. As it was explained to me, the planetary conjunction in the sky would take place with clock regularity—once every sixty years for two consecutive periods and then a 250-year pause. The reason why the gods selected these two sites in the sky is beyond my understanding. Gods can be as whimsical as we humans. My first chance for departure came sixty years later. By then my parents and all my immediate siblings had been dead for a while. What reason did I have to abandon such a paradise?"

"So why did you leave now?"

"Must a man have a reason to return to his hometown?"

"No."

"All my roots are here. The ashes of my forefathers probably enrich the flowers and trees I behold right now. I belong to this land."

"I see your point. It's late. Let's go home. You can stay with me until we find a place for you."

When our conversation was over, a crescent moon hung in the sky wrapping the town in a dim silvery mantle. The soft rapping beats of the sea reverberated and lured the surrounding into a trance. We returned home by Genoves Park. It was closed, yet somehow I still could hear the happy giggling of children playing. Through the iron railing I could see the lighted promenade hemmed by rich vegetation and tall palm trees. The scenery fascinated Plinio, but the emotions had tired him out. We walked back to my condo in silence.

When we got home, I opened a sofa bed in the family room.

"Plinio, I don't have any luxury to offer you but you can stay here with me for as long as you need ... until you find a place."

"I am much obliged for all the care that you are bestowing upon me. I shall accept your hospitality tonight."

"I'm glad you are staying. You know, I'm grateful to you. Today I learned much more than I could ever learn at the museum. I can hardly wait for my mother and my girlfriend to meet you. They're going to flip out."

I prepared some snacks and we went out to the terrace. The moon had moved higher in the sky, which now teemed with stars. An occasional motorcycle or car rode down the road adjacent to my building and broke the silence. Far away we could hear the laughter and loud voices of a few youngsters walking on the beach.

"Behold Jupiter and Saturn. It is now almost a single star," Plinio said.

"I can't see it."

"Gaze there towards Taurus."

I was struck by the large celestial body.

"To me they look like a single star. Do you think you can get back to your land?" For a moment I felt a little stupid that at my age I could actually believe in his fantasyland.

"No, the time has passed."

We stood quietly, meditating on the meaning of those words. The celestial vault hovered over us so peacefully that it seemed under the spell of a lullaby. I observed that his golden ring had an inscription.

"Plinio, I have seen rings similar to yours at the museum."

"Oh, yes, this one has great value for me."

He pulled it out and laid it on the palm of my hand. The ring shone so brightly that it looked as if it had been polished recently. The inscription read: "L PLINIVS F"—his name.

"My father gave it to me when I was a lad," he said after a brief pause, "I remember his words when he handed it to me, 'Let this ring serve as a reminder that although you are a knight's son, gold should never corrupt your soul.'"

"Your father was a good and wise man."

"There are still good people in Gades. You are one of them and I am proud of you."

"Plinio, don't get sentimental on me. I just gave you a sandwich and a snack. I mean, I haven't spent any money."

I was dying to ask him more about the Temple of Hercules, which had been built near Gades 3100 years earlier, right after this city had been founded by seamen coming from Phoenicia—an ancient civilization that had thrived along the coast of Lebanon. The temple was considered one of the most important places of prayer in the ancient world. It disappeared off the face of the earth 1400 years after it had been built. No one knew for certain its whereabouts. The temple was so venerated that even Julius Caesar visited it several times long before he became Emperor. Their priests were renowned for their ability to interpret dreams. Caesar had had one that unsettled him—he had seen himself making love to his own mother. The priest concluded that the dream augured him a great future; that his mother signified Mother Earth and that he would be granted control over the entire world. A few years later he ascended to the throne of Rome.

"Plinio, I have been waiting for you to mention the Temple of Hercules. A lot has been written about how important it was."

"As a child I used to go to the Temple of Hercules with my father and brother to offer sacrifices as women were prohibited to enter the sacred grounds."

His description confirmed what I had read. The temple was located so close to the waters that the sea waves lapped several yards above the foundation. There was a perennial bonfire, a golden tree with emerald fruits, Hercules' tomb, the statues of Hercules and Alexander the Great, two wells of potable water that filled with the low tide and emptied with the high tide, and two large quadrangular columns that stood on either side of the main door.

"I read that those columns were made of an alloy of gold and silver," I remarked. "Other historians mentioned bronze."

"Templum Hercules, behold your glorious columns, red like the sunset! No, it was orichalcum."

I did not know much about this extinct precious metal. I had read descriptions of the orichalcum vessels at Solomon's Temple in Jerusalem. Most of the orichalcum, however, had been mined in Atlantis, where one of the walls encircling this mythical island had been built of this ancient mineral. He pulled from under his tunic a red metallic pendant in the shape of a winged horse and as bright as a ruby stone.

"Orichalcum."

He let me touch it. It felt cold and was heavy like lead.

"Plinio, where did you really come from?"

He stood up and picked up a globe that stood on my bookshelf and pointed to an area in the ocean right in front of Cadiz.

"I came from Atlantis."

His words sent my heart pounding. Since I was a child I had read that Atlantis had sunk in front of Gades twenty-three thousand years ago. Plato—the famous philosopher and writer—narrated the story of this legendary land in his *Dialogue of Critias* four centuries before Christ was born. The existence of this island had been recorded and kept by Egyptian priests for several millennia before they passed it on to Solon, the Greek statesman who had traveled to Egypt and brought the information to Greece two centuries before the knowledge became public to the rest of the ancient world. Plato was explicit about the location of the island when he mentioned the real estate that was assigned by its ruler— god Poseidon—to one of his heirs:

"Gadeiros obtained as his lot the extremity of the island toward the pillars of Hercules facing the country which is now called Gades."

He went on to describe the paradisiacal life on this island. Several generations later, when the inhabitants set their eyes on greed and power, their gods punished them with a cataclysm that sank the island to the bottom of the ocean.

"So, Atlantis was destroyed, wasn't it?"

"Yes, it was. But the god of gods preserved a small underwater paradise to reward a handful of righteous men and women with gift of a joyful life till the end of the world. That was the land that I was blessed to encounter when I fell unconscious from the boat."

The sensation that I was living a dream came over me stronger than ever. At times I thought I was standing next to an apparition. Yet I could feel him and converse with him as I would with anyone else. He was human. He had eaten the same as I had. I stirred from this trance and posed a question,

"What else you know? Where was the temple built?"

"At the end of the Cortadura Beach, off the entrance to the channel where the ocean water joined that of the bay, about ten miles from Gades. The entire temple is now underwater."

"Yes, that's the consensus of most historians."

My eyelids were droopy from tiredness but my mind was alert trying to digest all the information I had gathered in the past hours. Plinio realized my tiredness.

"Let us rest. The sun has been gone for so long."

"Yes, tomorrow I'd like to visit the area where the temple was erected ... ooah...." A yawn interrupted my words as I covered my mouth with my hand. "I'll ask my boss for another day off."

I left Plinio sitting on the sofa bed and I must have fallen sound asleep quickly because I did not hear any noise until the daylight broke. A few seagulls fluttered and squeaked around my window and a few pigeons cooed nearby. The sea waves kept on their ever present soft hissing as the voice of the early risers echoed down on the streets. I looked everywhere in my apartment but I could not find him. I went on to my terrace to see whether he had gone down to the beach. It was deserted. Then I found a handwritten note on my living room table. Next to the paper were his golden ring, his orichalcum pendant, and his two shiny silver denarii. As I read then the note, line by line, the words popped off the page. The two coins and the jewels became dull and worn out before my very eyes. This is what he wrote:

"*Carissime Pepe:*

I apologize for leaving without biding you farewell; but my time on earth is about to come to an end in the waters caressing our hometown. This note, therefore, should serve as my warm goodbye to a true friend. Do not hold any grievance against me or bear sadness for my departure from the world of the living, for I have accomplished what I was obliged to do. You should know about the mission, which brought me back to Gades, because you contributed to its success as much as I did. I shall explain. There was a relic in the Temple of Hercules that only the high priests knew of—a gold table hidden deep under the main altar. Its whereabouts were kept absolutely secret under the threat of eternal damnation. It bears an inscription written in the language of Atlantis, which reads as follows:

'I, POSEIDON, HEREBY ISSUE THIS TESTAMENT WHICH I HAVE INSCRIBED ON THIS GOLD TABLE WITH MY OWN HAND. THE GOD OF GODS PROMISES THAT NO DESTRUCTION OF THE ISLAND OF GADES SHALL EVER COME TO PASS, AS IT HAPPENED IN ATLANTIS, AS LONG AS THIS GOLD TABLET LIES SAFEGUARDED ON DRY GROUNDS AND GOOD PEOPLE INHABIT THE LAND.'

"As I saw the waters rising over the past half a century, I realized that the demise of the island of Gades lay in wait. On May 28, 2000 at 6:04 PM, my opportunity arrived to leave Atlantis since the conjunction had occurred in Taurus. My decision stood firm and clear and I was granted thirty-six hours of life to accomplish my mission. Before I met you I had already completed the first task. After our meeting all the conditions had been fulfilled.

Vale amice, omnes di vobiscum—farewell, my friend, may all the gods be with you.

"Lucius Plinius Flavus."

When I finished reading, the imprint of his ring on the note disappeared as if flattened by a steam iron. I watched in awe the remnants of the coins and jewelry, which had by now crumbled into a fine metallic dust. I stood alone in the middle of the room holding the completely erased sheet of paper in my hand.

THE RUBY RING

The ruby before my eyes shone like the sunset in Cadiz, Spain, where rouge sparkles climbed upon the crest of sea waves and took an easy ride toward Victoria Beach, the golden sand turning red like polished copper. The stone was mounted on an 18-karat-gold ring to emphasize its beauty. As I held it in my palm, I heard my Aunt Raquel's words,

"*Guardalo*—keep it—your late uncle would have wanted his ring for you."

Her eyes welled up and I felt sad, but I did not weep. A ten-year-old boy should refrain from shedding any tears, even if his godfather had died. Men don't cry. I remembered my uncle wearing the beautiful ring, his thick and hairy finger wielding the precious stone with every word he pronounced as if using its glitter as sign language. The ruby behaved like a mood stone. If he laughed it glowed bright like a mirror in the sun and when the conversation turned quieter, its glimmer dulled to the hue of embers. I wondered whether my uncle had noted in my eyes how the red rays flashing from his finger had mesmerized me.

I clutched the gift tight and ran to the privacy of my room. I tried it on each finger. Even my right thumb was not big enough to fit tight, the band sliding down the way a horseshoe might fall down a peg. I sat on my bed, turned the dazzling ring around, and checked the stone and the metal inch by inch. It felt cold. It lacked the warmth of my uncle's finger. I didn't know why I expected to sense him. With tears in my eyes for the first time since his death, I got a piece of cloth and polished the ring. The stone glittered with brilliant yet icy sparkles, and the gold took an intense yellow like the sun at midday, but never warmed up. I opened a small drawer in my nightstand, drew out a small red box where I kept a few coins, removed them, blew some lint away, and laid the ring inside.

I did not open my box again until I turned seventeen. As my high school graduation ceremony approached, my aunt called me up.

"Now the ring would look nice on your finger," she said. "Wear it."

My finger had grown bigger and now it fit me well. The ruby gave off light like the day I had first stowed it away. But there was nothing jolly in the shining red color of the reflection. It was still cold. It brought back the same sadness I had felt on the day of the bequest. I thought of my cousin who had grown up without his father and of my aunt's loneliness. My uncle's presence lingered in my mind. I reminisced about the time he bought a boy's bike. He knew that my parents could not afford to give me such an expensive present.

"Share it," he said as he hugged my cousin and me. "Love each other like brothers."

A few times he had taken us for a walk, fed us with exquisite shrimps, and given us tiny glasses of anisette laced with raisins. On one of these outings I heard him say a maxim that he would repeat over and over,

"*La familia es lo que vale. Lo demás es cuento chino*"—that is, "Family is what really matters. The rest is nonsense."

I questioned why such a good man had suffered such a random death. He was standing between two parked cars when a van smashed into one of them, crushing him between the two vehicles. His end came instantaneously.

I kept the ring on. At times I perceived that I had revived my uncle; that he walked next to me anywhere I went. Little by little my eyes grew accustomed to seeing the beautiful ruby on my finger. It did not, however, feel like my own and added to my responsibilities, for it compelled me to be as good as my uncle, a savvy entrepreneur who had built his own company from scratch.

Three years passed and the ring became as much part of my hand as my nails. The color fit me well. It promoted health and its bright red scintillations fired my burning desire for knowledge. By then my aunt had remarried and the token of my uncle's affection did not mean much to her anymore.

"Is that your uncle's ring?" she once asked me as if she had forgotten what it looked like. "It seems darker. Did you replace the stone?"

I realized that life went on, people changed, and no one expected a young woman to remain married to a memory forever. Good and hardworking, the new husband lacked my uncle's charisma and passion for life. He won my cousin's and my respect but not our affection. Besides, son and late father bore such a striking resemblance, that every morning when the son shaved himself, his mirror image reminded him of his father. As for me, the ruby ring tied me to my uncle like a boat to its moorings. Through the lustrous stone I still sensed the love that he had once professed to me. Even now that my uncle's shortcomings registered with me for the first time, I was proud to wear his precious jewel.

"*Tu tío hizo cosas malas,*" my aunt had said. "He would go out and gamble away every single cent he had. If he had lost, he came home drunk to forget all the money wasted. And if he had won, he came home drunk to celebrate his booty."

I listened without reacting. She needed to justify having fallen in love with someone else. I did not know why, but her words brought to my mind the evening my uncle took her to dinner at the new skyscraper in my hometown, a 14-story building, El Trocadero. My uncle wore a dark gray suit and a red tie, and my aunt a below-knee-length black dress with a round collar fringed with black lace, high-heeled patent leather shoes, and a dark-blue velvet purse with a gold closure. Her dark eyes sparkled more than his ruby, for in those days dining out was as infrequent as winning the lottery. Her statement did not change my opinion of him. He stood in front of me perhaps more real, more human than ever before. I thought that there were no perfect men; that our mind bestowed perfection only upon some of the dead.

As time wore on, my golden ring wore down. After ten years the metal had grown so thin that its edges dug into my skin. It was the only thing of my uncle's that had sharpened, because all recollections of him had dulled with the passage of time. My cousin no longer saw his father in the mirror or talked about him. I felt he had finally died, for we live in the mind of our loved ones for as long as they hold dear our memories. My thirtieth birthday drew close and my life had taken a definite course. My daughter admired my glittering ring.

"*Papá*, can I borrow your prince ring?"

I put it on her finger and she stared at it fascinated. The stone never lost its gorgeous shine. You could count on it the same way you could count on a new daybreak each morning. In the late summer of this year I swam on Victoria Beach and when I came out of the water the ring was gone. A few days later a dream surprised me. I saw it on the bottom of the sea glowing like phosphorescent red algae, full of life, the waters caressing it, sweeping it back and forth on the sand. It dawned on me that it rested finally back where it belonged: on my uncle's finger. The sea had lent its hand to him. Dust to dust … sand and water … human life. The ruby ring once again shone with laughter.

VIEW OF CADIZ FROM SANTA MARIA DEL MAR BEACH

OLDEN SILVER PESOS

On the morning of June 2, 1904, Malos Pelos would have preferred being at home getting ready for the afternoon and evening festivity. Instead he kept digging sand to bury the discarded pieces of damaged tuna on Victoria Beach. The long beautiful sandy shore, which flanked the western isthmus of Cadiz along the Atlantic Ocean on the south of Spain, lay almost deserted on a hot late-spring day in June. It was Corpus Christi Day. As happened every year, a gold monstrance enclosed in a several-hundred-pound silver tabernacle was to be hauled out of the cathedral and paraded through the streets. Overhead, the route was covered with huge awnings to protect the faithful from the intense sun. Images of people walking down the main streets crowded his mind, their happy bustling, their faces tinted with the golden reflection of the radiance seeping through the yellowish canvas, children dressed in their best and giggling with delight, and the smell of fresh baked bread which permeated the surroundings. He was preoccupied above all with the feasting and carousing which followed the religious ceremony. Without pocket money, there was not much he could do. As he lamented the lot that God had assigned him in this life, his shovel hit a hard object. He cleared the sand and a bag appeared before his eyes. It was made of leather, which had been darkened by corrosion, and was still wet on account of the water that had covered it at the high tide. The upper part was corroded and the impact of his spade had punched a hole through it and a few old darkened coins had spilled out on the sand. The gash revealed a large number of coins. Next to the cache were broken pieces of empty leather bags with no trace of money around. He took a coin in his hand. It was as big as a silver dollar or the five-peseta *duro* and his finger pads went over the raised serrated edge and the blurred outlines of the figures and numbers engraved on the obverse and reverse. He could not read the inscriptions because he had never gone to school. A tap of the coin on his teeth resonated with a blunt clink and set off an eerie sensation traveling through his face.

"Silver coins," he said to himself.

He looked around. No one was watching. He grabbed a few fistfuls of coins and tucked them in his pockets, lifted the sack, placed it on a wheelbarrow, and eased his way toward the gravel road flanking the beach. Strong winds had piled up large quantities of dry sand. In a hollow between two dunes, he buried the treasure and camouflaged it with a few stones and dried brush. Out of the corner of his eye, a coworker by the name of Paco El Gallego saw him leaving quickly.

"Where are you going so fast?" Paco asked. "What kind of horsefly has stung you?"

"Please tell the boss I didn't feel well ... that I had to leave."

"He won't pay you for today's work."

Malos did not answer and rushed across the dry sand down Victoria Beach toward his home in the neighborhood of Extramuros on the outskirts of the city. The temperature had worsened with the presence of levanter, a strong easterly wind blowing from the Sahara Desert on the other side of Gibraltar Strait. The gusts fanned the crude smell of raw tuna and swept the water off the wave crests sprinkling it all over the beach as far out as the dry golden sand. The rhythmic sounds of the waves lapping on the seashore echoed everywhere. He passed the road that led to San Jose Hermitage, where he observed a group of workers getting ready to place the last tracks for the upcoming tramcar system from Cadiz to San Fernando, a nearby town. It reminded him of the mayor's words in the last election,

"Now that the Twentieth Century has just begun, this modern type of transportation will place the city of Cadiz on a level with the most advanced metropolises in Europe."

Words, words, misery, and more misery, he thought. My three little children don't even have a piece of bread to take to their mouth and I don't even have shoes to wear. Maybe my lot has now changed. He had no idea of the value of what he had stashed away in his pockets but he could always come back and get more from the hidden cache. At home he got the usual greeting from Pepi, his thirty-year-old wife,

"Wash up your feet outside before you set your hoofs in my house. We are poor but I refuse to live like pigs. What are you doing here so early? Didn't you find work today? So how are we going to eat today? Do I have to go and beg food from my brother? Oh, *Virgencita*, why did I marry you?" She continued whining as he kept his mouth agape waiting for the opportunity to speak. Finally she dried her hands in her blue apron, came up to him, and tossed a piece of dirty cloth at him.

"Here, don't forget to wipe between your toes. I'm tired of sweeping earth out of the house."

She hurried back to the other side of the room where she kept busy cleaning up kitchen pots. Her bad temper did not trouble him. He loved her anyway. Thin and nervous, Pepi could sting him with her sharp tongue and a few minutes later turn into a tamed lamb, huggable and tender like a fluffy doll. He nodded his head and laid his gray cap down as he watched the swinging of his wife's hips. After twelve years of marriage, she could excite him so much that sometimes he could hardly wait for daybreak to send his kids out and make love to her. He tried in the middle of the night, when the children were fast asleep, but she spurned him, hitting him with whatever she found handy. Now he sat on the step at the door rubbing his feet, his cropped hair short and straight, and his thick mustache stretching from cheek to cheek. He turned his head, pushed aside the brown burlap curtain at the entrance, and found her intent eyes on him.

"Stop bitching, don't be *malaje*—bad angel—I have something important to tell you," he said in a sweet tone.

He stood up and almost hit the low uralita roof. It was cool inside and once his eyes got used to the half light, the shapes in the crammed room turned into clear objects—the little wooden table with five rickety chairs; the three little mattresses lying over the bare redbrick floor; a bigger mattress on the opposite side of the room; a few metal pots hanging over a large earthen vat full of water at a corner; and a statue of the Sacred Heart of Jesus, who stood on a small seashell stuck into the brick wall, a few daisies with dandelions at the feet. Outside he could hear the sounds of the children playing in a big patio covered with dark earth and dotted with eucalyptus trees and wild brush. He emptied his pockets on the table. There were forty-three coins.

"Malos, what's that?" his wife said, her eyes wide in disbelief.

"Silver coins."

"Oh, Jesus, where did you get them? You didn't steal them, did you? What are we going to do with these coins?"

"I don't know."

"If the Guardia Civil find out, you can end up in jail for the rest of your life. This must be worth a lot of money. What am I going to do alone with the children? Oh, *Virgencita*, why does this man get into so many troubles?"

"We could hide them and wait for a while and see what happens."

"Where do you want to put them away?"

"I thought of taking out one of the floor bricks."

"What good is that going to do to us? Maybe you can ask my brother Mauricio. He knows how to read and write. He knows a lot of stuff."

"Mauricio El Loco?"

"Just because he was in an asylum for a few months doesn't mean he is demented. He just had mental fatigue."

"Mental fatigue? He was crazy. For all I know he is still crazy. He thought that he was a better matador than Lagartijo. I watched him get dressed with a tight jacket, put on a bullfighter hat, and spend the whole day shouting, *ole*! He swung a red cloth at a makeshift bull made with a broken chair and two brooms sticking out like horns as he warned the onlookers, 'Stay away, this is a killer bull!'"

"Oh, Malos, he was kidding, I know. You must understand. He went through a lot in the Cuban War. You or I would have been worse if we had gone through so much suffering. He watched a bunch of Negroes cut off the head of one of his friends, scoop his eyes out, and cook them. He had so many bad nightmares that he ended up in the asylum."

"Come on, I never heard anyone coming back from Cuba talk about cannibals."

"Yeah, yeah, I tell you, he said those Negroes prayed to Saint Barbara and offered her their enemies' blood. That's why we lost the war."

"We lost the war because the Yankees wanted Cuba for themselves and Spain was too far to fight them. Otherwise we'd have beaten the shit out of them."

"Malos, did you forget what happened to you when your father died? For two days you made no sense, 'Kill the damned black cat.' 'Throw the cat off the stone wall into the waters.' When I asked you to come with me to his wake, what did you say to me? 'Kill the damned black cat!'"

"I told you a hundred times, I got very nervous. A black cat jumped in front of me the day I witnessed my father's accident."

"'What accident?' she said. "Your father jumped from the top of Tavira Tower. Why do you look at the speck of sawdust in your brother's eye and pay no attention to the plank in your own eye?'"

"I was in shock. You didn't see or hear the terrible thud or how he looked like a bleeding sack ... no shape, his arms and his legs splayed like a sick chicken's."

"Well, maybe you have a better idea. At least we can trust Mauricio, you know. He doesn't talk to anyone."

"What am I going to tell him?"

"You'll figure it out."

Malos grabbed his cap, put the coins in his pocket, and rushed out of the house. As he approached the narrow Puertas de Tierra, the only entrance by land into the walled-in city, he heard the moos of the cows and bulls roaming a small beach, where they waited to be slaughtered at the nearby municipal stockyard. Gusts of wind lashed low clouds of dry sand against the legs of the animals and fanned around a sweet odor of decomposed hay. For a moment the stench made him forget the purpose of his errand and reminded him of the splendid bullfight scheduled for this afternoon. Six young bulls would be sacrificed in honor of the Holy Eucharist. He would have given anything to be one of the renowned *novilleros*, whose names had been tirelessly extolled by the public at large and mentioned in the newspapers every day. There was nothing like being a bullfighter. He had dreamed of it so many times. His body was fit for it—tall, thin, and erect like a spear. He knew the art, for he could fly and spin the red cloth next to his body with majesty. But his dreams had been shattered years earlier when he and a couple of friends jumped over the fence of a makeshift bullring at a small village's festivities and a large bull came toward him. He saw the animal's dark fiery eyes and felt his blood escaping his face and rushing through his body. His legs failed to obey him until one of his friends shouted at him and roused him. From then on he resigned himself to be a mere spectator whenever he could afford to attend a *corrida*. He put his hand in his pocket and heard the reassuring tinkle of the coins. Maybe, I'll get enough money to buy a ticket for today's *novillada*, he thought.

As he passed through the wall surrounding the city, the cannons at San Felipe's Jetty began the salvo that indicated the beginning of the procession at the cathedral. It was eleven in the morning. He hurried up through Mirador Street and reached El Campo del Sur by the Plaza de Toro La Hoyanca—a wooden two-story bullfighting ring—where a group of aficionados loitered around awaiting the upcoming event. The wind blew with vengeance and he had to hold his cap with his hand. His mind was so preoccupied about the coins that he lost awareness of his surroundings until he reached San Juan de Dios Plaza. The streets were lined with the faithful in anticipation of the holy procession. The well-to-do sat on reserved seats while the populace afforded standing room only by leaning against the façades of the buildings.

In the plaza, he jostled for a place under the main balcony of City Hall. Luxurious decorations stood before him and made him feel like a starving child gazing into a pastry-shop window: giant glass chandeliers, bouquets of roses and carnations, large pots in bloom, garlands of flowers, rainfalls of petals, replicas of the Arabic arches of the Alhambra of Granada and the Alcazar of Seville, Japanese and Chinese motifs, multicolored lamps, façades and balconies adorned with golden and red tapestries of velvet and silk, Spanish flags, and colorful electric lamps suspended from the fringes of large Filipino mantillas stamped with red and white designs.

"These politicians!" he said to himself. "If they cared about their constituents instead of wasting the money in these festivities, I wouldn't have to worry about anyone's silver coins."

Malos stood on his toes and scanned over the broad gathering of people before him. Up the street a three-story silver baroque *custodia*—a portable altar— as big as a carriage glittered with great splendor. Images of saints, angels, leaves, escudos, flowers, and scenes of Greek mythology and the Bible were carved into or attached to pillars. It was perched on an ornate silver cart with large silver candelabra on the angles, which supported a large apple-shaped cupola with a sphere and the figure of a crowned angel, and a large thirteenth-century, silver-gilt, gothic tabernacle in the center. Escorted by a sergeant and nine soldiers, the whole structure rested on the shoulders of a group of devotees who carried it on a wooden float. The mayor, the military governor, and the bishop marched in front while a martial band and a detachment in full formation filed behind. Overwhelmed by the display of silver before him, Malos stuck his right hand in his pocket and fiddled with the coins. Their surfaces were rough and the sensation made him feel poorer than ever.

Mauricio's home was only a few blocks away from the San Juan de Dios Plaza. Yet Malos could not venture crossing to the other side of the street because the procession cut the city in half and the entire route was flanked by troops in full regimentals. Their golden buttons, epaulets, and rosettes glittered in the sun. For a moment Malos considered going back home. Suddenly a racket erupted. A woman's dress caught fire with the tip of a cigarette and the flames spread upwards as the people stampeded away. A group of soldiers left the formation to put the fire out. Amidst the chaos, he skulked to the other side of the street.

Malos tapped open the door to Mauricio's apartment and found him polishing his leather boots. His only suit lay on a bed with a white vest, a white shirt with a couple of silver cufflinks and his white panama hat adorned with a dark ribbon. The walls were graced with colorful posters announcing bullfighting events and a pair of horns hung over the head of the bed. He kept on brushing and looking down as if no one had walked in.

"Malos, happy are the eyes of those who can see you," he said. "What are you doing here on Corpus Christi? If you come to ask for money, I have none. I've spent everything I had to buy the ticket for today's bullfight."

"No, I came to get your advice on something?"

"My sister sent you, didn't she?"

"Yes, but it was my idea too."

"Since when am I considered so important in the family? I haven't seen your children for a while, not since Luisillo made his First Communion. I'm the crazy uncle who was in the madhouse, right?" He opened his eyes wide and sneered.

"This morning I found a bunch of old silver coins," he said, placing the coins on the bed. "I don't know what to do with them. I thought that since you work for the city you might know someone who could buy them."

"Wait, wait! Put them on the table, I don't want you to mess my suit. Let me see. You didn't steal them, did you? Well, you are an honest man, not an adventurer like me. Anyway you know I'll do anything to help you and my sister."

Mauricio took one coin and went to a small window that overlooked the large Constitution Plaza. The sun was high behind his window and lit up the façade of the church presiding over the spacious square. Pigeons fluttered around the snake-shaped marble columns flanking the main door, some resting on the head and shoulders of the statue of Balbo the Minor, the great ancient Roman proconsul from Cadiz, which stood in the center of the plaza. The place was silent and empty. At this hour it used to be filled with the joyful voices of children playing, but this morning only a small group of stragglers headed toward the procession in a hurry. He pinched the edge of the coin between his thumb and index finger and stretched his arm out beyond the window frame. Sunlight illuminated the face of the coin. The silver was so dark that he had a hard time making out the inscription.

"Fernan ... Fernando the Sixth." He walked to a small closet, filled a

spoon with baking soda and mixed it with water in a little container.

"I can't make it out," he said as he rubbed the coin hard with the paste.

He went back to the window. On the obverse, the coin had two pillars with crowns atop and a banner wrapped around them where the words *Plus Ultra*—Farther Beyond—had been engraved. In between the pillars were two world globes floating over an ocean. The inscription "VTRAQUE UNUM"—Both Worlds Are One—surrounded the motif, and right under the ocean appeared the year that the coin was minted, 1750. On the reverse it had the Spanish heraldic shield and another inscription that read FERNAND VI D G HISPAN ET IND REX—Fernando the Sixth by the Grace of God King of Spain and West Indies. On the right side of the shield the denomination appeared clearly: 8.

"Eight *reales*," he said. "These are called both-worlds coins or *columnarios*."

"Where did you find them?"

"On the beach, at the tuna fishery."

"Are you sure?"

As Malos assented with a nod, Mauricio's face adopted a greenish tint as if he had swallowed a cup of bile.

"How many coins have you got?"

"Forty three."

"This is a serious matter. I know where these coins came from. I heard about these coins in Havana from an old Galician cook, Cayetano Ferreira. I remember his name well. These coins are cursed. Now you ruined me! You made me touch it, my God!" He rushed back into the middle of the room and tossed the coin on the table, his eyes opened wide and his face blanched in fear. He kept repeating, "I touched the coin. I'm doomed. We are doomed!"

For a moment Malos thought his brother-in-law had been stricken again with an attack of madness. Mauricio opened the lid of a large earthen vat, filled an aluminum jar with water, and poured it on his hands rubbing them with caustic soda over and over. Pensive, he sat on the bed with his elbows resting on his thighs and his chin on his hands.

"What's wrong?" Malos asked.

"What's wrong? I don't know what we are going to do."

"Calm down, Mauricio. Do you have any wine in the house?"

"Yes, please, look inside the closet. I have some sherry."

Mauricio gulped some wine, set the bottle back on the table, and although he wiggled his tongue to relieve the tension, his face remained pale and drawn. Malos sat on the bed and observed his brother-in-law as he waited impatiently for what he had to say. Drops of sweat had popped out on his brother-in-law's forehead and his frightened look turned gradually into an angry expression. He winced and settled down on a chair.

"You might as well have found a death sentence. Have you ever heard of the Black Mockery?"

"No."

Malos waited patiently for Mauricio's explanation but it did not come. His brother-in-law's eyes stared down as in a trance. His mind had gone back to the late 1890's, when he met Cayetano, an old seaman who sat at a corner of a bar in Havana bragging about his cooking. The boaster must have been in his 80's, for his face had shrunk to fine wrinkles, his dull blue eyes had deepened in their orbits, and the skin of his hands had thinned out to the texture of tracing paper. His tongue loosened by a bottle of rum, he was talking nonsense about his younger years as a sailor when a corpulent black man walked into the bar. No sooner did he see him than he began to scream out,

"He's back from the dead. Go away, cursed Negro bastard, you destroyed my life!"

He continued shouting and hitting the bottle against the counter as the astonished black man stood before him paralyzed. Mauricio, who sat at a corner with a corporal from his regiment, witnessed the incident. He stood up to calm the old seaman down as the newcomer sneaked away. Since Cayetano carried on, he took him to the military headquarters and locked him up in a windowless room for disciplining soldiers. The next morning after sleeping away his drunkenness, he sat with Mauricio over coffee and a conversation ensued.

"I'm from Cadiz," Mauricio said. "Where are you from?"

"I'm from Ferrol, but I know Cadiz well."

"A troublemaker *Gallegiño*, right? And when were you in Cadiz?"

"It's a long story, but it has to do with last night's incident. After being convicted of crimes that I hadn't committed, I ended up in prison at the Carraca in San Fernando, Cadiz, for ten years."

Malos became inpatient and interrupted Mauricio's thoughts.

"Come on, Mauricio, speak out. Tell me whatever you have to say about the Black Mockery. I don't understand. How can you be so frightened? These are just coins, do you hear me? Coins."

Mauricio did not answer. After scratching his scalp and passing his hands over his nape, he opened his eyes wide and resumed his story,

"Well back in the late 1700's, an English ship by the name of the Sea Wind put in at Havana Harbor with about 300 black slaves from the west African coast. Throughout the entire trip, the slaves had endured degrading treatment in the hands of Captain

Lawrence Brewer, who was in charge. Unable to survive the hardships of the voyage, about thirty men, women, and children were thrown overboard to feed the fish. These inhumanities went on amidst the deafening cries of the survivors. He reasoned with his crew,

'I am a Christian and although slavery is sanctioned by the Bible, I wouldn't do it to humans. Gentlemen, these beings aren't humans. These are beasts grown in the jungle. Do not forget it!'

The man had such a terrible reputation that even his name had been erased from the registers in Great Britain. His persistent trade of black slaves in foreign lands, in spite of the prohibition by the English Parliament of such commerce, prompted the members of this body to designate him persona non grata. And although the English flag waved from the mast of his ship, his business was considered closer to a pirate's than to a merchant's. Among the group of slaves aboard was a tribal prince, Tuba Motombo."

As he mentioned his name, Mauricio stood up as if he invoked the Devil himself. He paced back and forth, picking his chin, scratching his ears, running his palms over his cheeks as if besieged by an attack of hives. Malos watched this behavior as a child might for a first time watch a toy clown popping out of a box.

"Tuba was corpulent, with big muscles, and his countenance shone with pride and intelligence," he said as he went on with the story, looking Malos straight in the eye for a moment and staring again toward the window. "During the long trip, he had learned a few English words as he received his share of lashes and humiliations. Nothing broke his spirit, much to the captain's disappointment and anger. He had learned from a medicine man the art of witchcraft. His fellow captives knew of his powers and had the conviction that he would eventually use it and destroy everyone who had harmed them. After a couple of weeks at sea, Tuba suffered his countrymen's disdain because they saw the time passing by and their freedom evaporating quicker than ever. Captain Brewer convulsed with great guffaws when he saw the blacks fighting among themselves.

'These beasts have too much energy,' the Captain said. 'Cut their food and water and whip them until they shut up. But don't kill anyone.'

After several weeks, the ship arrived in Havana."

Mauricio looked at Malos again. This time a sad smile marked his face. The beautiful island, the Pearl of the Caribbean as Spaniards called it, had always drawn so much attraction from him that as soon as anyone including himself mentioned the name of his beloved island, tears would well in his eyes.

"It was a sunny day and the Negroes became excited when they saw the profuse tropical vegetation that reminded them of their homeland," Mauricio continued as he wiped his tears away with the sleeve of his white shirt. "The captain whipped the slaves with more vengeance than ever. A couple of hours later, he had hauled his merchandise out to a barrack for their quarantine. After the period was over, he took them to a market where his prospective customers could admire the cargo. Men, women, and children were in chains and exposed naked to the public. It had been hard to transport Tuba. He did not want to move and whippings and insults did not make him budge. Six big seamen restrained and dragged him down the streets. The black prince stood with his eyes looking ahead into the emptiness with an expression of contempt on his face. Jose Mendoza y Ledesma, a rich landowner, inspected the human cargo and after rejecting a few slaves, he purchased the rest and crammed them into carts. It was a good deal. On the island a trained slave cost about 400 pesos—3200 *reales*— but he had paid an average of 200 apiece for the newcomers. Cayetano helped his boss with the transaction and witnessed how two coworkers handed the captain a coffer filled with eight leather bags containing a total of sixty thousand silver coins of both worlds or *columnarios*. They were minted in Mexico and each was valued at one peso. The captain opened the coffer and looked at his treasure as a big smile broke out on his face. The deal was sealed with a handshake. At that very moment

Tuba managed to free his right foot from the chain and rushed toward the captain and his new owner. When the captain heard the metal clanking and the screams of the menacing slave, he pulled out a knife and drove it into his heart. Tuba cried out a few words in his native tongue as gushes of his blood dripped into the open coffer below, staining the coins."

Mauricio stood up, grabbed the bottle of sherry, and tipped plenty of wine down his throat, ending the huge swigs with a roaring belch. He stood before the window contemplating the empty plaza as if he had finished recounting the story.

"Is that all?" Malos asked perplexed. "Well, just take the blood out … blood doesn't blend with metal. You can wash it off."

Mauricio ignored his words and proceeded with the story.

"Before the deal Cayetano had enjoyed some drinks at a nearby tavern where a few crew members of the Sea Wind had boozed away their salaries. In an attempt to recruit him, one of the slave traders who spoke Spanish bragged about his exploits and the money he had made. He was tempted but declined. Cayetano and several subalterns hauled the human cargo to the plantation. Free of their chains the blacks now looked less somber. They were fed well and housed in comfortable barracks. A few months later the Galician cook learned the meaning of Tuba's words from an old black slave who had worked for his boss for several years: '*La maldición caiga sobre todo aquel que toque estas monedas, que una muerte violenta le arranque la vida.*' That is, let the curse fall upon any one who touches these coins, so that a violent death gouges his life out.

"Cayetano was a restless man. Ever since he had heard the men from the Sea Wind boast about their adventures and the money, his mind churned with the idea of working as a sailor. On one of his trips to Havana he embarked on a ship that was on its way to Rio de Janeiro. In this town his boozing binges and the rhythm of the mulatto women's hips roped him in and left him without a single peso. He ended up cooking for a Portuguese who owned a tavern, paid him with booze and women, and let him sleep in the kitchen."

"Make it short, Mauricio, please finish the story," Malos said. "Who gives a damn about his women and booze? You were talking about the Black something."

"The Black Mockery ... be patient ... let me continue, I'm almost there. Well, anyway, there, in the tavern, Cayetano met a compatriot from Pontevedra by the name of Benito Soto. An ambitious young man, he could dazzle anyone with the aplomb that shone in his eyes. His voice was so warm and convincing that few could resist his arguments. He had an evil side. His eyes could cast a cold gaze at you and paralyze you the same way a snake would its prey. As the boatswain on The Defensor de Pedro, he had the responsibility of recruiting men for a trip that would take the ship to the Portuguese colony of Minas on the West Coast of Africa. Benito hired Cayetano to care for the kitchen. Aboard were about thirty men under the command of a Portuguese captain appointed by the Emperor of Brazil to transport black slaves. At their destination Benito and a few of his Spanish friends mutinied and took over the ship. It was January 1828. Promising great wealth to those who joined him, he left the captain and all his supporters on land and sailed off with fifteen men in search of vessels with rich cargo. Cayetano went along with his compatriot because he was afraid to stay on that inhospitable coast. A few days later the self-appointed captain turned into a cruel leader. A Galician sailor got him so upset that he shot the insurgent in the head and threw his body overboard. Three weeks later the mutineers boarded the Morning Star, ransacked the boat, killed most men and children, raped the women and then murdered them too. A few male and female passengers who survived the carnage were tied up and left to die in the hold as water rushed in through the holes torn in the hull by explosives. Cayetano..."

"How could you trust what this guy said? He was a crazy killer," Malos broke in. "C'mon, Mauricio, just find me a buyer. You'll get a cut. I don't want to miss the *novillada*. It's getting late."

"Let me finish or go away and leave me alone! Cayetano assured me that he didn't do anything. He swore before God that he didn't participate in the massacre and that right then he decided to leave the pirate boat as soon as the occasion arose. After their butchery the name of the ship was changed to La Burla Negra—The Black Mockery. One day, not far from the Canary Islands, they came across a heavy ship with an English flag. Cayetano happened to be on deck when some shouts alerted the crew. As the Black Mockery closed the distance to their intended prey, he aimed his monocular and saw a golden mermaid protruding over the water at the end of the bow. It was the Sea Wind. Benito maneuvered his boat, aimed the five cannons, and fired. Captain Brewer and his crew surrendered. The pirate captain took the prisoners to his ship and kept his captive counterpart tied up to the stump of the main mast while his men sacked the ship. After cutting the captain's right ear off, he demanded the location of the valuables. The captain did not budge. He tore the captain's left ear off and chopped off his left fingers one by one. Once the pirate reached for the captain's genitals, the victim bowed out. Under a plank in his berth was a big chest with eight leather bags full of silver coins. When the pirates gathered the cache in front of their leader, Captain Brewer opened his eyes and broke into a loud guffaw.

"'Yes, take them,' he yelled. 'Take the damned coins. Take them all, you dirty pirate, sign your own death sentence!'

"Benito drew his pistol and shot him in the head. Cayetano recognized the origin of the bags because the initials of his former employer JML—Jose Mendoza de Ledesma—were marked over them. When he whispered to his compatriot about the curse, he laughed at him. After all the prisoners were hanged and their bodies thrown overboard, the Black Mockery set course to the Azores Islands where she put in for repair. The pirates reversed the name back to El Defensor de Pedro and continued their trip toward a fiord near Benito's hometown. Smugglers purchased their merchandise at a good price, and shortly after the ship hoisted anchor and sailed toward the south of Spain. On a pitch-black night Benito faked a shipwreck off the coast of Cadiz, ran the ship aground at Santa Maria Beach, and ordered his crew to disembark. The last one to climb off the ship, Cayetano saw Benito take the leather bags full of coins from the coffer. The pirate loaded his treasure on a small boat and sailed off alongside the seashell-shaped coastal recess into the straight long expanse of Victoria Beach. From the shore the cook watched how man and boat cut through the sea until darkness swallowed them. Things didn't go well. The crew had too much money on them and began to carouse and revel in orgies with prostitutes, tossing their cash away in handfuls. Their behavior caught the attention of the local authorities, who detained them. Benito managed to escape and travel a hundred miles until he reached Gibraltar, the British colony. A big surprise awaited him. The English police apprehended him, accused him of piracy, and backed their claims with the most unlikely witnesses—the women and men that Benito abandoned tied up in the hold of the sinking Morning Star. As it happened, they were able to remove their restraints, staunch the seawater that gushed in, and straighten up the vessel. The ship floundered along for two months until their arrival in England. Benito ended up hanged, his head cut off and exposed to the public."

"Well, the authorities would have hanged him anyway, touching or not touching the coins tinged with blood, wouldn't they?" Malos said. "I'm sure most of his crewmates were also hanged."

"Yes, except for a few lucky fellows like Cayetano Ferreira, who went to jail for a long time."

"You aren't going to believe in superstition. If these coins are tainted with blood, you polish them up and they'll get as good as new."

Again Mauricio was not paying attention to what his brother-in-law was saying. His pacing accelerated. He walked toward the window, back to the bed, sat, stood up again, back to the window, looked at the empty plaza, scratched his head, sniffed, made a few gestures with his mouth, shook his head, and turned around as if performing a crazy dance. Malos followed his steps with his face twisted in a wince of disappointment. When he was about to scoop the coins back into his hand and leave, Mauricio spoke again,

"Maybe there is a possibility of washing off the terrible curse. We should talk to Paca la Gitana."

"Paca, the old gypsy? Are you going to trust what that mad woman tells you?"

"It's our only chance. You don't want me to die like a dog, do you? You don't want to go through an agony that you would not wish on your worst enemy?"

Malos was not at all convinced, but he went along because he needed the money. They walked into a small building on Las Viudas Plaza, climbed several long and narrow flights of stairs, and reached a small landing right in front of Paca's apartment. The door was ajar and the somber trembling light of a pair of candles hovered over an empty room. They knocked on the door and a red curtain opened across the room. The smiling thin figure of Paca walked toward them with the light glancing off her mouth full of gold teeth. Her long green dress with black dots swept the floor, and the red powder on her cheeks become more and more conspicuous as she approached them.

They sat at a small table. Smelling of wilting flowers, the room was painted in white and had a light-blue ceiling with a score of dark-blue stars and a white moon. The main wall boasted a big radiating sun and a woman's face. On the opposite wall a big yellow disc with a red wheel and arrows pointed toward some Latin and Greek letters. She picked a deck of cards and placed it on the table. Malos observed her long knotted fingers, each with two golden rings, except for the right pinky, which appeared completely encircled by a golden snake with a long red tongue of ruby stone. Mauricio explained to her their situation.

"Well, that's different … we don't need cards. I have seen many soldiers from Cuba. I have enough experience with those voodoo curses to fill up a library. I must warn you … they are tough. You must be ready to sacrifice anything to save your skin."

"We are, Paca, we are," Mauricio said.

"How much are you going to charge us for your service?" Malos asked in an unfriendly tone.

"Not much … I'm here to help people. But I have to eat too," she said, her brown eyes sparkling with a condescending expression.

Without any delay, she lit a black candle shaped like a horseshoe and burned frankincense in a small red container. She smashed two clovers of garlic in a small wooden mortar adding some olive oil and holy water, which she claimed was from the Jordan River. She asked them to place thirty coins on the table. Malos was reluctant to do it, but Mauricio scowled at him. He put them on the table, counting them one by one as the gypsy quoted a Biblical passage,

"The graven images of their gods shall ye burn with fire, thou shalt not desire the silver or gold that is on them, nor take it unto thee, lest thou be snared therein, for it is an abomination to the Lord thy God. Deuteronomy 7:25."

The old gypsy placed her hands together in prayer and raised her eyes to Heaven. Malos sneered and shook his head while Mauricio paid attention to the invocation. Paca's murmurs finally grew into a clear voice,

"In the name of the Lord Jesus, I take authority over Abaddon and Appollyon, rulers of the bottomless pit, and I command this African voodoo curse to be broken, and all demons responsible for its execution to be expelled out in His name."

"Would you just wash the coins up and stop this nonsense?" Malos said.

"Quiet!" Mauricio whispered in his ear. "You unbeliever! Do you want to die? Do you want your money?"

The gypsy took the paste of garlic and spread part of it on the soles of Mauricio' leather boots and Malos's rope sandals and instructed them to smear the doors to their apartments with it. She stood up, covered Mauricio's eyes with her hands, and then Malos's, and when she took them off the thirty coins were gone.

"Oh, you rascal! What did you do with my money?" Malos cried out.

"Ask the demons ... what do you want me to do? They set the price!"

Mauricio sat agape because he could not believe that she had stolen the coins. While she had her hands on Malos's eyes, he could swear the coins lay on the table.

"Stop it," Mauricio said.

Too late, his brother-in-law had seized the gypsy by her hips, lifted her up, and turned her upside down while the old woman screamed. Her dress and petticoat fell over her head like a hood and uncovered her white underwear and both sides of her dark wrinkled buttocks.

"Help me! Help me!   You stupid brute! I don't have your coins!"

As he shook her, a bunch of coins click clacked on the floor and rushed out into the confines of the room like scared little mice.

Malos picked all the coins up, placed one in her hand, and left.

Flabbergasted and with the events still fresh in their minds, both in-laws walked down the stairs, where the old marble steps had been worn down to thin blades with ragged borders. Mauricio inadvertently misplaced his greasy sole on the edge of one of them, slipped and pitched headlong downstairs with a horrendous scream,

"*Maldito*, Tuba!"

Impotently, Malos watched his brother-in-law roll down and, with a solid thud, hit his head against a large cobblestone on the street. Mauricio's eyes stared into emptiness as a pool of blood formed around his head. Moments later, he turned his head to the side and was gone before his brother-in-law reached the ground level. The gypsy opened the door to her apartment when she heard the outcry, but she did not go down. Malos lifted his eyes up toward the landing and saw her forbidding face contracted into an expression of hatred,

"You, cruel brute! I told you thirty coins as it was paid for Christ!"

Malos felt like running upstairs and ending her life. The way he glared at her! Trembling, she felt her skin turning into a rolling pin, scrambled back into her apartment, and locked the door up. Screaming, he ran upstairs jumping two steps at a time.

"*Maldita* witch! Here are the other twenty nine coins!"

"Go away, you crazy heathen. You killed your friend!"

Malos carried his brother-in-law's body in his arms and rushed by the construction site of the Great Theatre on his way to Moreno de Mora Hospital, about 300 yards away. Blood and sweat drenched his clothes as his brother-in-law's head bobbed up and down and his lifeless right arm dangled like a pendulum. Construction was at a standstill, the streets were empty, and the sun raged in full force. Seconds seemed like hours but finally the new hospital, white and elegant like an ornate mausoleum, stood before him at the seashore of La Caleta Beach. He bore so much distress that only the blood and the death in his arms filled his vision. An old doctor with round spectacles, comma-shaped lips, and a long face came over and pronounced Mauricio dead as he kept puffing smoke from a cigarette hanging from his mouth.

Malos rushed home by Campo del Sur Road, feeling as if a nightmare had enveloped him in a ghostly world. Everything seemed unreal. Yet nothing had changed. The sea lapped against the walls with the same insistence, the strong rushes of levanter blew papers and dust down the streets flanking the waters, and the high-flying seagulls were swooping over their prey with precise accuracy. Even the cupola of the cathedral and Sagrario Tower next to Santa Cruz Church looked as majestic as ever. He dug into his pocket and took out the thirteen remaining coins. He held them in the palms of his hands and looked at each of them again and again, scrutinizing them for any possible clue that would reveal the drops of blood. He saw nothing—just old coins as dark and dirty as black magic. He raised his hands and tossed them away. The coins plummeted and hit the water with a splash, causing ripples that ran into one another.

"*Malditas* coins!" he murmured to himself.

As he approached Puerta de Tierra, the entrance into the walled-in city, he walked by the bullring, where aficionados waited outside to enter and occupy their seats. Every few yards the red and yellow Spanish flags waved from the poles at the perimeter of the venue. People queued in long lines to buy tickets. Children dressed in tatters walked about carrying earthenware vessels with spouts, hawking and offering them to the thirsty public for whatever they thought fit for the service. A few peddlers pushed their rickety carts filled with candies, peanuts, and hazelnuts. Smell of roasted peanuts permeated the air. Everything reminded him of the approaching celebration, of how he interrupted Mauricio's day, and of how he severed his brother-in-law's life as he was getting ready to enjoy the afternoon event. Sadness overcame him. What a terrible fate! And all because of those cursed coins, he thought.

When he was about to reach home, a couple of civil guards accosted him. The one with a big mustache and a prominent belly addressed him,

"Mr. Malos?"

"Yes, what can I do for you?"

"Your boss, Mr. Jose Zarandieta, has filed a complaint. He said you have some silver coins that belong to him."

"I don't have any silver coins!"

"Mr. Malos, one of your coworkers went to the area where you were digging and found a couple of old silver coins. He notified your boss and mentioned that you left in a hurry earlier than usual. Anyway, now he has a bunch of people combing and digging the beach for coins. People are swarming the place. He is paying three pesetas for each coin ... a lot of dough, a day's salary. Your boss thinks you might have quite a few of them."

"As I said, I don't have any coins."

"Anyway, you look terrible. What did you do, kill someone? You better accompany us to our headquarters."

The sergeant was not in a good mood. His thick eyebrows knitted and his big brown eyes with dark circles grew inflamed as he raised his hand and pushed Malos against the wall.

"Stop lying to me!" he yelled out. "Tell me the truth or we'll lock you up and throw away the key."

"You don't scare me," Malos replied. "I've already had enough scares in my life. I already told you what happened. I had some coins but I handed them to the gypsy and I tossed the rest into the sea. Those coins are cursed. The people should stop digging or something terrible will happen to them. No one should go near them."

"Did you hide any coins?"

"Why should I hide any cursed coins ... did anyone see me hiding any coins? I'm telling you the truth. People are going to die like my brother-in-law. Stop them! Please, stop them!"

"Shut up! I'm the one giving orders ... you want me to slap you across the face? Insolent!"

"*Maldito*, Tuba!" he hollered over and over, raising his eyes. "Do you want my life too? Take it!"

Malos spoke about a black prince sorcerer, cannibals in Cuba, pirates, killings, the hangings, a witch, the blood on the coins, a gypsy, his brother-in-law's freefall to death. He talked on and on. His eyes seemed to bulge out of their orbits. He fussed with his hands, with his hair, paced back and forth, pounded his chest like a gorilla, laughed with roaring guffaws, and a few moments later cried his eyes out. Copious amounts of fresh sweat diluted the crust of sweat and blood over his body and clothes, giving off a horrendous stench. The sergeant pinched his own nose closed and drew away.

Later that day a couple of civil guards brought the gypsy in for questioning. She denied ever meeting Malos or knowing anything about the coins. She wore a face of indifference as if the questions did not pertain to her. When the civil guards confronted Malos again, he continued with assertions about Tuba and the curse. Nothing stopped him.

"Mr. Malos, do you want your wife to come in?" the sergeant asked. "She is outside waiting."

"It wasn't my fault. I didn't kill Mauricio; it was Tuba, *maldito* prince of darkness! The coins are cursed ... stained with blood."

"Officer Zuloaga," the sergeant said, "please, take this man to the madhouse and lock him up until he recovers his senses."

The Manicomio de Capuchinos was a psychiatric institution run by monks and attached to a convent of the same name. Blending with the adjacent buildings, the small two-story structure was on Campo del Sur Road. Fronting the seawaters, the flanking wall lacked any apertures except for a small window, which belonged to the cell assigned to Malos. The main façade had a high arched portal crowned with a tabernacle, a balustrade with several pinnacles bordering a flat roof, and four large ornamented bar windows overlooking a private interior courtyard. It housed a chapel that was famous in Spain for the Murillo's paintings. Malos was in solitary confinement and watched closely by Brother Manuel, his caretaker. Tall and thin, the old monk was a reborn-Christian bullfighter who patiently endured his rants and raves.

"*Señor* Malos, don't you want to get well and go home?" the monk asked.

Malos liked him. He had a matador's elegant bearing and when he smiled, a large scar crossing his cheek anchored the right side of his mouth.

"I got this scar in Bayona, France," he explained to Malos. "The bull almost beheaded me. But God knows His ways—"

Talking about bullfighters, the monk would now and then distract his patient. But moments later, Malos would reverse back to Tuba and the curse. From the window of his cell, he could see across the water to the beach where he hid the bag with the coins. The reminder brought attacks of panic upon him. He would scream over the top of his lungs and dart back and forth in the room. Three orderlies had to wrestle him to the floor and tie him down to his bed with leather restraints.

Nightmares besieged Malos. In one he saw someone standing on the beach where he had hidden the bag. It was a huge black man with deep circles around his eyes, his mouth open in a roaring laugh, and his front teeth stained with blood as if he had just devoured raw meat. Hanging from each of his hands was a head with blood dripping from the ragged neck stump. Malos tossed and turned but did not wake up. The right hand held Mauricio's head. He could make out his face as clear as when he sat in front of him. His mouth, adorned with two gold teeth, had contracted in a sardonic grin and his eyes, opaque like a blind person's, had drifted wide apart. He could not recognize the face of the head dangling from the left hand. The black man placed his trophies on the sand and proceeded to dig up a large bag. He lifted it up and tipped it down. Instead of coins a large gush of blood splashed out onto the sand, staining everything bright red and spreading out to the water. The killer picked Mauricio's head up and crammed it into the bag and then turned around to lift the other head. At that very moment, Malos noted that it was alive; that above a big mustache and a large nose, its eyes moved up and down, left and right, like a doll's. Something else caught his attention: a crescent-moon-shaped scar that bore great resemblance to the one over his right eyebrow, which had resulted from a fall from a chair when he was a child.

"My head!" he screamed.

He jumped out of bed and reached for his neck.

After a couple of weeks his wife visited him. Malos was locked in his cell sitting on his couch facing a wall, his eyes staring at the bloodstain left by a mosquito, which he had squashed with his rope sandal. Pepi saw him through a barred window in his door. He kept rocking his body and murmuring,

"I have to kill you. I have to kill you. The black sorcerers sent you to suck my blood. I have to kill you."

"Malos, I am Pepi. My love, look over here toward the door."

"Go away! You, gypsy witch!"

"I'm your wife."

"Wife, wife, wife, she didn't touch the coins ... clean, clean, clean."

"Stop it, Malos! Do you hear me?"

"Clean, clean, clean."

Once a week she returned to see him. Until her fourth visit he didn't engage in any conversation. At first his attention span was very limited and after a few words, he would shut his mind and ignore her questions. After five weeks of confinement he recognized his wife and began to make a little sense. The situation made his wife nervous and easily upset, for no money was coming in and food was now scarce.

"Malos, would you stop this nonsense? The children are hungry. You need to get well and go back to work."

"Pepi, tell the children I love them. I'm doomed. I'm as good as dead. Stay away from me. Kill me, please. Bring Mauricio's gun. Don't tell the monks, just come over and shoot me. I don't want the black sorcerers to cut my head off. They'll tear me apart. Bring me potatoes with calamari. I'm hungry."

After his wife's previous visit, Malos began to stick his head out the window to look at the sea. The neighborhood children sneered at him,

"Madman ... nuts, can you see the fish flying? Ha, ha, ha, would you like some silver coins? Here!" A rainfall of stones hit the wire screen on his window.

Impervious to their harassment, Malos stood staring into the emptiness of the ocean as if watching for a menace approaching from afar. After a while his impassivity wore down the little punks, who grew indifferent to his presence. After two months, he started to follow their games: spinning tops, tossing horseshoes, hopscotch, marbles, skipping rocks. One day a child pitched a horseshoe, stepping over the throwing line, giving rise to a big hubbub among the players until Malos shouted from above that the cast was a dead shoe. Astonished, the children gazed up at the madman and realized he had a tongue and could talk. From then on, they relied on him to be their referee. It was about two months after his confinement he heard the children singing at the parapet atop the stone wall holding back the seawaters. The lyrics of the song intrigued him.

"People in Cadiz have talked so much
Of the olden silver coins ...
Of how everyone swarmed the seashore ...
It is the funniest thing I ever saw.

The beach bustled like a state fair,
Oh God, it was miserably unfair!"
Some dug out more than thirty coins,
While others got none to spare …"

The few words that Malos exchanged with the children made him think that maybe not everyone who had touched the olden silver coins had died; that somehow the curse might have been broken. After this epiphany, his conversations with his caretaker turned more rational and for the first time he could talk about Mauricio's death. Initially he did it with a panic-stricken expression but then a few days later, with a calmer demeanor. Pepi visited him and to her surprise he answered her questions,

"Malos, how do you feel?"

"Fine. How're you and the children?"

"We're okay. For God's sake, get well and come back. We are worried about you."

"I want to leave this place and work and make love to you and kiss my children. Can you see how dirty are those seagulls' beaks? They are swooping down and snatching all the silver coins. Now that the curse is over, the damned birds are stealing all the coins."

"It's good you're looking forward to making love. That's a good sign. But please, Malos, think twice before you open your mouth. The birds are feeding on fish. Their beaks are white and clean."

After a couple of weeks, his reasoning turned clear and the image of the sack filled with coins popped into his thought. He avoided mentioning it to anyone for fear he would be transferred to a jail. It took another month before Brother Manuel deemed his patient free of mental illness and scheduled his release. The night before his release, a great storm with high winds lashed against the coastline. Whistling like a locomotive, gusts thrashed the waters, which pounded against the stone wall, jumped over the parapet, and flooded the road. A few hours later the dawn broke. The sea lay still like a mirror reflecting the spinning beams that shone from the nearby lighthouse. He could hardly wait.

By the time he arrived, the beach was deserted. The area where the two sand dunes stood hiding his treasure had now turned into a large ravine as high as a man and as wide as two adjacent large rooms. It extended about a hundred yards as it became increasingly shallow, leveling out at the seashore. He stepped down to the bottom and looked around for any signs of the coins. There was none. He stood spellbound by what he saw. The wet sand had been furrowed into long parallel grooves made by the pebbles carried in the receding sea waves. Other stones, polished over millions of years, lay anchored in the sand as if studding a magnificent tapestry with precious gems. Around the stones the waters had carved detailed embroideries. He took a deep breath, raised his eyes to heaven, and went home.

ALWAYS READY

George Gordon Meade, the man who saved the Union, lies in his deathbed at home in Philadelphia. It is November 2, 1872, two days since he took ill with double pneumonia. His end approaches. The word Cadiz comes to his mind, the way his parents and older siblings pronounced it, with emphasis on the first syllable, Cádiz, his birthplace in Spain on December 31, 1815. He has no personal recollection of this city because he left when he was one and a half years of age and never returned. Yet, his knowledge and admiration for his hometown have grown over the years. His late mother enjoyed recounting its glorious past—in her own words it was "a land of ancient legends and history, of bullfighters and artists."

His birth in Cadiz was not a chance occurrence. His dad, Richard Worsam Meade, had moved from Philadelphia and set the family residence there eleven years earlier. Through the open door of his bedroom, the General lays eyes on a large picture of his father, which presides over the adjacent family room. Framed in dark wood rimmed with gold paint, the portrait shows him sitting in a mahogany armchair. His double-breasted black coat and high white collar impart on him an air of distinction. His face is asymmetrical as if drawn at different stages of his life. His right facial folds are hardly noticeable as compared with the left, and his right eye bears a smile rather than the stern expression of his left. The General takes after him, his quixotic body shape and dignified manner, his long straight nose, his thin face. His personality is also similar. He can crack a joke or tease a relative or friend with the incisiveness and hilarity *Gaditanos* are famous for. He believes in due diligence and the naked truth without any trappings, exhibiting hot temper aimed at those who have neglected their duties. He shares the same commitment his father had toward the Modenese inscription on their family coat-of-arms: *"Toujours Prêst"*—always ready—that is, ready to defend just causes. This pledge could be traced back to his grandfather who supported George Washington's army with a donation of two thousand pounds sterling, a huge amount at that time; his father backed the Spanish loyalists with his personal wealth, and the General has stood up against any unfairness toward the weak, such as the occasion when, as a young lieutenant in the warfront, he criticized his superiors for abandoning Mexican informants at the mercy of their own army.

His father was a ship owner and merchant in Philadelphia. On his early trips abroad, he became acquainted with the major role played by Cadiz in the maritime commerce. Responsible for eighty-five percent of the trade between Spain and the colonies, this city had grown into a cosmopolitan metropolis of 100, 000 inhabitants, half of them foreigners or immigrants from other Spanish provinces. The frequent wars between Spain and Great Britain promoted commerce under the flags of neutral countries, benefiting foreign merchants, particularly those from the United States. Businessmen swarmed Nueva Street in the heart of the town, which could only be compared to Wall Street today. Exports and imports were booming when Richard Meade arrived in 1803. He opened a shipping agency and established his residency at 4 San Carlos Street, right in front of San Carlos Arch, one of the gates of the stone wall surrounding the ancient city of Cadiz. Overlooking the bay, his building had three stories and a flat roof from which he could watch his merchant ships arriving in the harbor. The upper floor housed a staff of servants, the lower served as storage, and the middle accommodated the family quarters, where ample rooms boasted magnificent balconies crowned with pediments. His wife and two daughters joined him shortly after.   During the first few years, the family survived a devastating epidemic of yellow fever and a blockade of the harbor by the British Navy, whose floating city of war vessels could be seen from their roof. Spain and France reacted by assembling a large armada, which fought the English off the coast of Cadiz at the Battle of Trafalgar on October 21, 1805. It ended with a terrible defeat for the allied fleets. The crippled ships took refuge in Cadiz, where the surrounding wall and heavily armed fortifications prevented enemies from setting foot or approaching its grounds.

His father's business thrived in Cadiz. His earnings afforded him and his family great luxury, marble from Italy, a rich collection of paintings from the most renowned artists such as Murillo, Goya, and Velazquez, parties with the cream of Cadiz society in attendance. He was appointed naval agent for the U.S. at the harbor of Cadiz in 1806. On May 2, 1808, a war erupted between the former allies, Spain and France. On this date Cadiz still remained under blockade by the British Navy. The vessels of the maimed French and Spanish fleets were still anchored in its bay. On May 29, the people of Cadiz joined the Spanish uprising against the French. His mother had been reluctant to recount to him the incidents she lived through that day. It was not until April 1847 that the subject came up in conversation. He had just returned from Veracruz, Mexico, after participating in the Mexican War, and had stopped in Washington to visit his elderly mother. He laid his blue hat and his sheathed sword atop a round mahogany tea table on a scrolled tripod, which stood in front of a fireplace. The polished golden buttons of his blue uniform shone in the penumbra of the drawing room. The area was filled with memorabilia, portraits of his father, his mother and his grandparents, his father's writing desk with his feather quill pen dipped into an inkwell—the way he left it before he died—a large bookcase boasting books with black covers and titles in golden letters, and two large tapestries depicting the birth of Jesus and the adoration of the three kings. A soft smell of aging, like decayed carnations, wafted through the air as mother and son sat across from each other. Her blue eyes shone with love and tenderness, gracing a face without a single wrinkle and a complexion as splendorous as the white magnolia petals blooming outside. Even her blond hair, which had turned silver, kept its youthful sleekness and bestowed upon her an aristocratic air.

His mother informed him of the loss of *Caritas Romana*—Roman Charity—a famous masterpiece of one the greatest painters of the seventeenth century, Bartolome Esteban Murillo. The work depicted a starving old man with his hands tied behind him being breastfed by his daughter on one of her visits to his jail. His mother had brought the painting to the U.S. on her 1810 trip abroad and bequeathed it to the Academy of Arts of Philadelphia before her return to Cadiz in the spring of 1811. A pyromaniac set the building ablaze in 1845, destroying numerous pieces of art, among them the *Caritas Romana*.

Richard Meade had bought the painting in Valencia and brought it to Cadiz a few days before the war between Spain and France broke out. It had belonged to Manuel Godoy, the queen's lover and prime minister of Spain under Charles IV. Eight months pregnant with his sister Margaret, his mother sat in the drawing room when the nearby crash of a cannon ball frightened her. The noise shook the walls and brought down this painting, which almost hit her. A group of loyalists assaulted the house of the military governor of Cadiz, Francisco Solano, about sixty yards from her home. Trained in France, the governor found himself in a quandary. On one side lay the British Navy, Spain's traditional adversary that was still unaware of the uprising in Madrid, and on the other was the French Armada, his former friend and new unsuspecting foe whose ships were anchored amidst the Spanish fleet. The outraged people demanded that he order a cannonade against the French. Since he failed to act promptly on their request, they forced their entry into his residence. He killed one of his pursuers as he escaped through the roof and hid inside a secret closet in the building next to the Meades'. The assailants did not relent. Some threatened to set fire to the entire block if the governor was not handed to them. After locating him, they dragged him into San Juan de Dios Plaza, about one and a half miles away, and killed him. A few days later the French Armada surrendered.

His father sided with the Spanish loyalists. A year and a half later a large contingent of French troops surrounded the city, the only bastion in Spain that Napoleon had been unable to conquer. The French shelled the city from across the bay, but most of the bombs ended in the bottom of the waters as *Gaditanos* laughed at their enemy.

"With the metal of the bombs thrown by the French, our ladies make rollers for their curls," the people sang.

Cadiz refused to capitulate. Richard Meade sent his family to Philadelphia for a brief absence from home, but he stayed behind. The land blockade was complete and the city was only accessible by sea. He freighted two hundred and sixty vessels, supplying the townspeople and the garrison with eight million dollars worth of staples, including flour, rice, bacon, rye, corn, cod, and biscuits. At times up to fifty of his ships were docked in the harbor. The siege lasted for two and a half years, but Cadiz never gave in.

The Spanish government defaulted on its payments for the supplies. Military conflicts and the loss of the colonies had impoverished the country, and the minister of finance and his corrupt associates had preferred to pay their friends. The abuses of power angered Richard Meade. He accused the Spanish State Treasurer of embezzlement, because he had approved the purchase of spoiled cheese from a friend to supply the armies without a fair auction. The stinky goods ended up in the bottom of the sea. When his complaints fell on deaf ears, he wrote an article, charging the regency in power of ineptitude and dishonesty, and published it in 1812. It landed him in jail. After three months he was released on bail. When the war was over, the king recognized his contribution. Yet, only two thirds of the debt was satisfied. The Spanish government guaranteed payment of the balance due to him with treasury notes payable in silver coins.

Four years later—a few months after General Meade's birth—
a court appointed Mr. Meade sole assignee of the estate of a fellow merchant that had declared bankruptcy. Cash proceeds were
used to pay local creditors. Instead of depositing the rest into
the Royal Treasury—around 52,000 dollars—he pocketed the
funds and replaced the amount with government treasury notes.
When the court ordered him to pay in cash, he refused. He was
locked up again. This time all his pleas fell on deaf ears. It was
not until his wife and children returned to Philadelphia in 1817
and she appealed to Congress that he was released in 1818. A
Spanish royal tribunal reviewed his contracts and established
that the sum owned to him was 374, 000 dollars, of which 75,
000 was compensation for his unfair incarceration. Per agreement between both countries, this debt was to be paid by the
U.S. government out of the five million dollars retained from
the purchase of Florida from Spain. His father pursued the case
and after years of aggravation he died in Washington on June 25,
1828, at the age of 50. The money was never recovered.

The loss of the family fortune has never embittered the
General. He has always been aware of the silver lining to the mis-
hap: it forced his mother to choose a military career for him.
According to her, his successful destiny was sealed at his birth.
Her description of the happy event was so vivid that he has pictured his first breath like a rush of happy air pushing its way into
his lungs as if spurred by the rapid strumming of a flamenco
guitar.

"On the day you were born," she said, "from my bed I could
see the moon silvering the waters of the bay. It seemed as if a full
universe of twinkling stars was dancing on the surf. Then I saw it
... a shooting star dashed through the sky from north to south. It
was an omen of the great future awaiting you."

The General was baptized Catholic at the Church of Our Lady
of the Rosary on January 8, 1816. The temple was built at the
foot of Santa Maria quarters in the sixteenth century. It boasted
a high and svelte square-shaped tower and a rectangular façade
with a two-pilaster portico. Upon this entrance was a hollow with

a half-a-shell-shaped roof, underneath which an image of Our Lady of the Rosary stood with baby Jesus in her arms. The main nave housed a stunning neoclassical altarpiece, which spanned its entire width and height. It was made of multicolored marbles and adorned with four large serpentine black marble columns. The font was located at the entrance. It was there where Gordon Meade's godmother, Christine Gordon Prendergast, held him in her arms as the parish priest scooped up holy water with a shell and poured it upon his head. Outside, the beauty of a cold and sunny day enthralled the attendants.

Friends gathered for a celebration at the Meades' home after the ceremony. The wide and spacious San Carlos Wall lay before their eyes. It had recently been built with oyster-stones and embellished with a magnificent gate graced by a royal crown. This access into the city was right in front of the Meades' home. Bustling with merchant ships, Cadiz harbor was beyond this wall and farther out to sea were numerous vessels anchored in the bay, waiting to unload their precious merchandise. A north breeze had swept away all the clouds and a pristine blue sky had fused with the intense azure of the calmed ocean waters. The color contrasted with the white hue of the fishing villages, which surrounded the bay like a white pearl rosary on a devotee's hand.

Forty days after his birth, his mother and a servant took him for a stroll by La Alameda, a promenade along the waters that was blessed by the fragrances of the sea and the trees in blossom. His family owned a stroller, which looked like a miniature adult carriage pulled by a small pony. The expensive rig had come in handy ever since his father bought it in London for his sister Elizabeth, whose birth had taken place in Cadiz ten years earlier. Other siblings born in his hometown included: Richard, 1807; Margaret, 1808; Maria del Carmen, 1810; Catherine, 1811; and Salvadora, 1812. Catherine died as a child and her tomb remained in Cadiz. The General has never known the details of her death. It was an issue too painful for his parents to discuss. Yet, somehow, in a strange way, he has been comforted by the thought that some of his family ashes nurture the earth of his

birthplace. He loves his brothers and sisters. Yet fate managed
to create a deep breach between him and Elizabeth. During the
civil war, she became an avowed secessionist and a staunch sup-
porter of the South. Her two sons died fighting against the North,
Frank confronting his corps at Chancellorsville and Edward a few
months earlier. Ever since, she kept her distance from the General
until her death a few months ago, despite all his loving letters.

The walks by La Alameda Promenade were soon exchanged
for frequent visits to Santa Catalina Castle across the bay in
Puerto Santa Maria, where his father had been incarcerated on
May 2, 1816. He had free movements within the compound but
grew more and more despondent, witnessing the months pass
and his shipping business dwindle down to almost nothing.

In June 1817, his family moved back to Philadelphia to lobby
for his father's freedom. From then on his mother never stopped
praising Cadiz, despite all the difficulties she had endured over
there. She missed the murmur of the sea; the ocean breeze, which
seemed to whisper in her ears words of love; the daily sunlight,
which wrapped its colors around streets and plazas; the fizzing
embrace of the impetuous Atlantic surf and the timid waters of
the bay; the svelte palm trees and the ancestral dreams that dwelt
underneath gigantic dragon trees; the scent of jasmine in the
nights when the full moon silvered the cityscape; the surrounding majestic stone wall, which made the old town look strong
and invulnerable, and yet it also lent it an air of coziness and
serene retreat; the echo of history raising to the surface with each
footstep upon the ancient ground; the whitewashed whiteness
of the city as white as the seagulls soaring high above its sandy
beaches; the bustle of the food market in *Plaza de la Constitucion*,
where people of all walks of life shed their loneliness; the joyful wittiness of its citizens, whose town's millenarian experience
made them look at life through the prism of laughter; the elegance of *Calle Ancha*, which became the point of encounter for
the Spanish elite; and the blazing splendor of the sunset, which
flamed the horizon and rouged the sky as pink as a baby's rosy
cheeks.

This was the same sky where his mother saw the shooting star that presided over his birth. My shooting star, he ponders ... Gettysburg. Memories of this battle spring to mind like tiny green plants on a burned field. He has never thought of his victory as an act of heroism. It was just his duty. His forefathers' pledge of equality for all men was at stake, and thus far their statement had been ignored. Men were then called upon to put their life on the line to defend their beliefs.

His appointment as commander of the Army of Potomac on June 28, 1863—three days before Gettysburg—still strikes him as a stunning surprise. He agreed to the new post despite the gigantic challenge that loomed before him. In three days he had to pull together an army in disarray and face a victorious and formidable enemy, over one hundred thousand strong. Defeating Robert E. Lee would entail effort, planning, and discipline. The man was a natural leader and his army had fought with courage. General Meade realized that he had no choice but to infuse the same fortitude in his own soldiers. The importance of the upcoming battle could not be overstated—win and the Union would be saved, lose and Washington would fall into enemy hands. His troops were exhausted from long marches, sickened by sunstroke, dispirited by the last two defeats in Fredericksburg and Chancellorsville. Some of his divisions would have to trudge seventy-two miles in two days with hardly anything to eat or drink and engage the enemy under dreadful conditions. The whereabouts of most of his men and his enemies were unknown to him. Yet, he was not afraid of danger, for he saw his new position in the light of faith.

"It appears to be God's will for some good purpose," he wrote to his wife, "at any rate, as a soldier, I have nothing to do but accept and exert my utmost abilities to command success."

The General's thoughts are interrupted by the light touch of a cloth dabbing the perspiration from his forehead. His wife stands next to him, her soft eyes set on him as if cajoling the illness out of him. There is no fear in his blue eyes. He smiles. He has witnessed so much dying, pain, and suffering in this world. All those boys in the trenches and fields of Gettysburg died with their mouths buried in the mud. Their bodies lay deformed and flattened like discarded sacks of bones, while their rifles stood next to them intact as if waiting for them to resume the fight. The stench of death has ever since permeated his senses. Pits were filled with bodies, most of them unidentified, and corpses covered with only a few shovelfuls of earth. What a lonely death in the midst of a desolated field with no loved ones to take notice and cry over their loss. Only God was there. He reminisces about the final prayer of his men and the words of Father Corby. The priest stood on a large boulder on the second day of the battle as the decimated Irish Brigade dropped to their knees and bowed their heads,

"Remember the sacred nature of your cause, the defense of the dignity of man, whom God created in His own image ... in the name of the Father, the Son, and the Holy Ghost, Amen."

So many soldiers died that day that the General now views his own upcoming death as his inevitable turn, an event postponed by the grace of God. He prays. His wheezing and rattling sounds interrupt his invocation, for his chest feels like a coop full of fighting cocks. Fatigue catches up with him. The previous night he did not get a wink of sleep. Shortness of breath and bouts of coughing kept him up. Over and over he presses down with his arms against the bed and expands his chest. His ribs collapse and squeeze the air out. He looks to his right and sees his wife sitting on a rocking chair at his bedside. Sleep has overcome her. Beautiful Margaretta, the mother of my seven children, he thinks, with her charming smile and her peaceful eyes capable of changing any windstorm in my life into a pleasant breeze. She has always been there for me. He wishes he could lean forward and caress her gray hair. To him it still feels sprightly and plush, like the rich long curls of her younger years. He reminisces about his foreboding words on their last stroll, just before illness struck him.

"If I die," he told her, "my only grievance against life will be that it took me away from you for too long."

The maple tree outside his window now stands almost bare, for only a few yellow leaves cling to the knotted twigs as if life had taken a hiatus. This autumnal image does not portray his life. His is one full of happy children and grandchildren. Between wakefulness and sleep, his mind drifts to the last day at the Battle of Gettysburg. His front line held up. Those boys dug themselves into the breastworks and rifle holes, and nothing, not even the pounding of the formidable Confederate artillery, made them flinch. With the dead and the wounded populating the trenches, they kept up their spirit. He remembers the denuded trees broken and burned, the moist soil reddened, the stones cracked, the rivulets of mud and blood. But then, bigger than his hope for mankind, a red sun peeked through the heavy clouds above the horizon. History was about to turn over a new leaf.

"Victory at last!" he heard himself, crying out.

His smile fused with a tear sliding down his cheek as he contemplated the barren field strewn with the dead and the wounded.

The relief the General felt at the conclusion of this battle was great, but does not compare to the serenity that he now experiences. He has accepted his impending death and the life that God assigned to him. Forgiven are the ungrateful acts, such as President Lincoln's belated thank-you letter for his success at Gettysburg. It was tainted with a sense of disappointment for allowing General Lee and his army to cross the Potomac River and escape to Virginia. Did the President know about the state of his exhausted army and the loss of valuable officers? Did he know how many of his men had no shoes or food? General Lee was in retreat, but a wounded lion could lash out with his claws. Rifle pits and infantry parapets could be built in a couple of days. Perhaps if the President had seen with his own eyes the earthworks thrown up by the rebels and the readiness of their artillery, he would have understood the mortal trap that Robert E. Lee had prepared for his army.

He has also forgiven the press for the undeserved criticisms leveled against him. The reporters did not like him, because on one occasion his temper had gotten the best of him. The incident

happened before Gettysburg, because he felt that a war corre-
spondent's criticisms of him were unfair. He sat him backwards
on a mule with a notice on his back that read "Libeler of the
Press", and paraded him off the camp as drummers played the
Rogue March. The reporters avenged his temper tantrum against
their fellow newspaperman. As usual history ended up being a
deformed tale narrated by a few rather than the true accounts of
witnesses.

A thought interrupts the memory of those unpleasant
moments:

"My ... son ... Gordon ..." the General whispers.

"Do not talk, my dearest. He is on his way," his wife said.

"I ... must ... speak ... to ... him."

The unfairness of others no longer fazes the General. He
has come to terms with the fact that no one can be absolutely
happy with his or her performance in this life; that each of us
is an unfinished chapter. His conscience is set at ease, clear of
any regret. He has striven to achieve his best. He now realizes
that his major victory lies at home, at 1836 De Lancey Place in
Philadelphia, where his loved ones stand next to him during his
last hours. No criticisms, no ungratefulness, no recrimination.
He loves his wife, children, and grandchildren so much. His son
George's voice interrupts his thoughts,

"Papa... General, did you call me?"

"Please ... bring me ... the picture ... of Cadiz," the General
says.

"Cadiz?"

It is a copy of an original work by Alfred Guesdon that was
lithographed in 1853 and shows a panoramic view of his hometown as if seen from a globe floating above the building where the
Meades used to live. His son George gave it to him as a gift a few
years ago. The image depicts an impregnable citadel at the sea:
the surrounding stone wall bristling with cannons, the heavily
guarded gates of access into the city, the bustle of the harbor and
the peacefulness of the bay, the stately custom house and government buildings, numerous churches with svelte bell towers,

the recently built cathedral towering over the scenery, and shell-shaped La Caleta Beach whose entrance from the sea is guarded by Santa Catalina Castle at its north end and San Sebastian Castle at the south. The latter fortification is located at the tip of a long jetty where a lighthouse rises above the waters.

"Do you ... spot ... the lighthouse?" the General asks his son after he has walked into the room with the gold-framed lithograph.

"Yes, right here, Papa. The stone tower is round and tall ... similar to the one you built in Florida."

"Mine ... is red. This is ... white."

"Most of the buildings in Cadiz are white."

"I wish ... I had ... built ... another one ... there. Do ... you ... see ... the ... building ... with ... the big ... cupola?

"Yes, the cathedral.

"I remember ... my parents ... talking ... about ... the large ... cathedral ... that was ... being ... built ... which ... seemed ... like ... it would ... never be ... completed."

The construction of the Cathedral of Cadiz began in 1722 and ended in 1838. The church had an elaborate baroque lower half of pale-brown marble and jasper stones, and an austere neoclassical upper half, much lighter, of cream-white limestone. Graced with elaborate reliefs, the lower half of the façade boasted a pairs of Corinthian columns and a large portico. An enormous yellow cupola crowned the main structure, which rose next to ocean waters and was flanked by two high towers. The interior harbored expansive naves, tall columns, high arches, and numerous chapels full of religious statues and paintings of renowned artists.

"General ... Papa, you did not call me to talk about Cadiz, did you?"

"No ... but a man ... should always go ... back to ... his beginnings ... when confronting ... his final days. A Chinese proverb ... says, 'Though a tree ... grows so high, the falling leaves ... return ... to the root.'"

"You will recover. You are strong."

"No ... I will not. We are ... soldiers. We can ... look at death ... in the face."

"What do you wish to tell me?

"The new list ... of benefactors ... for Fairmount Park ... is in my desk drawer. Hand it ... to the mayor. In a few days ... General ... I mean President Grant ... will be reelected ... send him ... a letter of congratulation. At my funeral ... there will be politicians ... who will wish ... to honor me in death ... when they have failed ... to support me ... while I was alive. Do not let them. You know ... who they are ... do you not?"

"Yes, Papa."

"Colonel."

"Yes, General."

"I love you."

The effort winds him. He listens to his son's steps leaving the room as he so often did when they were together during the war campaign. If only he could hug the sounds of his tread, put them away in a safe nook in his mind, and caress them forever. The rhythmic cadence of his son's heels carries him back. Why do his thoughts always return to the hallowed soil of Gettysburg as if he had buried his heart there? He sighs. Out of the stench of death and the smoke of gunpowder, the spirit of man sprung anew from this battlefield. The spilled blood cleansed the bigotry and prejudice harbored in the heart of those who had looked down upon their colored brothers and sisters. The freedom of man stood reaffirmed, slavery banished, the Constitution amended. The General's ribs waver. His belly flutters. His navel tightens up. There is not enough air and opening the windows does not help. Why did he ever think that dying would be a simple task? It is hard work. He prays that God will take him in His arms. He sinks into a coma and four days later, when his life has burned out like a candle, death arrives. The General rests in peace.

PORT OF CADIZ WITH REPLICAS OF COLOMBUS CARAVELS

UNDER THE
CRESCENT MOON

The low tide revealed a solitary cove surrounded by large stone blocks and isolated from the road and Santa Maria del Mar Beach by a ravine. Dressed in white, a youngster's svelte figure stood above the ocean waves that eased toward the narrow strip of sand.

"Fatimah!" Alvaro exclaimed to himself.

She turned her gaze upward toward the opening of a cave as if she had heard him. Her eyes were black and shone with happiness as she shifted her vision toward the immense sea. It had been so long since he had seen her. He had no doubt; those were her eyes. They bore the same expression as the last time they had met. It remained engraved in his mind. She had the small black spot next to the dimple on her right cheek, the little upper lip that protruded over her mouth in a faint perpetual smile, and the waist-length black hair that now waved in the soft breeze. Oblivious to everyone, she strolled and bent to pick up little seashells. They were white, pink, light blue, white and pink, round and pointed, smooth and corrugated small snails and tiny oysters. She admired them in the palm of her hands for a while and then gingerly set them down on the shore's edge as if each was made of fragile glass.

Her image brought back memories of his first visit to the red-bricked castle overlooking Qadis, his hometown. The 321 Muslim year—933 AD—was in full swing. As a child he had always marveled at its four large square towers crowned by bat-tlements, which stood tall over a thick wall that rested on the cliffs high above the turbulent seawaters. From this tower, *Hajib* Al-muminin, Lord of the city of Qadis, kept a close eye on the activities at the great mosque and the bazaar. His subjects' reclu-sive living quarters were attached to the *medina* like partitions to the core of a walnut.

Alvaro often walked by the thick wooden door that led inside the castle. He wondered what could possibly be inside. So when his father, Count Julian Ibeniegas, informed him that he would be joining him on his upcoming visit to the castle, the youngster's excitement grew as the day approached. At sixteen he had been working with his dad for a couple of years and had learned the trade of money lending, a business frowned upon by Muslims, since the Koran prohibited any interest on loans. The *Hajib* engaged Count Julian to provide this service in the territory under his jurisdiction.

"Remember my son," his father said. "Moors are very touchy when dealing with money. Watch what I do when I greet the *Hajib*. You must learn proper protocol."

Escorted by a couple of armed guards Alvaro and his father walked inside the castle. They went through a long lobby with a few windows, which was illuminated by candles set in small wall niches. After a while a large sunlit room shone before them. It took a while for Alvaro's eyes to adjust to the bright surround-ings. Overhead, the ceiling was ornamented with mosaics of circles and rhombuses of delicate red beads fixed on a base of golden floral designs. The white walls were covered by an elabo-rate lace-like foliage pattern, which ended at the corners with a narrow fringe of Arabic calligraphy. Alvaro read the inscription to himself,

Ashhadu an la ilaha ill-Llah; Muhamma rasulu Llah—I bear wit-ness that there is no god but Allah; I testify that Muhammad is God's messenger.

The white marble floor of the salon contrasted with the three long black onyx columns, which stood up close to the main wall.

Over these pillars balanced three pairs of parallel horseshoe-shaped arches with alternating red and white stripes. Underneath the colonnade, the *Hajib* sat accompanied by two of his advisors. The sun flooded the place through three trefoil arches. Alvaro's thoughts of admiration were interrupted by his father's voice.

"*As-Salamu Alaykum,*" he said, bowing as he pushed Alvaro's head down too.

"*Alaykum As-Salam,*" the *Hajib* answered. "How are things in your temple? Are the parishioners of Santa Maria Church happy? Are they unhappy with the *jiziyah*?

"No, *sayyid*, we all think your religious tax is reasonable. We all are grateful that you allow us to celebrate our religious services."

"I heard the Jews are lobbying to lower the tax. Maybe some-day you will all see the light and convert to Islam. Anyway, you have brought me a visitor."

As Alvaro subtly bowed, he observed a grave expression in the *Hajib's* little blue eyes, which hid under bushy long eyebrows. His stern husky voice and long nose were incongruent with his short height.

"Yes, *sayyid*, my son Alvaro, he is going to follow in my footsteps."

"He is young. His eyes are full of curiosity and cleverness." The *Hajib* turned around and ordered one of his subalterns, "Yusuf, take this young man to the garden. Let him enjoy its beauty while I discuss some business with his father. No one is there, correct?"

"No, *sayyid*, no one has yet come down from the harim."

The portals of the salon opened to a garden dotted with bushes and almond trees that flanked a long rectangular pond. The branches had bloomed. A myriad of thin little twigs danced over the water like marionettes. The gentle rippling sound and the hush of the wind in the trees were punctuated by songs of canaries, while goldfinches trilled over the constant chirping of flitting sparrows. A delicate almond fragrance permeated. Alvaro reached the middle of the patio and saw a young woman. She sat on a corner of the pond as if she were a statue adorning the place. Her hands played with the white petals that floated on the water. She heard a rustling sound and raised her head, quickly covering her face with her veil. He had been able to steal a glance at her face. Her lips were strawberry red, her complexion white with a nacreous resplendence, her eyes dark and full of life, and her cheeks pastel pink, the right bearing a small black spot next to a dimple.

"You should not be here," she said. Her voice was sweet and melodious like the tunes of a lute. Her subtle lily perfume and the almond fragrance fused into what Alvaro thought would be the scent given off by a heavenly apparition.

"The *Hajib* invited me to visit his garden. I saw you before you covered your face. You are beautiful."

"You are not supposed to see me. I do not care. You have seen your Christian girlfriends, have you not?"

"I have no girlfriend."

"I am sure you have met several good-looking Christian young women."

"I have not met anyone as gorgeous as you."

"The veil is not that important. It is just a custom. There isn't any single verse in the Koran stating that women must wear veils. The *shariah*—the Islamic laws— do not require it either. We must cover ourselves from our neck to our ankle; that is all."

"Then why do you keep it on now?"

"What is it to you? You are a Christian, anyway. I am not supposed to chat with Christian young men."

"We are not conversing. We have not been introduced."

"I know who you are. I saw you coming in with your father, the money lender. What's your name?"

"Alvaro. What's yours?"

"Never mind, I cannot be seen with you."

"Why not? I am your guest. You can show me your garden."

"I am sorry, not without my father's permission. Excuse me, I must leave now."

"As you wish … I hope to see you again soon."

She rushed away, brushing against the lower branches of the almond trees, which scattered her path with a flurry of petals. Then she turned around and said,

"Fatimah. That is my name."

That evening Alvaro could not keep his mind off Fatimah. He lay in bed with his hands folded under his head gazing at the ceiling. This behavior was most unexpected for him. He was not a youngster prone to unrealistic daydreaming. He was a studious young man who enjoyed classic Greek, Roman, and contemporary Muslim authors. He kept abreast in astronomy, geography, mathematics, philosophy, literature, science. He looked forward going to Cordoba and partaking of the most advanced center of civilization of his time. The city boasted the largest library ever, over 400,000 volumes. Sages from Moorish Spain and all over the Muslim world flocked to its institutions, where the cultures of sciences and literature flourished. Ancient texts were translated into Arabic and preserved for future generations.

Yet, those few minutes had been enough for her beauty and demeanor to captivate Alvaro's imagination. Fatimah had dazzled him. An irresistible desire to see her again took root in him. Every Thursday when the sun was about to set, he would gaze at the glittering blue minaret, which overlooked the ocean on one side, and the rectangular court-and-hall mosque made of terracotta on the other. His eyes were riveted on the little balcony where the muezzin made the calls for prayers. Its railing faced east because, according to gossipers, the Moors wanted to turn a blind eye to the huge Roman Almerana Tower. The ancient structure stood half a mile to the west and rose about one hundred and fifty feet. For many centuries, it served as guidance for vessels that had sailed into Qadis Bay and its harbor. Atop the tower was a togged and bearded idol with a large key in one hand and a staff in the other. Some townspeople thought that this statue irritated the Muslim hierarchy. The truth was that the rulers considered its presence a proof of their policy of religious tolerance. Alvaro would wait for the muezzin to stand on the minaret, face Mecca, and chant the first invocation,

"Allahu Akbar!"—Allah is great!

He did not wait for the four repetitions of the *takbir* or for the other six praises to Allah and His Prophet that followed. He rushed out toward the castle and stood at a corner behind a cart, watching the *Hajib*, his favorite, and his twelve daughters ride on litters shouldered by slaves. The young women had their faces veiled and the carriages boasted red silk canopies, which were kept closed during the entire trip. It was a short distance from the castle to the great mosque. Hiding, Alvaro followed them and occasionally was rewarded with a glimpse of Fatimah's shadow through the curtain. Sometimes he could swear he had seen her turn around to look at him.

Alvaro had been right. Fatimah was aware of his whereabouts and kept her eyes on him. Her sister Zaynab, who rode next to her, reprimanded her,

"Fatimah, do not look at that youngster. He is a Christian. If Father sees you, he will impose a serious punishment on you both."

"Oh, Zaynab, I have not cast my eyes on anyone."

"Father wants to marry you off to a good Muslim, a wealthy and valiant warrior."

"I do not know if I can share the man I love with another woman."

"What kind of thinking is that? You are a Muslim woman. You must follow the teachings of the Prophet (*salla-Llahu Alaihi wa-salam*—peace and blessing be upon him.)"

"The feeling is inside of me. I do not think I can get rid of it."

"Have you been talking to Christians?"

"How could I? None of our servants or slaves are Christians, you know that."

"When the time comes you will do what is right. Those feelings will disappear. Otherwise, I would not want to be in your shoes."

Kind and loving to her servants and slaves, Fatimah was a goodhearted young woman, whose emotions burst out in response to any unfairness or injustice. Weakness, fickleness, and vacillation were not part of her personality. On the contrary, her opinions and decisions were steadfast and sound as demonstrated in an incident at the harim: A young slave from Galicia stole a gold bracelet from her. The jewel was found among her possessions. According to the *shariah*, she was to be punished with amputation of her right hand.

"Rania, if her hand is cut off, she will not be able to sew for us and what good is that going to do us? She embroiders like an artist. Maybe she has not stolen it from my jewel box or my room. We have no proof. It must have fallen from my wrist. We should consider it an act of omission … she did not inform the owner."

"She knew it belonged to you. She confessed."

"She confessed under duress. I do not believe in those confessions. When I talked to her, she said she found it on the floor outside my room."

"She should be warned and from now on she should be sent to work outside the palace salting fish until she earns enough money to buy me a new bracelet. She will do her regular duties in the evening."

"That will take at least three years."

The truth was that Fatimah believed that the punishment should fit the offense. Severance of a hand far exceeded the seriousness of the crime.

Back in the palace, Fatimah daydreamed of Alvaro, his smiling green eyes, his humility and confidence. She had stood next to him for a few seconds, and yet realized that he was different, that before him no one had ever treated her as an equal. Her interactions with the opposite sex had been disappointing. The suitors in love with her revered her like a princess, but those who disliked her or were indifferent considered her inferior. The latter relied on the *shariah* to wield their superiority over her, since canons valued a woman's testimony as half that of a man's. Almost a year had gone by and the occasion to meet Alvaro again had never arisen. Whenever he visited the palace with his father, she rushed down to the pond, but he was never invited to stroll around the garden again. Both searched for each other and wished their eyes could penetrate the thick walls. She grew depressed. Dark circles framed her eyes and her radiant face turned pale. Everything around her seemed gray, as if the sun had abandoned the land to never return. She spent hours alone in her room, overcome with extreme fatigue. Raina, the maidservant who had raised her since her mother's death twelve years earlier, became concerned. She called the family physician, Rabbi Joseph. After he examined the patient, he walked out of the room and entrusted her maidservant with a blue ceramic jar that was the size and shape of an acorn.

"Take this infusion of *atropa*—belladonna," he said. "Give her only a drop every day. This is a powerful potion that will stimulate her heart and bring color to her skin. But, like all good remedies, if ingested in a large amount it will surely kill her in a matter of minutes."

Fatimah overheard the doctor's recommendations. Later, when Raina tried to convince her mistress to take the medication, she declined. In fact she got hold of the container and refused to hand it back to her. She went along with the prescription of biweekly milk bath, but her languor and doldrums persisted.

"Fatimah, my little girl, I have not seen you smile for so long," Raina said. "What is wrong with you?"

"I am bored. I lack the strength to live."

"Oh, my little girl, I would do anything to remedy your malady."

"Oh, Raina, would you? Would you take me to see Alvaro, the moneylender's son?"

"My child! Do you want to bring disgrace upon us? He is a Christian. If your father finds out, my head will roll."

"Just once … please. I just want to see him once more."

Rania relented and a few days later, under the false pretense of running an errand she left for the bazaar. She visited it at least once a month to find out whether any new material or dress worthy of her mistress had arrived. This time she left instructions for no one to disturb Fatimah until her return, on the pretext that she had just taken her infusions and needed a long rest. Her young mistress dressed as a young boy, hid her long hair under a turban, and joined her. The maidservant cast her charming smile at the guards who let them get out of the castle without any questions. They rushed through the bazaar. Fatimah had looked down at the market from atop the castle. But up close it was so different—the bustle of shoppers, the smell of merchandise, the fragrances of flowers, the vivid colors, the melodious calls of the hawkers. There was a world outside her golden cage. A feeling rushed inside her as if infusing her with life. Led by her maid, she slinked through a labyrinth of alleys, where dirt and the stench of human misery pervaded. She had no idea people could live in those conditions. Her eyes were not meant to see humans crawling out of their abodes like cockroaches from their holes. Maidservant and mistress walked through an arch that opened to a small plaza. The neighborhood changed. The small homes were now clean, the walls whitewashed, and the facades full of flowerpots. Farther down they arrived at a big house with a blazon attached to the upper part of the main door. The escutcheon had a white background and three horizontal blue stripes. Under the motif was an inscription in golden letters: "Julian Ibeniegas, *Comes Julianus*". The title of Count of Julia alluded to Alvaro's ancestral command over the city of Gades, *Augusta Urbs Iulia Gaditana*, from the day the Roman Empire had disappeared in 476 AD to the time Arabs had invaded Spain in 711 AD. The conquerors had renamed the city as Qadis.

Raina knocked on the door, and an old black woman with a big belly and soft eyes ushered them into a reception room. The housekeeper did not suspect anything unusual about their visit. Townspeople often called to finalize a loan or inquire about it. Inside the house, Fatimah felt butterflies in her stomach. The whole room smelled of dry wood and a high ceiling was held in place by dark, thick wooden beams. Her eyes took in every single item, a dark wooden table with four chairs, a large image of Christ atop a mahogany console, a picture of the Madonna cradling Baby Jesus, and a large portrait of an old man with a Bible in the right hand and a crucifix in the left. She analyzed his face.

A stern air anchored his eyes and lips and set off his Andalusian features. Alvaro resembled him. Fatimah kept her head cocked to one side to examine the picture as Alvaro approached them. The young mistress signaled her nursemaid to step out of the room. After exchanging greetings he looked her straight in the eye as if he had recognized her.

"Excuse me, young man, I have met you before, have I not?" he said.

"Alvaro, it is I, Fatimah. I came to ask you, why do you follow me every Friday? You have no right. We belong to different worlds. You should respect mine and I should respect yours." Her mouth quivered and her eyes shone with excitement.

"I know I should not do it but I need to feel you passing near me, to feel your closeness, to inhale the same air you breathe."

"I must go. I cannot stay away too long or my father will find out I have left the castle without his permission."

"Will we see each other again?"

"No, I cannot leave the premises. Maybe you will stroll by the garden again. I will be at the pond in the early morning every day before anyone gets up and in the evening when the moon is over the castle and everyone has retired to the harem."

"Wait, I have something for you," he said. He rushed out of the room and fetched a cage holding a pigeon. Its white feathers, rich and luscious, contrasted with the orange-colored beak and legs. The bird looked at Fatimah with its green eyes, bobbing its head and making a cooing noise as if greeting its new owner.

"It is a gorgeous bird," she said.

"Delilah will keep you company and if you ever wish to communicate with me, she will fly back home to her old nest. She is a carrier pigeon … the best."

Alvaro tried to use his astuteness and cunning to get back into the castle. But his visits failed to yield any results because the *Hajib* allowed him to stay with his father and participate in the business discussions. Desperation began to catch hold of him. He even thought of embracing Islam so he could have a chance to ask for her hand. His mind tried to justify it,

"We believe in the same God, do we not?" He asked himself. "They believe in Jesus and Our Lady. But they do not believe Jesus is the Son of God ... that He died for our sins and resurrected on the third day. To them, He is just a prophet."

The apostasy could be readily achieved. All he had to do was to go to the mosque and repeat three times the *shahadah* in front of witnesses. He even learned the prayer by heart,

Ashhadu an la Ilaha illa LLa, wa ashhadu anna Muhammad rasulu LLah—I testify that there is no God except Allah, and I testify that Muhammad is His messenger.

But he could not do it. His mind and his heart kept on fighting a pitched battle that never seemed to end. Father Raimundo heard him in confession.

"You do not want to lose your soul. Forget that woman," he said.

"Father, I have no soul. I am nothing without her."

"My son, for centuries fellow Christians have suffered and fought for the rights to practice their religion. They lived in catacombs and died so that you can profess your faith ... and now you are thinking of giving it up."

"Catacombs!"

"What did you say?"

"I'm sorry. I was just thinking aloud."

"Go home and pray to God and Jesus Christ."

The mention of catacombs brought back memories of a story he had heard several years ago. Like Rome, Gades had boasted underground tunnels, which had branched out in a net of passageways crossing the city from side to side. Those tunnels had their hub at the Roman Theater, whose ruins had lain buried beneath the castle for the past few centuries. The townspeople called the fortress Al-Maab, the Castle of the Theater. As far as he knew no one had any idea of the location of these tunnels and their openings. The passages might have collapsed over the years.

Alvaro, however, suspected where it could be located. He sat down with a few talkative old-timers who recounted stories passed down from their ancestors. One caught his attention. As a

child, one of the storytellers heard his father mention that he had
discovered the mouth of one of these tunnels on a small beach
near the town. He did not specify which one. As far as he knew
no one had ever crawled in or even gone nearby for fear that it
housed the lair of a killer dragon. Besides, the old storyteller
thought that the cave had probably collapsed during an earth-
quake a long time ago.

Aboard his white horse and accompanied by his greyhound,
Alvaro searched the outskirts of the town. All his efforts led
nowhere. He dismounted his horse and walked on a beach near
the town, longing to meet Fatimah again. The sea waves were
placid after a long night of fierce storms and high winds, which
had caused avalanches and cracks in the upper terrains. He sat
on the dry sand and let his greyhound Lentus roam around while
his white horse Sentinel stood patiently nearby.

Alvaro's mood was somber because of the fruitless search. He
pictured Fatimah waiting by the pond, but the vision made him
feel lonelier than the peak of the single rock that poked out of
the water far off the beach. He brooded over his lot when his
dog approached him, wagging its tail. The whimpers and determined look in the animal's eyes revealed his eagerness to secure
his master's attention. His jaws held something in their grasp as
saliva dribbled down his black lips. Instinctively, without looking at the animal, Alvaro held his palm out to receive the offering
while he caressed his beloved pet's back with the other hand. In
his fist lay a rough piece of metal that smelled of wet soil and
something else that felt like a small twig. He examined them. It
was a finger bone with a golden ring, which had been polished
by the dog's saliva. The bone was studded with cracks and the
ends were disintegrating. The signet ring bore a round seal with
the carved figure of a Roman goddess.

"A Roman's skeleton! Where did you find it?" he questioned
as he jumped on his feet.

He traced the paw prints up toward a steep slope separating
the beach from a path that led to the town. The dog followed his
master with his small tail erect, as if proud of his discovery. At

the foot of the slope, almost hidden by large rocks, he could see a big hole that the mudslide had unburied. Pushing with all his strength he moved one of rocks. He wormed himself into the pitch-black cave with no end in sight. His deep breath drew a rush of foul humid air into his chest. He had just discovered one of the mouths of the Roman tunnels. He got out, repositioned the stone, and left.

The afternoon wore on, yet dusk never seemed to arrive. Now and again he mapped out in his mind the locations of the cave and the castle, the distance between them, and the direction that the passageway must follow to communicate with the fortification. From time to time, sweet thoughts of Fatimah interrupted his ponderings, easing his mind. When the sun hid beneath the horizon he stood ready. After crawling inside the cave, he lit a candle. Close to the entrance were a skeleton and a rusty Roman helmet. The bones of the right hand lay scattered. The remains belonged to the owner of the ring he had examined the day before. The spacious tunnel was made of coquina stones. He could walk without hunching over and stretch his arms out far enough that his fingers barely touched the walls. It was humid and a strong bitter odor, like a mixture of smoke and sweat, permeated the passage. Now and then, he saw occasional recesses with rusty and corroded candleholders. Cobwebs filled the corners. A few cockroaches stood in their tracks surprised by the unexpected visitor.

As he plowed forward, some of the scavengers scurried up to the ceiling and others flew over his head. A couple of beady eyes sparkled in the darkness as the tunnel veered toward the left. A long tail hid beyond the bend. As he probed deeper the flame flickered and became dimmer. Heaviness in his throat and chest set in. He welcomed the presence of rats ahead of him, for it meant that at least some air was seeping in. A few steps farther on, he noted a large puddle. From the ceiling, large drops of water plunked down on the dark gleaming surface with a loud metallic click. The flame of his candle surged. Blinded by the light, a horde of rats darted past him brushing his legs while emitting high-pitched cries. He stayed put.

After trudging along for perhaps another four hundred yards, he reached a bifurcation. He picked the left branch and kept going. Farther down, a pair of dried-up leather sandals lay on the floor next to a rusty sword. Unlike the Muslim design, its blade was straight and crumbled into small pieces under his foot except for the dark guard and pommel. He squatted down to examine it closely. It bore a blurry Latin inscription which read *Gades Erculi Victori*, "Gades to Hercules the Victor," alluding to the legend of the Greek god who visited Gades in ancient times. He put it down and ploughed along for another couple hundred yards in the midst of a sepulchral silence. Not a living creature stirred. Next to him, his own ghost-like shadow crept up the wall toward the ceiling. It trembled with each one of his steps as the screeching noises of rats and the overhanging cobwebs returned. A cloud of cockroaches flew overhead. He ducked, but they carpeted his face for a moment, the bugs impervious to his swatting and gesticulations.

He advanced about ten feet and bumped into the dead end of the passage. A small stoop led to a corroded contraption attached to the wall. It was made up of a large rusty dentate wheel and a long metal handle. He yanked at the lever several times but nothing moved. He tried once more and this time a sharp snap was followed by a hesitating wail of the wheel. A large rock moved. It revealed a crack through which he could see the garden of the castle. The door opened enough for him to slip through.

A crescent moon had begun to climb the late evening skies. The spring freshness greeted Alvaro and relieved his fatigue. Crickets were strumming their legs and an almond fragrance filled the air. Fatimah sat at the pond alone. Alvaro approached her hunching over under the trees and whispered her name. Her expression lit up when she saw him and approached his hideout. He embraced her and covered her hands with kisses. They lay on their backs next to each other holding hands and looking at a sky teeming with stars, which shone more brightly than ever before.

"Venus lies close to the Moon," she said.

"They are seeking each other like us"

"This is far too dangerous. If my father finds out … he loves me, but he will follow the *Shariah* to the letter and execute us."

"Our love is a gift from Allah. Why should he steal from us what He has blessed us with?"

"Go away now. Soon the guards will start their rounds. I will see you in four weeks. My father is taking my sisters and me to Cordoba to visit our cousin Abd ar-Rahman, Al Nasir, the Caliph."

After a few days, Alvaro felt emptiness inside him, for his beloved was so far away. As the weeks passed, the void turned into uneasiness and later into a ghastly sensation. It was a terrible foreboding that some misdeed might come to Fatimah. His sleep became restless. He dreamed of an open country covered with bare soil where several people lay dead devoured by wild animals. The beasts had been so fast that none of the victims had stood any chance to survive. It was a clear day and a small crowd of frightened onlookers regarded the corpses. Alvaro could not understand their fear because he saw only a pack of inoffensive white dogs roaming around. In the middle of the field, a young woman rushed close to him, seeking protection. Unexpectedly, the dogs charged him and suddenly turned into black bulls. He feinted to his right and fooled the animals so they stampeded past. To protect her, he turned around to embrace the young woman, but she was gone. He looked up and observed a white dove flying high in the sky. The dream unsettled him for a few days. Once the waiting period came to a close, he set forth for the secret tunnel.

That night he found her in the garden. She wore a long white dress, which made her look more beautiful than ever, and her eyes sparkled with love. High in the sky, a crescent moon witnessed the warm embrace of the young lovers. The world was at rest. The stars twinkled overhead, and the garden was carpeted with the dried petals of flowers that had fallen from the almond trees and had been replaced by lush green leaves.

The silence enwrapped them like a veil, but in the midst of their passionate breathing, they could hear the rippling sound of the fountains, the yawn of a sleepy guard, or the occasional tweet of an insomniac sparrow. Alvaro felt her tears slip over his hand and noted sadness in her expression. Something was rending her heart to pieces.

"My darling, I am the Caliph's betrothed," she said. "A sumptuous wedding will take place in two weeks. I know my father wants the best for me, but ..."

"That is a great honor for you and your family ... and a terrible loss for me, I must confess. But if you are happy, I will be happy for you. "

"I do not love him. I do not want to be one among many wives and concubines. I love only you."

"I care for you with all my heart. But if he loves you and you give him a male son, you will be his favorite. You will become the new *al-Sayyida al-Kubra ... the Great Dame.*"

"I do not want that. I want to live a quiet life ... my husband, my children and just enough wealth to sustain my family. I do not want to share my husband with anyone. There is nothing that I yearn more than living a simple life with you. I dislike power and influence. They do not lead to happiness and are enemies of love."

Alvaro told Fatimah about his nightmare, about the dogs turning into killer bulls, about the dove flying away from him, about his fears of losing his life's one love. He hugged her and kissed her. She shuddered. He drew a small silver knife, made a small incision in his hand, another in hers, and pressed the two wounds together. Their droplets of blood fused in a warm embrace. They looked into each other's eyes and promised eternal love.

"Nothing will separate us," Alvaro said. "I'll love you beyond this life. If something happens to me, wait for the almonds to bloom under the crescent moon. I'll return to you."

"You must go. The Caliph has added more guards to protect me."

"We have no time to waste. I am coming back tomorrow. I will prepare two fast horses to escape to the Christian Kingdom of Leon."

"Not to Leon. Abd ar-Rahman Al Nasir is a blood relative of Ramiro's, the king of Leon."

"Then, we will travel farther north."

Fatimah handed him a handkerchief embroidered with her name that smelled of perfume. Alvaro caressed the dainty silk and rushed away. She raised her eyes to heaven and closed them in a prayer. Footsteps sounded nearby. Guards approached the pond just as she saw his shadow reach the wall that led to the tunnel. She stood up and walked toward the palace to divert their attention. He scrambled back inside and fled by the skin of his teeth. Upon returning home he was missing the handkerchief and concluded that he must have dropped it during his escape.

The guards found the handkerchief pinched between two large stones in the wall. Their attempts to pluck it out failed, so they dug it free with their knives. The captain of the guards informed the *Hajib* about the newfound evidence. One of the guards also believed that he had seen the shadow of someone running toward the wall. He discounted it because he saw the *Hajib's* young daughter walking toward the palace. No one thought anything unusual. Everyone knew of her eccentricity, of her penchant for spending the late hours of the night in the garden alone. It was clear to them that there was a secret tunnel into the castle although no one knew how to open the door, short of tearing down the wall. The captain of the guards handed the handkerchief to the *Hajib*.

The embroidered name of his daughter on the handkerchief brought him to tears. The idea that she could be part of a conspiracy against him seemed too incredible. She loved him. Besides, she, the Caliph's betrothed, could use her power to destroy him by merely expressing her desire to her beloved. Why would she resort to secret passages and accomplices? It made no sense. He forbade the captain and the guards from discussing the incident with anyone and decided to reinforce the vigilance. Constant

surveillance should be kept over the wall where the handkerchief was found and all efforts should be directed to finding the
mechanism that would open the secret passage. The old archives
should be opened and the castle plans scrutinized. He instructed
them to watch his daughter closely as soon as she walked out of
the harim, and organize additional patrols to scout the environs
of the castle as far as the beach. The tasks were to be carried out
without raising any suspicion. He then held the handkerchief at
arm's length from its upper edge and let it hang down away from
him as if contaminated with a contagious disease. He looked at it
with sadness, handed it back to the captain, and said,

"Get rid of this."

Fatimah noticed more activities than usual in the castle. At
first she blamed it on her new status that called for more protection. Her sleep was restless. The prospects of leaving her family
and her homeland for a foreign country loomed large before her.
There was no hope of ever returning as long as the Caliph lived.
But she could not envision herself in the arms of such a cruel
man. The ogling expression in his blue eyes aroused such loath-
ing in her. Her father would never pardon her either. To him
she would be dead. Her love for Alvaro towered over any other
feeling.

"*La ilaha illa Llah*—there is no God but Allah," she said.
"Please, grant Alvaro and me happiness and togetherness. Forgive
me for marrying him and forgive him for not embracing Islam.
But he loves You and follows the teaching of Jesus, Your Prophet,
(*Salla-Llahu Alaihi wa-salam*—peace and blessing be upon him.)
Let our pure love be our prayer to You."

In the early hours of the morning she felt her invocation rising
to heaven as solitary as a lonely pilgrim in the middle of a desert.
As the stars faded away and the sun rose hopeful and vibrant,
her mood turned eager with excitement. She smiled and giggled
with a nervous laugh. Her cheeks glowed with a pinkish color as
her eyes shone with love. Sensations, alien to her, surfaced from
the most recondite areas of her heart. She desired him. She could
hardly wait to make love to him. Her passion fused with fear

as the moment of leaving for the garden approached. Her sister Zayna observed her mood.

"The Caliph's betrothed finally shows happiness and excitement in her face as the wedding day draws near," she said.

"Oh, Zayna, my sister, I am happy but I will miss my family and my hometown Qadis ... the crimson sunset far away in the sea, the resplendence of the moon, the stars twinkling on the surf."

"You will have the power to enjoy anything you want. You are now the most important woman in the caliphate of Al Andalus. Did you notice how the castle has been reinforced with more sentinels? I overheard something about a secret passage into the castle ... something about an intruder."

"An intruder?"

"I heard a guard talking."

"Zayna, do not be prone to gossips. It is not proper for a lady from a noble family like you."

As soon as her sister left, Fatimah wrote a note:

"Alvaro, my love, I just learned that our trysts and the secret passage have been discovered. My father has not said anything to me; he must be plotting against us. You must hide and stay away from me.

Let Allah grant you a long and happy life.

Yours forever,

Fatimah"

Fatimah folded the note and crammed it inside a tiny basket attached to Delilah's right leg. The pigeon raised her head proudly, her eyes stern like an eagle's, turned her neck left and right, and stretched her wings as if she had waited for this moment all her life. Her owner cradled her on her outstretched hand, leaned over the ledge of her bedroom window and gently nudged the bird on. The pigeon took off at great speed.

As Delilah flew high, Alvaro was still at home getting his accoutrements ready for his trip. He had spent the previous night awake. Leaving his father alone, now that he had reached old age, caused him great distress. Today at lunch, father and son sat at the long dining table opposite each other. The servant brought a cold soup with tomato, parsley, and cucumber. It was fresh and delicious but Alvaro did not feel like eating. He went through the motions but desisted. He did not seem to be sick, so his father smiled to himself, looking down at his plate. The old man remembered how weak appetite led the flurry of symptoms when he fell in love for the first time. The accuracy of his assessment became evident when his son did not even touch the plate of veal glazed with a mixture of honey, almonds, and raisins. The dish tasted so good that had he been in his usual state of mind, he would have licked his fingertips afterwards. Besides, his eyes shone with the warm expression of love. Alvaro, who had always enjoyed a conversation with his father at the table, remained silent, his lips quivered as if ready to reveal the name of his love.

After staying a while in the dining room, Alvaro stood up, kissed his father on the forehead and, following a respectful bow, retired to his quarters. Back in his bedroom, he pondered the biblical forefathers who were called to make similar sacrifices such as his father was about to endure. Their children set off from them to populate remote areas, bearing the absolute certainty that they would never meet again here on earth. Fathers and offspring submitted to God's designs. But, he realized that those children departed with their elders' blessing. His father was entitled to an explanation. He wished he could bid him farewell in person, but that was not a choice. He wrote a note explaining the reasons for their elopement. It ended as follows:

" ... *meu Sidi—my Father— I know that your love is unselfish and you value my happiness far and beyond any concern. I implore you; bless us in the name of God. I will send you news as soon as we set foot on safe Christian land.*

Your son who worships and loves you,
Alvaro"

He kissed the letter. He thought how fortunate the paper was, for it would feel the touch of his father's fingers when he, most likely, would never again. He sealed the envelope and laid it propped against a blue cushion on top of his white-and-blue bedcover. A large crucifix hung on the wall overlooking the room. A prayer came from his lips almost instinctively. He opened the cash drawer in a built-in cupboard and withdrew all his money. He slung two blankets over his shoulders, picked up a pair leather waders with one hand, seized a small cage with two carrier pigeons with the other, and went down to the stable.

At this very moment Fatimah lingered at her window watching Delilah fly above the towers in the direction of Alvaro's home. The bird barely cleared the walls of the castle when a barrage of arrows zipped through the air. The wounded pigeon spun around, swooped down a short distance, regained control of one of its wings for a split second, and nose-dived into the sea. A shiver ran down her owner's body as she backed away from the window. Outside a racket broke out. Guards rushed around trying to locate the window from which the conspirator had launched the carrier pigeon. Others climbed down the cliffs, searching for the bird in the water. The weight of the arrow had sunk the impaled courier deep into the sea. Fatimah stayed in her room waiting for them to come and detain her, but nothing happened.

Everything turned calm again in the castle. The sun cast a purple-red veil on the horizon. The day waned and the murmuring breeze from the sea coddled the town like a baby in its mother's arms. But, the serenity did not envelope her mind, which raced with fear for her beloved's life. The voice of the muezzin calling to prayer pierced the silence of the evening,

"La ilaha illa Llah"

She kneeled on her golden prayer rug facing Mecca and implored Allah for help. As she stood up, she could see through the pink silk curtains of her window overlooking the garden that the palm trees were gently swaying in the wind. The salty taste of her tears rekindled her forebodings. She composed herself and opened the gold clasp of a wooden chest. She picked out a long white silk gown with a high collar and a rose with its stem embroidered on the left side of her bodice. Two horizontal stripes of tiny roses circled the borders of the dress and its wide sleeves. From her jewelry box, she selected the Caliph's wedding gift: a diadem, a necklace, and two bracelets, all set with large rubies surrounded by small diamonds. A shoulder-length white-lace veil studded with tiny pearls and a pair of red ballerina shoes embroidered in gold completed her attire. She stepped out of her room and summoned Raina. The maidservant was struck by her mistress's appearance and the determination glowing in her eyes. She asked her where she was going in her best so late in the evening. She replied with an order,

"Please, call the captain of the guards. I need to see him about an important matter."

Fatimah and Raina walked down to the salon where the captain was waiting. The young man stood at attention with his arms folded on his chest as if ready for combat. His thick black beard and dark haughty eyes emphasized his warrior's countenance. The maidservant stayed behind at a prudent distance as the mistress approached the captain. He bowed respectfully and for a moment shifted his gaze back and forth between the mistress and her servant.

"I must depart immediately for Cordoba. I need to talk with the Caliph," Fatimah said. "It is unsafe here. My carrier pigeon was killed. She was on her way to deliver a message to him. Line up your men outside and I will pick my own escort. He will be furious when he learns of this incident. Someone is plotting against me!" Her external sternness belied her internal fears. She prayed that the captain would bow out and allow her to leave soon enough to get to the beach and warn Alvaro.

"Your Highness, we have orders from the *Hajib* to disallow any communication with the outside or grant any exit permit without his approval."

"If you value your head ..."

"My head has no value. I am at your service Your Highness. You are free to go anywhere in the palace. It is now safe. We secured the secret tunnel and did away with the intruder," he said as he bowed to excuse himself.

"What intruder? You must be bluffing!"

He pulled out a piece of cloth and said,

"We found this on him. Do you recognize it?"

Upon seeing her handkerchief, she stood like a statue, an icy coldness overtaking her body. After the moment of bewilderment, she mustered her strength and plodded along toward her room. From her window, she observed the huge stone door to the tunnel wide open. In the twilight, its entrance was darker than a dragon's maw. She opened her jewelry box again and rummaged among golden rings, earrings, pendants, and pearl strings. Down at the bottom was the blue acorn-shaped bottle with *atropa* that her physician had prescribed a year earlier. She plucked it out and uncorked it. It was full and gave off a nauseatingly pungent odor.

She swallowed the potion in a single swig. It had a cloying aftertaste. She smacked her lips and lay down on her couch. An eerie silence followed. She kept her eyes open, expecting something to happen, but only a great peaceful feeling engulfed her. She daydreamed of paradise where she would meet Alvaro, amidst angels, florid landscapes, delicate fragrances, and oceans of love. A little breeze parted the blue silk curtains of her windows and the last purple-red clouds of the evening burst forth before her. The tops of the palm trees swayed in the wind. Her face felt aflame, her heart pounded, the room spun around, and the golden heptagonal and floral designs of the wall tapestries transformed into snakes and scorpions. The creatures wiggled and crawled off the fabric toward the ceiling and floor. She placed her hand on her mouth to stifle a cry. A convulsion seized her body rendering her unconscious. Her arms, legs and face jerked uncontrollably as the air trapped in her lungs burst out with a loud scream.

At this time Alvaro rode along the beach on Centinel, with a second horse cantering next to him. Under the light of the crescent moon, the starry night stirred alight. The waves drummed on the rocks, the surf bellowed, the breeze murmured. He slowed down. Paced by the trotting, his mind ran away with him. Now that the departure from home was behind, he felt liberated. He thought of his beloved, of their impending embrace, of their forthcoming happiness. A cave carved in the rock by high tides and bad weather served as a temporary stable. He tied the horses to a rock, laid down the accoutrements, and hurried toward the mouth of the nearby Roman tunnel. Centinel growled, but Alvaro's distracted mind did not heed the warning. He scrambled inside the tunnel, lit a candle, and a barrage of arrows assailed him.

The news of the deaths of Fatimah and Alvaro was announced to the townspeople as two unrelated events. Her death was blamed on an acute illness and his on a hunting accident. Large crowds attended their separate funerals. A few days later, their parents met in private at the palace. Count Julian read the note left behind by his son. Both old men had a hard time containing their tears.

"You and I understand that this union would have never been possible," the *Hajib* said. "Allah has willed their death. Let us be content with His will.

The fathers were not contented and their suffering ended only with their own lives, which happened in less than a year. Fatimah and Alvaro had been interred in the same cemetery, each in the area reserved to those of their faith. Their corpses were laid to rest at odds with each other, hers on her right side facing Mecca, and his on his back facing heaven. Little by little the real story of what went on the night of their deaths reached everyone's ears. Rumors grew that Alvaro's ghost lingered in the tunnel. Gossipers claimed that his imploring voice rose to God praying for the return of his beloved. Some even swore that he walked on the beach, scanning the horizons searching for her. Others recounted that when the crescent moon shone in the sky, his spectrum left the abode and sat inside the castle at the pool waiting for Fatimah.

The story turned into a legend that passed on from parents to children as they sat idly chatting in the lull hours of the evening. Sometimes it gained new credence when recent sightings came to light. A few neighbors reported a young man in a long white tunic with rectangular neckline and wrist cuffs decked with embroideries, the details of which could not be distinguished in the moonlight. His hair was dark and he seemed to float or slide over the seashore, his robe unruffled by the breeze. Some even claimed to have seen him walking through walls or entering the mouth of a cave where no one had ever dared go for fear of dying.

Now after so many lifetimes have gone by and the spring of the year of Our Lord 2003 shines in full bloom, local fishermen report a distinct sound. It's a winsome feminine voice, which has ridden the sea waves stirred by the East wind and has spoken in Arabic, invoking the holy name of Allah. They believe that like the wind, the words come from North Africa from as far as the Sahara Desert. The visions coincided with the moment that Alvaro first saw Fatimah picking up little shells. She basks in the happiness of her return to her homeland, the pristine foamy waters carpeting the rocks, the dance and shrills of the seagulls high in the sky, the minty scent and cool caresses of the sea breeze. Even the air floats full of lights, twinkling as if embedded with tiny crystals. Her mortal remains have been away ever since her father moved her grave to the land of his ancestors across the ocean in the neighboring continent. He wanted to end the story of the young Christian's ghost waiting for his daughter. The stratagem did not work. Now, Fatimah feels her beloved's closeness and longs for him. She remembers his promise, and as she gazes at the little scar on her right thumb, sensations of her blood mixing with Alvaro's erupt alive again: the warm taste in her mouth, the music of rippling waters, the sweet fragrance of almond flowers—everything enwrapped in the moonlight. Her prayers have been answered and now she waits for the crescent moon to reign in the sky for the covenant to be fulfilled. Shaped like a cutout segment from a cotton cloud, the moon's timid silhouette rises in the east, as a bold sun dips into the water. The anticipation of their tryst grows with the waxing tide. After the seabirds have retired to their sandy beds and Venus has awakened blinking like a somnolent bride, a smiling moon witnesses the anxious lovers' eternal embrace.

"*Gloria in excelsis Deo*—Glory to God on high," a masculine voice praises in tenor tones.

"*Allahu akbar*—God is great," a woman's exclamation echoes nearby.

Some witnesses observe a couple in white walking hand in hand on the beach under the silvery lights of the Muslim moon. The lovers cast no shadows in the glorious night. Yet a strong almond fragrance trails in their wake as they glide over placid waters toward the distant horizon, where they fuse with the mist joining the ocean and the sky.

AN ERRAND FOR GOD

His voice sounded warm and soft, but I could not see Him.

"Don't forget what I have asked you to do!" He said, reminding me of the errand He had entrusted me with.

There was a big screen of flowers, red, yellow, white, pink, purple, and other colors that I had never seen before. There were roses, daisies, carnations, chrysanthemums, orchids, and other big and small flowers that I could not recognize. In the beginning I believed I had dreamed the whole event. Being a neurologist I started to discern the facts.

I examined my face in a mirror. Cold sweats covered my forehead and my lips looked as pale as marble. I felt heaviness in my chest and a light flutter lingered in my heart. I knew that I had a heart ailment, which had been kept under control by a distinguished cardiologist, the best in this country. Nevertheless, I concluded that I had had a near-death experience, a transient cardiac arrest. In the past I had found patients who reported dramatic stories during these episodes: floating freely out of their bodies, trips through a long tunnel with intense light at the end, paradisiacal visions, celestial music, luminous beings, panoramic views of their own life. Some even claimed to have seen the blinding light of a Supreme Being. I only saw the screen of flowers and heard His voice,

"I am Papa Dios"

He said His name in Spanish, for that is my first language. Then He gave me instructions,

"You must tell others what I look like."

"I cannot see You. The flowers are in the way."

"I have already shown Myself to you before."

"God, even if I could see You now, You are picking the wrong person. I can only draw the rough outlines of ducks and donkeys."

"Well, that is one of the reasons why I chose you. I don't like people to venerate My image."

Initially the more I thought about my vision, the more I considered it to be a real experience. I thought about what the Bible says about seeing God. On one hand, Psalm 105:4 reads, "Seek the Lord and His strength; seek His face evermore!" On the other hand, the sacred book also says:

"So the Lord said to Moses, 'I will also do this thing that you have spoken; for you have found grace in My sight, and I know you by name.'

And he said, 'Please, show me Your glory.'

Then He said, 'I will make all My goodness pass before you, and I will proclaim the name of the Lord before you. I will be gracious to whom I will be gracious, and I will have compassion on whom I will have compassion.' But He said, 'You cannot see My face; for no man shall see Me, and live.'" (Exodus 33:17-20)

I believed these biblical verses were conclusive: we should look for His face all our life, but with the certainty that we would only see Him after our death. If I had really seen His face I would not be alive now. Yet maybe my near-death experience had qualified as a true death and, therefore, I had been allowed to see Him for a moment. But the harder my mind strained to recall His image the bigger the void in my memory.

My cardiologist adjusted my medications and after a week my heart was ticking properly again. I felt great. My recollection of the event became remote. I began to doubt the accuracy of my diagnosis. The idea that everything had been a dream took root. We doctors cannot judge ourselves well, so my uncertainty about what I heard and saw grew more and more as time passed. But illness often finds its way back to continue the inexorable destruction of our bodies. A year later I experienced another episode. This time there were no flowers, but I heard His voice again,

"How could you doubt your own diagnosis ... you, a neurologist with so much experience?"

After I came to I felt the same telltale signs and symptoms—the sweating, the paleness, the chest pain. The existence of my near-death experiences was now clearer to me than a midday sun on a cloudless day. I felt ashamed and incompetent. His words reverberated in my mind,

"You must tell others what I look like."

"God, let me see—"

The rest of my request went unsaid for I found myself sitting in my armchair again. This time there was no screen of flowers, and yet I was not able to see Him.   The conclusion burst upon me: I had not looked at Him face to face during my near fatal episodes; I had not even caught a glimpse of Him. Since He had not given me any clues, His errand loomed as insurmountable.

I figured that He had credited me with more intelligence than I really had; that I would realize when and where I had seen Him and get down to the task at hand; and that He must have made Himself visible in the face of someone close to me, perhaps just for an instant.   It was a type of transfiguration. I tried to recall faces during the happy episodes in my life. I approached it like any diagnosis, step by step, beginning with my childhood and working my way up. I rummaged through my foggy early years, my mother's face as she washed dishes and cleaned the house, my sister's as she sang louder than our neighbors while helping my mother with her daily chores, my father's smiling face in his security guard uniform as he alighted from his bicycle and walked into our home after a twelve-hour working day, my brothers' awed faces when we discovered one of the old underground tunnels that had been used by the people in my hometown to escape from pirates' sieges.

I continued with my school years, my graduation, my marriage, the birth of my children and grandchildren. All to no avail. I looked into my bad times, of which I had plenty too—my grandmothers', aunts', and uncles' deaths, illnesses in my family, serious stresses in my medical practice. Those memories were even foggier. Our brain does not like to keep sharp images of bad memories. I could not see His face anywhere. At night I invoked Him and prayed, trying to obtain a clue. His answer was a deafening silence. As weeks passed I found no solution to the puzzle. I became more and more frustrated.

"Why are You doing this to me?" I kept asking. "I know you are God but You are ticking me off! If You want to take me, take me. Why do You subject me to this mental torture?"

After pondering for a while I concluded that the adult human brain might not be able to perceive His face. As we get older we lose the ability to ascertain the real meaning of what is going on around us. We listen to other people's words and their mere phonetics obscures the real messages. As we look at their faces, we see the details of their physiognomy yet miss their true expression. As children, however, we receive information like antennae that can sense and see beyond the tangible reality.

I had already delved into my childhood unsuccessfully. My brain needed some help, some sort of evocation to access the memory storage. I boarded a plane and headed to Cadiz, my hometown in Spain. As I drove across the bridge overlooking the Bay of Cadiz, I instantly felt freshness on my face, as if my hometown had sent me a welcome kiss. One would think that such an ancient town would have a stale breath. On the contrary, I felt a surge of young energy, the sensation that its people were elated to embrace their prodigal brother. Now small, Cadiz boasted the pride and grandeur of a city that had been one of the most important metropolises of the Roman Empire. If only stones could tell stories—

After greeting my relatives, I got down to work. I walked through Puertas de Tierra, the two large arches in the stone wall that had surrounded the entire city—most of it still remained standing. Now two tall spiral columns towered before the fortification. Erected in 1945, the year I was born, they sustained the statues of St. Servando and St. German, the patrons of the city. When I was a baby, there was only a small door in the middle. My uncle Jose had been one of the workers who had torn down part of the wall to make room for a road connecting the old town to the outside communities. I was four or five years old when I wielded a small pick and helped him chisel the cement mortar off the surface of the big stones that he had just removed. He sat down rolling cigarettes, smoking, and watching me doing his job. His face was one of musing happiness. My uncle loved me, but he was not too fond of working. He would rather tell jokes and drink with his friends at one of the many neighborhood taverns. No, I thought, God would not look like him—or would He?

If anything, I thought that I might find His face under the disguise of my late aunt Mercedes, Jose's wife. She had always been busy, cleaning houses, mopping floors in government buildings, cooking, washing. Her face had a bluish discoloration caused by her heart disease, which would eventually end her life. She always wore a broad smile and I never heard her raise her voice. I spent Holy Thursday nights at her home on Botica Street, where I slept with my cousins while waiting for the procession of Jesus of Nazareth to parade by.

It was not until five in the morning that we heard the drums and bugles of the music band escorting the venerated image. Dressed in a purple tunic with gold embroideries, the figure of Christ bore a heavy cross on His right shoulder as His eyes brimmed with resignation, and His long black human hair waved in the wind. It rested upon a large gilded wooden float with baroque adornments. About forty *cargadores*—volunteer loaders—shouldered the heavy altar to atone for their sins or beseech for a desperate cause. My cousins and I woke up, got dressed, and stood on the balcony to watch the procession file through Barrio Santa Maria, one of the poorest neighborhoods. I watched my aunt implore Jesus and thank Him for all her blessings. Engrossed, she gazed at the image with an expression full of piety. Was her face His face? I did not think so. So many artists—Rafael, Murillo, Tintoretto, Michelangelo—had captured that sort of face so many times in paintings. I reasoned that God disapproved of any drawings of His face.

As soon as the procession had passed our balcony we rushed outside to bear witness to its arrival before the local jail, the Royal Prison, a block away. The stone neoclassic building boasted small barred windows and an impressive entrance with four marble columns. On its façade an inscription read:

"Hate crime but be compassionate with the offender."

It was customary to release a prisoner to commemorate the yearly procession. The face of this man was one of joy as the guards freed him. Yet his eyes shone with sadness and anger. No, God would not look like him. Once the procession approached Santa Maria Chapel, its final destination, a crowd blocked the last one hundred yards of the official itinerary. The faithful scrambled to postpone the end of the religious parade for fear of their upcoming apprehension—as strong as the unholy withdrawal from a potent drug—which would overtake them as soon as the float carrying the Nazarene crossed the threshold of the main chapel door amidst the cadence of the Spanish national anthem. It would mean the end of that year and the beginning of a drawn-out countdown until the next Holy Week. They were not about to allow it, not yet. Other volunteers replaced the worn-out *cargadores* underneath the float and, ignoring diocesan regulations, turned it around, swinging and moving it along the road with such grace that the figure of the Nazarene seemed to be walking. They carried it back to meet that of Our Lady. The latter had trailed behind and was now before the Royal Prison, about two hundred yards away.

After placing the two images in front of each other, they rocked them to the rhythm of the trumpets and drums as if at a pagan ritual dance. The crowd broke into applause and cheers. Everyone's faces bore signs of exultation. But even here I could not see God anywhere. I was disappointed. The scenery might have been perfect for the facial features of God to have become visible to my eyes: the sea waters spread over the rocks with layers of white foam, the silvery glade of the moonset undulated on the surf, the soft sea breeze wafted into the plaza and narrow streets next to the chapel, the twilights of dawn cast a dainty pink veil upon the horizon, the cathedral's yellow dome gleamed under a twinkling sky. Yet neither Mother Nature's nor man-made creations were enough for Him to show His face.

After a while the procession finally came back to its temple, where it had begun ten hours earlier.   The place was packed. Emotions surged to a crescendo. Taking turns, several people burst into singing *saetas*—flamenco religious songs—as the image paraded along the final stretch. My cousin Juani was one of them. I observed her expression as her eyes filled with devotion and the veins swelling on her neck. She gestured with entreaty and her voice grew beautiful and moving. Yet, where was the face of God?

I walked on the street where I was born, 15 Mirador Street, in Barrio Santa Maria. It was now well paved with granite blocks and the houses rehabbed and painted in white. When I was a child, the street had been covered with ballast stones and the houses had been dilapidated. I could still hear the bustle of the tough life of those years. My house no longer existed. Instead of the new building that stood before me, there had been an old two-story townhouse, where my grandmother had lived on the first floor. It was a three-room apartment that my relatives called *La Accesoria*. The most lateral was used as a living room and a kitchen and opened onto the street.   The rest were bedrooms. We counted ourselves among the privileged, because we had our own toilet bowl in one of the rooms. There, behind the brick wall, where the house used to be, I envisioned my grandmother Micaela's face after coming home from a long day's work in her fish shop at the Plaza de Abastos. Could God have shown His face through hers? She had a big heart. At her home there was always a piece of fried fish for the poor in the neighborhood. She did not let them go hungry. She died and one of her daughters, my aunt Lola, replaced her—the same look, the same big heart. Still I could not see His face on either of them.

Antonia, my late paternal grandmother, had resided across *La Accesoria*. She lived on a fourth floor and was so old and fragile that I never saw her step out of her home. I thought that maybe she might have known the answer to my quest. Otherwise how could she have smiled all the time? She went blind sewing clothes to put food on the table for her children after my grandfather died of the Spanish flu a couple of months before my dad was born. Maybe she had seen His face. Maybe He was close. Or was her face His face? Again I could not picture it.

I walked the streets of the neighborhood back and forth and even visited the new house that replaced the old *Posada*, which translates to inn in English. I had lived there with my family for two years. My mother would set a mousetrap and every morning I would wake up to find five or six mice inside the cage. Bigger than cats, huge rats promenaded around our kitchen as if they owned the place. Life flaunted its ugly side. I had been only three years old, yet looking at the remnants of the old building brought about fresh joyful memories. My younger brother's baptism was celebrated in the inner courtyard amidst music and dance. From the second floor, I saw the happy faces of those present. There was a short elderly man with white hair who played his accordion, pressing it, stretching it out, and then swinging it like a rocking chair. The instrument gave voice to celestial music. Yet I could not pinpoint His face.

Frustrated, I went to visit Santa Maria Chapel, just a block away, the place where the image of Jesus of Nazareth was venerated. Built upon leveled ground in the early sixteenth century, its façade fit like a wedge into the upper end of a narrowed high-sloping street. The main portal was made of oyster-stones, and featured two pairs of large pilasters, upon which rested an entablature. The façade stretched upward to a svelte tower with a belfry and a pyramid-shaped roof covered with blue and light brown ceramic tiles. Inside the church, a carnation fragrance welcomed me as flower bouquets lay at the feet of the altars. The main nave shone with a stunning, baroque, gilt wooden retable, which was graced with an image of Our Lady of Dolores, a crucified Christ, statues of saints, and elaborate leaf decorations. In an extension of this nave the image of Jesus of Nazareth stood in a niche at the center of a shrine. Every Friday parishioners went there to pray and kiss the image's feet. It was Monday and two nuns were fixing the cloak of the image. The statue stood naked. It had no body. The face, hands, and feet were all attached to a wooden frame. His image was not there.

Back in Chicago, tired and fatigued from my trip, I sat in my backyard. A couple of squirrels scurried along the fence and jumped to the trees. A pair of cardinals checked for food in the feeders. The sun was out and my wife's flowers were blooming. Lying next to me, my three-year-old granddaughter Lucia had fallen asleep. I observed her nacre-like eyelids and the beauty of her long eyelashes, her rosebud-shaped lips, her nostrils subtly opening with each soft breath, the tranquility of her expression, the contours of her arms perfect like a baby doll, her smooth hands, the tiny shiny stars glued on her thumbnails, the four dimples in between the svelte fingers of each hand. She was shear perfection for everyone to admire.

After a while Lucia opened her big precious eyes and, as she noticed me looking at her, she smiled. I saw my own image reflected in her honey-colored eyes followed by a subtle burst of colors as if her eyes had transformed the image into tiny butterflies and flowers. There, beneath her dancing eyelashes, beyond this chorus of colors trapped in the smile of her pupils, lay a mist of quintessential sweetness, a serene yet immense energy, a rhapsody of tender feelings. And inside this ethereal mass, as in a chapel, was the face of God. I saw Him for an instant. He had no eyes nor mouth nor white hair, just flaming tongues of pure, immaculate love.

CATHEDRAL OF CADIZ, SAGRARIO TOWER, AND SANTA CRUZ CHURCH

THE OLD MAN
AND THE DOG

I read in a major newspaper that five dogs had received official recognition for their heroic feats and were inducted into a hall of fame. The article reminded me of another dog that I knew as a youngster, whose deed would most likely be unsurpassed. The story went that Manuel, his owner, after his retirement from his job at the Zona Franca harbor in Cadiz, had found himself alone and bored. Darkened by faded-green shades, his apartment was on the first floor of the five-story building where his former cow-orkers and their families resided. He spent most of his days in his family room in a rocking chair, falling asleep as he listened to the radio or moping his hours away. Hanging from the wall in his living room was a large picture of his late childless wife. She was dressed in black with a tight bun on the back of her head. Ten years had gone by since her death and looking at her still brought tears to his eyes. Sometimes he even confused the squeals of his rocking chair with the murmurs of his weeping. The place had a kitchen but he never cooked. His meals consisted of a can of soup or a sandwich with thin slices of *mortadela*, ham, or cheese. Sometimes he made coffee. His small bedroom was in disarray, with sheets and blanket lying crumpled over a plain mattress. A sagging pillow was perched at the edge at the head of the couch, and a couple of cushions sat untouched on a chair ever since his wife left them there. A strong reek of humanity hovered.

The building was located on the outskirts of Cadiz, Spain, in the middle of a desolate field. It was bound on the west and south by a high brick fence, on the east by a dusty path next to a railroad, and on the north by a large dry field. The open land extended for over a mile and ended at a small recess in the Bay of Cadiz. No building could be seen within half a mile. Early in the morning his tall lanky figure would leave the house, wood cane in hand, a little slouched over, long nose, stern face, and a brown hat on. He strolled around the solitary building like a ghost, limping with his arthritic right knee. There was nothing there but arid land. Thorny shrubs and a few green weeds clung to life by tenuous roots. An occasional small snake, mouse, or rabbit scurried about. Only once had he ventured to cross the railroad tracks to enjoy marshes, small ponds, and eucalyptus trees, which graced the wet meadow on the other side. He sat under a tree and took in its fresh scent. Trills and songs of colorful goldfinches filled the air amidst the happy hubbub of the sparrows, jumping, flitting, and flying between the ground and the trees. On his way back home he brooded over minor problems, ignoring an approaching train that almost hit him. The near-mishap put an end to his thoughts of extending his walks to greener pastures.

Manuel had been born in the countryside and had moved to Cadiz thirty years earlier when he could no longer survive in Chiclana, a nearby small agricultural town. Two years after his retirement the depression became unbearable. He decided to close his apartment for a while and move back to his home-town. He picked up a few belongings and stowed them away in a banged-up cardboard suitcase, which he had kept since his induction into the army as a youngster. A bus took him back home. It was only a 40-minute ride, but the last time he had made this trip was fifteen years earlier when he attended his sister's funeral. His job had absorbed him completely. By now all his relatives had passed away except for his niece Micaela who lived abroad. Yet, nostalgia drove him to reclaim his past.

Manuel settled into a small inn near the river that divides his hometown in two. The stream had slowed to a trickle and the stink of stagnant water pervaded the surroundings. The town felt foreign to him. Buildings now sprawled far beyond the old boundaries and the bars and cafés that he used to patronize no longer existed. Even the fresh food market had moved to a different location. A walk to the small farm where he had grown up revealed fallow fields and a herd of cattle grazing on sparse grass. A strong stench of manure irritated his eyes. His house was gone and those of his former neighbors were dilapidated and empty. Shrubs and brambles overran them. The sun still shone high over the faraway gray mountains as it always had. A sweltering heat cracked the terrain, baking the crisp air, and drying the spines and cones, which carpeted the ground beneath the surviving pine trees. Nearby, whitewashed small houses adorned with flowerpots faced lush orchards that brimmed with oranges, pears, and apples. He asked about his old neighbors' whereabouts, but his inquiries failed to yield any results. The new tenants and landlords had never heard of them. He visited his parents' and his older sister's graves in one of the walls at the local cemetery. The weather-beaten inscriptions on their marble stones were effaced. Weeds grew and bloomed over the dusty edges. A feeling of impotency over the passage of time came upon him. He missed his apartment and a few days later he was back in Cadiz.

Routine set in again. Every morning he strolled toward the municipal slaughterhouse along the dusty path next to the railroad, and breathed in air tainted with the smell of the doomed cattle. The pungent odor brought back childhood memories.

"The world definitely spins around," he once said to himself. "After so many years I'm right back where my life began ... walking the countryside, smelling the cattle."

He sat down on a large square stone close to a bridge, which arched over the railroad tracks and then merged with the only road into the city. He enjoyed a cheese sandwich for breakfast. The place lay amidst prickly pears, but it was quiet. Silence was broken only by the clatter of the occasional car or truck passing over the bridge and the chugs of the passenger or freight trains marching along at their scheduled times down to the minute. He did not have any use for a wristwatch. Warning him of the approaching dawn, the express train rattled along past his window on its way to Madrid at six in the morning. When the Talgo arrived from Seville at ten, his daily walk began. At noon the Rapido sped through, and at 1:30 a regional from Jerez made its way into the town. He then headed back home.

One day in early May he set off for his usual ramble. Winds from the west had swept away most of the clouds leaving a pristine blue sky, and a bright sun began to warm the earth. He walked with the collar of his navy-blue jacket turned up and his scarf protecting his throat. Hunger pains struck him. He reached for the sandwich in his pocket. As he began to munch, he noticed a dog following him about twenty yards away. It was a medium-sized young male with a retriever's profile, dark golden fur, and brown patches on its flanks. The dog had the face of a beagle, long droopy ears, big brown eyes, and a white line between his eyes that extended down to his muzzle and belly. Manuel stopped to see if the dog would pass him by. He didn't. The animal paused, lifted his right leg against an electric pole by the railroad and peed. The old man turned around and proceeded along the path without realizing that the dog trotted after him with its tongue hanging down. As soon as he stopped, the dog sat down and stared at him from the distance of a few yards.

"Cluck, cluck, cluck," Manuel clicked his tongue against his teeth after swallowing a bite and said, "Go away, dog! Go away."

The dog sat, wagged his tail, and looked at him as if trying to understand.

"Oh! C'mon, go home! I don't like dogs." The old man was not in a good mood this day. He was never in a good mood.

The animal's long and thin tongue quivered with his breathing as his eyes shifted back and forth from the small piece of sandwich to Manuel's face.

"Oh, I see. You are hungry."

He tossed the food to him. The animal jumped up, caught the morsel, and gulped it down, his shiny eyes gazing at his benefactor. Manuel ambled on but now and then he turned around, surveying the path to make sure the stray dog had gone away. The dog sat for a while, eyed him from a distance, licked his lips, and scratched his belly frenetically with his hind leg. The third time the old man searched the dog was gone.

Manuel thought the animal had continued its daily foray. He pictured him digging into garbage cans, loitering around butcher shops or the slaughterhouse for a piece of gristly meat. Canine hunger might drive him to the tenements in El Cerro del Moro or Puntales, where a few goodhearted old women or children could feed him their leftovers. Maybe some young punk kids would stone him for fun or a dogcatcher who had his eye on him would lurk nearby, ready to end his days.

He felt sorry for the animal. Yet a pang of disappointment overcame him at the recognition that the dog was little different than his fellow man. As soon as the dog had gotten all that the old man possessed at that moment—the sandwich—he disappeared from the old man's life. His disillusionment made his mind go back to two years earlier when his niece Micaela had visited to inform him of her upcoming wedding. She asked him for money. He handed her all his savings, two thousand pesetas, an amount equal to his monthly pension, and a china set that his late wife had inherited from her mother. After that day she came over every few weeks to tote off some of his furniture to her home in Chiclana: four wooden chairs with ornate legs, a chest with a brass lock and a faded red coat of arms, a glass-top coffee table, and a floor lamp. Her words still resounded in his ears,

"Uncle Manuel, you live alone; you no longer need them. They bring you only bad memories."

Once nothing worth removing was left, she didn't return for almost a year. When she finally did, it was to say goodbye. She and her husband had decided to emigrate to Australia.

"The world is full of ungrateful people," he said to himself, still waiting and hoping for a letter or a Christmas card from her.

He then saw the dog on the other side of the railroad tracks, walking parallel to him. The animal trotted slowly, stopped every few steps, lowered his head, sniffed, sat and looked at him. The eyes gleamed in the sun like two firebugs. Manuel was a stone's throw from the dog, yet he felt a sense of companionship, which he had not experienced ever since his wife died. At that very moment, the sad reality of his forlorn life hammered him once again. He accepted it as something irremediable. He shook his head trying to chase away the intrusive thoughts. They stuck to him like those white snails that he saw clinging to the little leaves and branches of the shrubs flanking the path. By the time he reached the large stone block where he sat down, the sun began to heat the air. He removed his jacket and laid it next to him. The dog lolled nearby, staring at him.

"I don't know why you waste your time with an old man like me", he said. "I haven't had a dog since I was a boy. I loved my German shepherd. He was dark gray with long ears ... longer than yours. He was bigger than you, muscular, and had dark eyes. He had the solemn beauty of a brave bull. I don't mean to put you down. You are a good-looking dog too."

The dog jerked his head from side to side, scratched his left ear, and wagged his tail. His eyes remained fixed on his human companion. The animal lowered his head, laid it on his paws, and sprawled out comfortably on the grass.

"I remember his name, Chispa—Spark—we called him that because he was fast and witty. He played with me as if I were another dog. When I was four years old I used to climb on his back and when I grew older, we ran together around the farm all day. He knew what I wanted. In the morning he fetched my backpack full of books, walked me to the school, and then went back home. When I finished my school day, he would be outside waiting for me. We had a lot of fun. I remember when I went bird hunting. In those days meat was scarce, so if my father killed a pig or a chicken we sold it because we had no money. My mother fried the birds I caught, particularly, the large and meaty woodchat shrikes. In the morning, before starting my hunt, I stepped into my backyard and I dug out long worms to use as bait. I clamped them in the middle of their bodies with a pin from my spring-loaded wire traps and placed them down under bushes and small trees. Chispa did the rest. He chased the birds until they perched on the branches overlooking the traps. The wiggly worms attracted their attention. Those birds were always starving and as soon as they pecked at the bait the traps went off and zapped them dead. I felt sorry for the poor birds, but back then I was so hungry."

The dog reclined on the floor completely still, looking at the storyteller as if trying to understand what was being said. The animal's breathing accelerated and his tongue palpitated, drooping down longer and longer as the heat intensified.

"One day he got sick. I remember his eyes were red and teary. I put my arms around his back and petted him. I was crying. His breathing became faster and faster, heavier and heavier, as if there was not enough air to fill his lungs. He dropped his head and was gone. His death saddened me so much that ever since I have stayed away from dogs. Now you understand why I don't want you around me. You need to find another master because ..."

Suddenly the dog stood up with a growl, raised his ears, snarled fiercely, and jumped toward Manuel, snapping at the jacket which lay next to him. The old man cried out and dodged the onslaught.

"Crazy dog! What are you trying to do to me?"

He reached for his cane to stand up and defend himself. The dog had his garment in its mouth and was worrying it back and forth frantically. Dangling below the navy blue border of his jacket was something long, thick, round, gray, and cord-like. The cord wiggled. Its shiny scales and long zigzag stripes swung as blood dripped from the dog's mouth. As soon as the snake's body hung flaccid, the dog dropped it. The half-yard-long viper lay dead, the triangular head crushed in the middle. The needle-like tongue drooped limp, the vertical slit eyes shone open, and the tail lay curled like a corkscrew.

Awestruck, Manuel gaped at the snake and his savior. Blood oozed from two puncture wounds where sharp fangs had pierced the dog's muzzle. The animal whined in pain, the color of his eyes faded, and his wounds turned black and dark blue. The right side of the muzzle and cheek swelled up, displacing the ear upwards and backwards.

"Come with me. Don't cry,"

He caressed and patted the dog's neck and shoulders as the animal blinked, stuck his tongue out, and licked the caring hand.

"Let's go home so I can take care of your wound."

Manuel and the dog plodded along next to each other on their way home. The animal became short-winded and his loose tongue grew bluish and dry.

"I don't even know your name. Well, anyway, didn't your mother teach you not to attack snakes? I am old. My days are numbered. You shouldn't have taken such a risk for me."

The dog's legs trembled and almost buckled. He raised his brown eyes and seemed to gaze pitifully at the old man.

"That viper bit you hard. I don't know whether to name you. There's no point in naming a sick dog that might not make it. Well, I remember when one of my sheep was bitten in the leg by a snake. There were no vets nearby and my father said that it didn't matter anyway because they weren't helpful in these cases. I can still hear his words, 'Manuel, my son, fetch a couple of blankets, let's tie her legs down and flip her over, so her wound stays higher than her heart … and pray. If she survives the next 24 hours, she'll be fine.' He later explained that the venom weighed less than the blood, so if the leg was lower it could float up into the heart and kill her. But if the wound was higher, the venom would stay put. Anyway, I don't know why I'm talking to you as if you could understand me. People will think that I'm out of my wits … a senile old man."

Once at home the animal stood at the door for a moment, unsure whether to go in or wait outside. Manuel invited the dog in and he tentatively entered the apartment. The old man cleansed the dog's wounds with soap and water. The animal didn't utter a single complaint, but his eyes gazed at the healer with such gratefulness that their expression reminded Manuel of a little boy cuddled by his mother after she had kissed a boo-boo. To counteract the coldness of the floor, the old man spread a spare blanket under the dinner table and coaxed the dog to rest on its belly. A piece of rope served as a leash. He wrapped the makeshift leash with a towel to cushion the animal's neck and tied the free end around the tabletop with a loop to exert traction and keep the dog's head above the floor. The dog's pupils were so large that they filled the irises except for narrow greenish-brown rims, and its eyelids drooped halfway. The muzzle was cracked and dry. The dog was in severe pain. Manuel picked up the only blanket on his bed and put it on top of the animal. The dog shrugged it off.

"C'mon, let me take care of you. You are burning up with fever."

This time he swaddled the dog's furry trunk with the blanket and girdled it with his leather belt. His patient looked as pitiful as the wounded of a retreating army. Despite bouts of retching and coughing, the dog licked a crushed aspirin mixed with several tablespoons of apple juice from the old man's hand. Now and then he lapped water from a container atop a shoebox. A little saucer with milk sat untouched.

"Dog, you have to try harder. Milk can absorb poisons."

Any attempt the dog made to drink resulted in a white frothy regurgitation. For the next few hours, Manuel watched him closely. The blanket could not muffle the sound of the dog's chattering teeth as it endured repeated bouts of shivering. At times the dog's eyes drooped shut and made Manuel think that it had passed out. The old man patted the dog's withers and talked to him,

"Stay with me. This is no time for you to sleep. Death is treacherous and can slip inside you like water into a cracked roof."

The dog's eyes wandered and glanced at his caretaker woefully with a glassy luster.

"One should not be afraid of death. We all are going to die sooner or later. But you are a young dog. You have a life before you. At my age when I go to bed I always wonder whether I'll see a new morning. In the early dawn, when the express train to Madrid wakes me up, I thank God for another day. I fear pain, not death. I want to feel my death coming, to look at its face as it tears my life away. It is not that I have to say goodbye to anyone. I just don't want its dark shadow to close in on me and take me by surprise. A lot of people aren't aware of their departure from this world. But look at you ... only a dog and looking death straight in the eye—"

Suddenly, the dog closed its eyes. The animal sank into unconsciousness. It collapsed on the floor, its legs stiffened, its jaw clenched, and then its breath halted. The dog lay rigid like a board despite the old man's attempts to shake him awake. Manuel thought the dog had died. A few seconds later, the respirations returned, and the old man sighed with relief. The animal's legs rapped against the floor, and his mouth drooled copious amounts of saliva, as if life were overflowing from it like a waterfall from a river. A few minutes later, his eyes reopened.

"I thought you had kicked the bucket. Come to think of it, I don't know where you'd go if you died. I have been taught that we humans have souls and go to heavens if we have behaved in this life, but as far as I know dogs have no souls."

The dog shook his head and blinked a few times. After eagerly drinking water, he looked at the old man again, his eyes red and swollen from the convulsion.

"You look terrible, dog, but I still think you'll make it. If you don't, don't be sad because I' m sure that there must be a nice place for good dogs like you."

With an expression of extreme fatigue and resignation, the animal fixed his eyes on his caretaker.

"I mean, I'll be glad to have you up there with me. A lot of people love their dogs more than anything in this world. Some cannot even conceive of heaven without their loyal friends."

The night fell and Manuel stayed up, keeping the dog company until sleep overcame him. When he woke up in the morning, a complete silence had fallen upon the room. He wondered whether death had prevailed. But when he approached the limp motionless body, the animal licked the old man's hand and glanced up at him with life gleaming in his eyes. The threat had been defeated.

Free of the traction paraphernalia, the dog tottered out from under the table, shook his body, and sat next to his elderly healer.

"I'll name you Canelo since you are golden brown like *canela*—cinnamon. I hope you like it. Let me prepare something for you. You need to get your strength back."

Manuel cooked a beef stew. Except for a few pieces set aside for his own dinner later that day, most of the meat ended up on the dog's plate. The animal bolted down the food in a few minutes. The feast was followed by a bowl of milk that he lapped up eagerly. Both dog and old man were so tired that they did not go out for the next few days. The animal lay curled next to his master who reclined in his saggy armchair. The dog yawned so hard that his uvula dangled like a bell from the vault of his throat and his long red tongue slithered down almost to the floor. It was a peaceful rest. Now and then he opened his eyes, roused by the old man's roaring snores. The harsh rumbles could make the walls shudder and startle every resting creature around, including the sleeper himself. Manuel nudged his eyeglasses back up on the bridge of his nose and continued gazing at his magazine as if he had not missed a single line. His mind reveled in his inner comfort. He felt useful again. He looked forward to the next chance to take care of the dog, feeding him, bathing him, brushing his fur, and taking him out for his basic needs.

On one of their outings close to the building, Canelo caught fleas. The dog scratched his ears and his tummy with his hind limbs as if he were playing rock-and-roll with an electric guitar. Killing the fleas proved challenging. Armed with his reading glasses, Manuel searched the dog's belly and groin after the pet gracefully obliged by rolling on his back. Little dot-like bugs scurried out of sight from under his fingers. As a child Manuel had used his wet fingers to pluck fleas off his dog's fur and dip them into a bowl full of water. The minuscule creatures had swum themselves to death. He now counted thirty fleas and growled,

"C'mon, how did you manage to get so many fleas? I'm itching everywhere, my legs, my arms, my ears. I have no fingers left to scratch myself."

Manuel never found a single live flea on his own body, but the itching persisted for several days after the first bout of flea infestation. The animal basked in his newly found happiness. He capered around, jumped on his master's legs, licked his hands, yapped gratefully, and climbed upon his lap or sat next to him with eyes shining with love. The old man requited the affection by sliding a tremulous hand down over Canelo's withers and patting his forelimbs.

Positive changes began to take place in the apartment a couple weeks after man and dog's initial acquaintance. The sun peeked through the open windows and fresh air rich with the fragrance of the nearby sea flooded all the rooms. The illuminated old picture hanging on the wall somehow acquired a different hue, as if it now finally belonged to the past. The husband's love, respect, and deference to his late wife remained intact, but he no longer lived within the photograph. Free, Manuel sprang into a new existence. Aches and pains no longer troubled him as much. For the first time in many years, he saw himself smiling in a mirror. The neighborhood noise, which used to bother him so much, suddenly acquired a different meaning. He became aware of the playful children's voices, the women singing while cooking their food or hanging out their laundry, and the tolling bells from the faraway church. Even the clanging of the cowbells past his window, the murmur of the nearby ocean, or the whistling wind from the west enlivened his senses like a splash of cold water on his face.

Manuel and his dog spent day and night together. If he left the room and walked to the kitchen, the dog stood up and followed him like a shadow. If he went out to the bakery, the dog would wait outside the store until his master had completed his errand. His pet also accompanied him on his bimonthly visit to the local hospital, where the old man had been getting remedies for arthritis. The dog made Manuel feel safe. He ventured through a shortcut covered by a canopy of leafy trees and flanked by cottages full of palm trees. At one, a large green parrot with contrasting vivid red feathers was perched in a large cage hanging on the porch. Upon seeing the dog, it became agitated, jumped onto the wall of its cage, and began to cry out,

"Lola, Lola, a dog! A dog! Watch your cat!"

"Woof, woof, woof ..."

"Oh, stop it, Canelo," the old man said. "It's just a crazy bird."

They kept on walking and arrived at the hospital, the Residencia Sanitaria Zamacola.

The seven-story facility, shaped like a three-cornered hat, sprawled along the main avenue leading to the old town of Cadiz. The emergency room stood on the west side and the out-patient wing was on the east. A low iron fence separated both areas from the street. The facility bustled with patients and their relatives walking in and out through a huge entrance supported by three columns in the middle of the façade. Manuel disliked going there. He saw a woman in a black dress and a black head kerchief cry into her hands. A little girl quietly held on to the woman's skirt and an older boy sobbed by her side.

"I hate coming to the hospital, Canelo. There is so much suffering in this world."

The dog shook his head. The old man entered the outpatient department through a lateral gate as his pet sat outside near the fence waiting for him. A couple of hours later he came back and both returned home.

The new master realized that his young dog's muscles needed more physical activity than an old man's company could offer. So he kept the kitchen window ajar to let Canelo jump down and frolic around an inner courtyard shared by several families. Since there were not any other dogs around, most neighbors welcomed him. The animal often lingered near their windows, munched their treats, and after a while bounced back home to be with his master. In the morning the old man sat on the front stoop and played fetch with the dog. Canelo enjoyed the game and became a fast catcher. After a while Manuel tricked the animal by feigning to throw a stone but instead hiding it in his pocket. Immediately the animal barked at Manuel's his right shirt pocket. After making sure that the dog didn't see him, Manuel laid the stone out of sight atop a nearby high windowsill. The animal lifted his face, barked at Manuel twice, and after the old man showed the dog his empty palms, Canelo scampered around sniffing. Circling the area, the dog searched every single spot where he had previously retrieved thrown stones. Canelo ended up under the windowsill, jumping up and barking at the concealed object.

"I can't fool you, can I? You could have made your living as a hunting dog."

The company of his dog encouraged the old man to cross the railroad tracks again and expand his daily rambles. He went close to the bay waters. Little silvery snappers made ripples on the surface looking for food, and bass huddled together near the wild tomato plants that grew alongside the shore. He sat on the sea rocks, dug a few oysters, and ate them raw. Nearby lay Cortadura Beach, which was part of the sandy coastline that extended over a hundred miles up to the Rock of Gibraltar. A few young boys were catching crabs next to a stone fortification built two centuries earlier to stop the offensive of Napoleon's troops against the city. He strolled south along the beach. The dog jumped into the blue waters, shook off the cold water, and soaked his master to the skin.

"Stop it! Canelo, behave. It's cold. You are going to give me pneumonia."

After a short while, the old man and the dog turned around and walked toward Victoria Beach. The seascape was framed by the silhouette of the ancient city of Cadiz: the wondrous cathedral with its dome shaped like a giant topaz, rising above buildings as white as seagulls; the forest of spindly towers of nearby churches; the rampart of the Campo del Sur and its breakwater blocks, where the sea waves climb to the parapet.

At the beginning, Canelo had a playful tendency. On the daily walk with his master, he still sniffed and pissed on every smelly spot along their route. The old man's disgruntled murmurs changed this behavior. Over a period of few years, little by little almost imperceptibly, a transformation, a metamorphosis, evolved in both of them. The old man took on the patience and solicitousness of his dog. His walk rejuvenated as if he had drawn in energy from his young companion. He would stride with his gaze straight ahead, shoulders upright, a sprightly facial expression, and a firm step down the path. His limp became almost imperceptible as his cane tapped against the ground in time with each step. Likewise, Canelo's physiognomy, his demeanor, even the rhythm of his limbs resembled those of his human soulmate. As both grew older—the old man aging faster—the outlines of the man walking his dog fused into a single profile yoked together by an unbreakable bond.

There were disagreements too. The old man liked to dine with his dog in the kitchen, so he had arranged Canelo's food plate and water bowl in the corner. Yet the animal insisted on carrying the pieces of meat one by one to the family room and devouring them on the rug next to the window.

"Canelo, stop it! You are making a big mess!"

The dog froze, lowered his tail, and took a sidelong glance at his master. A few minutes later he approached him to make sure he still loved him. The next day brought a rerun of the same scene.

Their lives rolled on uneventfully for a few years, both dog and master basking in the sweet lull of daily routine. With the passage of time the old man's health began to falter. On bad days his gait turned a little unsteady, and his right leg limped more than usual. The dog could sense the old man's struggle long before it became evident. Canelo stopped and barked twice to signal that both should turn around.

"You noticed, didn't you?" Manuel once said. "I get fatigued. It's normal. I'm an old man. But don't worry I don't plan to leave this world yet. Do you know that a dog ages in one year as much as a man does in five? You might still catch up with me."

The dog gazed at Manuel with alert eyes. Canelo's tongue hung down. He shook his head briskly and continued on his way back home at a slower pace. Upon arrival, the master sat down and asked his dog to fetch his slippers and a pillow. The animal complied without hesitation, reclined next to him, and waited for the old man to feel rested.

One day they were returning from their evening walk as the sun dipped into the ocean. The sky blushed and an intense luminosity painted the clouds purple and the horizon pastel pink. The wind died off, leaves rustled on their twigs, and a cotton moon hung overhead as bird songs erupted from the trees and bushes around. Manuel watched his dog next to him. Canelo was a joyful figure with proud head and muffled steps. An extreme peacefulness flooded over Manuel. He felt that he belonged in this sea of serenity. That if he died at this moment, he would fuse with the other world in harmony, free of any guilt, reconciled with his deeds on earth. He did not reveal his thoughts to his dog. Sometimes he thought the animal understood everything he said. The feeling persisted with him all evening. After tucking Canelo under a blanket and caressing his forehead, Manuel went to bed and fell asleep, praying.

When the first daylight seeped through the windowpanes, Canelo became restless. His master, who should have been up, had not stirred awake. The dog jumped on Manuel's bed, licked his master's face, clenched the blanket with his mouth and pulled it down. No response. The old man lay still, eyes turned toward the window staring into emptiness, mouth twisted toward the opposite side, dry saliva on the corner of the lips, and limbs flaccid. Nothing moved but for an irregular heaving of Manuel's chest that barely disturbed the nightshirt. The dog paced around, baying, circling the bed back and forth, pawing his master's feet and hands, and barking at him. A high-pitched wail arose from deep in Canelo's throat. He sat and gazed intently at his master awaiting a reaction. All his efforts were futile. He pawed open the unlocked kitchen window, jumped down into the inner courtyard, rushed across the patio, and planted himself before the neighbor's window barking with all his might.

"I warned you, Maria," a man's voice growled as the curtains opened behind the windowpanes, "that Manuel's dog was going to snap one of these days. I don't like dogs. In the end they all screw up. They can live on a farm but not in a building."

"Oh, shut up! Canelo has never done this. Maybe something is wrong with the old man. Put something on and find out."

The neighbor found Manuel unconscious and dialed the emergency number. Two paramedics arrived and carried the old man on a stretcher, laying him down in the back of an ambulance. The dog stood outside. His eyes took in everything that went on around his master. As soon as the rear doors closed behind the patient, the vehicle screeched down the gravel path and drove off onto a paved road. Canelo took off after the rescuers. For a while he trailed a few feet behind as a cloud of exhaust enveloped him. Soon the driver stepped on the gas and the animal couldn't keep up. The siren's wail and the blue strobe light faded into the distance.

The ambulance sped along Industrial Road for about half a mile, turned left at a railroad crossing, and after rushing through an avenue, arrived at Residencia Sanitaria Zamacola. A few yards away an early sun lit up the rippling blue waters of Victoria Beach. A policeman stood on a small round platform in the middle of an intersection directing traffic. A tram, a trolleybus, and a modest number of cars rode along the avenue adjacent to the hospital. Clusters of patients and their relatives walked in and out of the building. A security guard sat at the door while next to him a male nurse in surgical attire smoked a cigarette.

The old man was taken to the medical ward, where he remained unconscious surrounded by tubes and life-support machinery. Canelo reached the hospital ten minutes later and sneaked in through the building's west gate. With his head straight, tail curved up, and tongue hanging from his run, Canelo tried to enter the facility through the emergency room door. The security guard saw him coming.

"Eh, eh! Dog, go away!" he shouted from a safe distance.

The dog didn't bark or growl but simply retreated to the hospital fence and sat down nearby to scratch his tummy and hips.

One of the paramedics who happened to walk out of the emergency room recognized Canelo.

"Jesus! This is the old man's dog," he said. "Poor animal, he must have run very fast to get here so quickly."

He fetched a bowl of water and placed it near the dog. Canelo lapped it up in a few minutes. The dog stayed there until well into the evening until one of the hospital security superiors showed up and threatened the animal with a club. The dog did not confront him. Canelo jumped over the fence and loitered nearby. As soon as his expeller's scent cleared, he climbed back and found refuge in the lee of the fence again. Whenever the security guard edged toward him, he stood at attention ready to jump away again.

"You're going to get me in trouble with my boss," the guard said. "Here, dog, here, come here behind the bush ... hardheaded dog!"

He threw a folded blanket on the ground. After a bit of coaxing and repeated cues, Canelo sat in the improvised hideout.

The animal stayed put around the clock except for his daily trips back home. He sought food from the neighbors and did his necessities at the sites where, over the years, his master had instructed him. On the third day, the old man, who had never recovered consciousness, died and was buried at the local cemetery. Still the dog continued his daily routine.   Soon among the hospital personnel the portrait of the faithful dog waiting for his departed friend broke the hearts of animal lovers. Even those indifferent to dogs grew fond of him. Likewise, Canelo's plight caught the patients' attention and after a couple weeks he became sort of a mascot. Some lavished treats and toys on him; others lured him into their homes or attempted to adopt him. Yet, no one could wheedle him into staying. The dog continued his daily trips back home but always returned to the hospital, where by now he had a green doghouse.

Petra, a pediatric nurse who had befriended the dog, had the brilliant idea of convincing him that his master was dead. One evening after visiting hours, she enticed Canelo into following the same route as Manuel's ill-fated admission to the hospital. The animal eased into the lobby, peeked around with a nonchalant attitude, and lingered sniffing at a corner where someone had spilled coffee. He disliked elevators.

"Don't you pick up the old man's scent?" she said, trying to coax him into one of them. "C'mon, let's go in."

Canelo's legs were riveted to the waxed floor. Nothing persuaded the animal until his rubber duck, which had been brought from the doghouse, was laid inside the elevator. The canine visit ended at the foot of his master's deathbed, which at the time was the only one empty in a ward full of seriously ill patients. The dog smelled the disinfected floor, raised his ears, wagged his tail, and skirted the bed. He whimpered and poked his nose against a nightstand drawer over and over. The nurse opened it. Stuck in a corner was a tiny vanilla envelope with the name of the old man written on it. It contained a scapular, which had inadvertently been overlooked when the rest of his belongings and those of the subsequent occupants had been disposed. The mission failed.

So did Canelo's visitation to the old man's gravesite at the Catholic cemetery a few days later. The dog roamed through the inner courtyards by tombs and mausoleums as if at a park. It should be mentioned in his favor, that he made no distinction between richly ornamented graves with large artistic statues of Our Lady or Jesus and those bearing plain headstones. Only on two brief occasions did his behavior intimate a change in attitude. He stopped, shivered like a wet chicken, and stuck his red tongue all the way out, panting. The first time it happened a few yards from Manuel's resting place, and the second in front of a mausoleum belonging to one of the town's late mayors. No conclusion was drawn. Overall, both experiences seemed to increase the dog's resolve to wait for his master. On following nights, the security guards on duty observed the dog having what appeared to be happy dreams. He would yip twice and his legs would drum against the floor of the doghouse in a frenzy of twitches that lasted for several seconds. The next day Canelo's demeanor bloomed as if he had enjoyed an outing with his master. His gait turned more cheerful, his tail rose in a proud curl, and his eyes beamed with a keener sparkle.

The failure of these attempts didn't dissuade everyone. A male nurse harbored the interesting notion that a dog with such a sense of loyalty and responsibility might behave like a human: once he found female companionship, he would fall head over heels for her and forfeit his quarters at the hospital. His fluffy white female poodle, with big eyes like a fawn, served as the bait.

"I brought you a friend, Fifi," he cooed to his poodle. "Isn't he a handsome dog?"

At the sight of the newcomer the unwilling seducer barked as if her life depended on it. Canelo did not flinch, walked over to her, and sniffed her scent. The poodle scurried off with her tail between her legs. She retreated behind a potted plant in the house's garden. Eyeing her, Canelo lay with his tongue lowered to the grass. A few times he got on his feet and took a few nonchalant steps toward her. She snarled. After a while he sidled toward the gate that opened into the street and sat waiting. The nurse let him go.

The following three days saw the same scenes repeated with clockwise precision. In their fifth meeting an encouraging change took place. The poodle lingered next to her new acquaintance, and both dogs roamed around, sniffing and licking each other. Canelo, however, ended each courtship session in front of the gate, waiting to return to his doghouse at the hospital. A month later they mated. Intercourse did not modify Canelo's behavior. When it came to falling in love, the male nurse concluded, dogs could hold on to reality better than humans. It was as if the animal could look beyond love's infatuation and smell trouble the same way a trained beagle could sniff and discover foodstuffs inside a closed suitcase.

The long months and years of waiting for his master took a toll on Canelo. His walk turned into a dispirited heavy amble, his eyes grew dim and tired, and his tail drooped down straight and limp. Aging had come upon him. Only the presence of children revitalized him. His expression became vivacious and his movements adopted the strength and alacrity of a young dog. Their meetings began with the children letting him lick their hands and faces. After these displays of affection, the dog flipped on his back with eyes shining and tongue palpitating, eagerly waiting for his young friends to scratch his belly. The long expanses of wet sand on nearby Victoria Beach at low tide became their final destination.

The sea sparkled and undulated like the spread wings of a giant butterfly. The dog enjoyed running toward the water to fetch a rubber ball as the wind swept the crests of sea waves and sprinkled him with salty mist. The romping children's happy hubbub kept him active before their soccer game began. He then lay on the dry sand and was lulled by the soft murmur of the surf. The warm sun dried the moisture off his fur as the stamina faded from his body. After a while, his tongue lolled out and he lumbered down the street back to the doghouse to continue his protracted vigil.

Several years had gone by since the old man had passed away and this morning, to everyone's consternation, Canelo did not wake up from his night's sleep. Grief and sadness spread as the bad news circulated around the town. The local paper featured a photograph of the dog. It showed him with his eyes wide open and his expression shining with intelligence. Mourners pored over the pages celebrating his life. A physician purchased a small white casket and buried the remains in the backyard of his nearby country home. Bouquets of flowers piled up at the door of the doghouse, red and white carnations, lavender and yellow orchids, golden daffodils, red roses, yellow narcissuses. Their perfume enveloped an assortment of toys, toy bones, rubber balls, rubber ducks, and cloth turtles. Patients had deposited them as if sharing the ancient Egyptian belief in an afterlife where personal objects would come handy. In the neighborhoods around the hospital, grownups remembered the dog with great sympathy, some shedding tears.

I thought the story ended there, for that is the way our lives and our pets' end. But a surprise took me aback many years later. On one of my trips to Cadiz, I visited a friend at the new Residencia Sanitaria Zamacola, which was now called Hospital Universitario Puerta del Mar. The new impressive building was twice as big as its predecessor, which had been demolished to make room for the new facility. The ten-story structure had wide halls, state-of-the-art equipment, and an elegant façade with a colonnaded main entrance. As I walked on Avenida Ana de Viya, I came across a small side street that had been named after Canelo. The street bordered the southwest fence of the hospital. Next to ceramic tiles marking the designation was a large metal plaque engraved with the relief image of a dog. The animal appeared resting on the ground with his face looking ahead and his expression awash with tireless perseverance. An inscription read:

"To Canelo,
the dog that waited for his late master at the door of the hospital for twelve years.
The people of Cadiz as homage to his loyalty."

The image on the plaque matched the memory I had of Canelo, his long ears, his sad eyes, his svelte muzzle. The artist had given shape to the essence of his character and the beauty of his virtues. I did not ask how this official recognition came about, but it made me happy to know that his legend would now last forever.

CROSSING
THE HERRING POND

I am waiting in a line at O'Hare Airport in Chicago. This is the first time I have flown, for my life has rolled on with routine predictability in my hometown, Cadiz, Spain. I have never felt an inclination to move anywhere else. Cadiz enjoys tasty tapas, great beach, excellent weather, plenty of sunshine, beautiful women, and a lot of *cachondeo*, that is, mirth and merriment. Revelers march on the streets and have fun at daylong or weeklong local celebrations several times a year. In addition, everyone partakes in the rest of the world's holydays, frequent three-day weekends and our own month-long vacation. After three millennia of existence, *Gaditanos*—the citizens of Cadiz— hold dear a motto,
    "Don't live to work ... work to live."
    Yet, my curiosity has become stronger than my fear of flying and reluctance to step far away from my hometown grounds. I have crossed the herring pond and come to the U.S. for a visit. I have gotten off the plane and rushed through corridors while holding on to my heavy carry-on luggage. I have been carried by a three-story-high escalator and several electrical walkways to a huge marshaling area. The place is as big as a soccer stadium and dotted with immigration officers in blue uniforms. The stern-looking officials steer everyone through intricate puzzle-shaped lines which crisscross the room from side to side, north to south and east to west, each queue separated by thick ropes and heading

toward a long row of stands, where custom officials sit stamping passports. The procedure reminds me of the way cows are driven at a rodeo or a livestock show.

You may wonder how I got into this pickle. It all began when I won the 2001 La Viña Chess Championship, a neighborhood in my hometown well known for its local artists. In the evening eleven participants gathered at the back of a bar, where two wooden tables and twelve rickety chairs were set up for the contests. The main wall boasted pictures of four successful matadors and four killer bulls side by side. The bar owner believed in giving equal opportunity in the bullring to men and beasts. Next to our area was a room, where a *chirigota*, a group of twelve singers, were preparing for the Mardi Gras annual contest. Their creative funny songs and pantomimes vied for the players' attention. Amidst this hubbub we cussed at one another in a friendly way while we made a move on a chessboard.

When I wrote to my cousin Mauricio in Chicago about my victory, he was elated. He praised me as some kind of genius and urged me to take advantage of the opportunity to hone my skills in the Windy City by visiting him. I accepted. My cousin is the genius, not me. Three years earlier he quit law school and left for Chicago. A few months later he became a *notario publico*—a notary public—with offices on 26th street. In Spain *notarios* hold real estate law degrees and their income ranks among the highest in the country. My whole family swelled with pride including me. We were all excited about my cousin's success, brandishing about the word *notario* like a Jehovah Witness does his Watchtower Magazine. I knew the word didn't have the same importance in English but, nevertheless, I didn't look down on his accomplishment. I was proud of him. To succeed in a foreign country while learning a different language must be challenging. Anyway, crossing the Atlantic Ocean on a plane wasn't as scary as I thought and the view of Chicago from the sky impressed me. Underneath fluffy white clouds the city looked like a chessboard with myriad parallel streets and never-ending crossing avenues. The shape augured a productive stay. I thought Chicagoans had moved their pieces around with masterful precision. The king skyscraper—the John Hancock—sat well protected by the lake border of this gigantic board. Inland, the queen Sears Tower lay in wait at the junction of diagonal and horizontal paths as if ready for a strategic assault against an opponent. Checkmate!

The long passport line is slow and I sit down on the floor. My memory drifts to Cadiz and its view from the sky. It is so different from Chicago. The tallest building boasts only fourteen stories, and the cityscape is tiny and shaped like a guitar. A few narrow thoroughfares run like strings and several parallel streets cross them like frets. Every little plaza, beach, church, and park is arranged in the soundboard-like area with such harmony that it calls to mind the guitar notes of a flamenco melody.

My thoughts are interrupted by my butt, which has frozen from the cold tile. I can now see an immigration official approaching me. Overweight and overbearing, she's sternly shoving her palm up over and over as if playing racquetball. By her expression I guess she doesn't like people sitting on the floor, yet there isn't any chair around. She says something but I only understand "sir and passport." I wonder what has happened to all the words I have learned in English class and from the records advertised on TV. My ears can't find them. I could blame my lack of word recognition on her accent, but I know better. I nod my assent to the officer. I stand up again in the turtle-speed visitor line as a Hindu man with a large white turban holds the queue up at the passport booth. A Hispanic-named official—who doesn't speak a single word of Spanish—stamps my passport. Sniffing beagle dogs threaten to piss on me. An inspector rifles through my underwear and my bottles of sherry, but he settles for a long chorizo sausage. These guys are going to eat sandwiches at my expense for a whole month.

Now I understand why my cousin said to me in his letter, "Come, Champion, come over to Chicago, Hawaillinois, USA." I exit the door that leads to the crowded waiting lounge and I can see him smiling with four floral garlands girding his neck and a couple in his hands. His girlfriend, Matilde, wears hula-girl attire and on my cousin's cue she dances with elegant cadence, her vigorous bust about to spill out from its bodice. Her belly quivers also; yet, my eyes on their own accord keep drifting toward her cleavage as she and my cousin slip the garlands over my head. I finally get hold of myself and take a good look at her beautiful eyes. They are large and dark like a gypsy queen's, and her big smile brightens up the whole airport. My cousin has good taste. For a moment I scrutinize my surroundings, expecting a big crowd to gather around us clapping and cheering us on. If this type of Mardi Gras scene took place in my hometown, the townspeople would surround us like the wild Indians did to pioneers' wagons in Western movies. I realize this is America and, as my cousin forewarned me, no one gives a darn—everyone minds their own business.

"Didn't I tell you, Paco? Look at this place. Isn't Chicago beautiful?" Mauricio says as he repeatedly slaps me on my back and Matilde plants a big kiss on my cheek. "Did you see the lake? Did you see the lake from the plane? One beach after another is brimming with beautiful women like my Matilde. Heaven, just heaven for a single man like you."

This is my cousin, talking on and on and not giving me any chance to open my mouth. As we walk outside in the parking lot, a towering city of concrete skyscrapers, bridges with mighty columns, buildings, and roads springs up before me. I feel the sun heating us with a vengeance as if an angry God has disapproved of our welcoming ceremony. The strong sulfur odor of jam-packed traffic reinforces this notion. Certainly our ritual didn't have any resemblance to the erection of crosses the Spanish conquistadors engaged in when they first came to the new continent five centuries ago.

My cousin loads my suitcase into the huge trunk of his brand-new, flashy red Ford Taurus. Mauricio scoops his girlfriend's buttocks, pushes her into the back seat of his car, and insists that I sit next to him. He has changed. I observe an incipient receding hairline at the temples and a few folds in his forehead. The changes belie his account of his effortless achievements in this country. Laughing at life, he stands out with his ever-present gleaming eyes, dimpled square jaw, and tall athletic figure, which he has always credited for his success with women. As far as I know he has had at least five girlfriends. We ride off onto an expressway and merge with the tide of cars. The road swells like a river about to spill over and flood the city grounds.

"There is nothing like a big American car ... you have room for everyone," he says. "Do you remember when your family and mine fit in my father's tiny Seat 600? Ten people got inside a car almost half the size of a Beetle. But, here in America everything is made big ... well, except suppositories. So don't you get your hopes up!"

He laughs as I observe in the rear mirror how his nonchalant girlfriend chews gum while she stares out the side window. Our conversation strays to Cadiz. My cousin misses the *Botellon*, the Big Bottle. Crowds of young people gather on Saturday evening in plazas inside the old part of the city and hang out all night until dawn, engaging in boisterous conversations over big bottles of wine, beer, and liquor purchased at local supermarkets.

"Every year the crowds get bigger. I don't go there ... I don't like drinking. I hear that most of the time partygoers are well-behaved, but occasionally a few troublemakers may get drunk and spoil the evening."

"I know ... I've been there many times," my cousin says. "We had neither jobs nor money. Young people couldn't afford drinking at a bar. The *Botellon* showed our desperation. That's why I left."

"As far as I remember you always talked about coming to the U.S. even as a child. You didn't need any reason."

My cousin smiles and slaps me on my back again.

Soon we arrive at my cousin's apartment. He lives on the eleventh floor in a tall old building on the north side of Chicago where Lake Shore Drive turns west and fuses with the big maze of downtown streets. The view is wonderful. Lake Michigan blooms, strewn with sparkles twinkling atop its blue surf all the way to the faint line of the horizon. There, a bank of white clouds hovers aloft witnessing the embrace of sky and waters. It looks like an ocean except, down on the beach, the hushed surf ripples without the seashell-like roar, and the mist doesn't prickle your nose like the salty sprinkles from the sea waves. The next morning I wake up to a silent apartment. My cousin is away attending to his business and Matilde is sound asleep. She has worked all night at a post office. I decide to go for a walk. Small waves lap softly against the shore, and flocks of seagulls and wild geese strut on the sandy beach. An expansive drive flows like a giant magic carpet at the feet of a cityscape of skyscrapers, each climbing higher and higher as if Babel towers vying to reach the heavens. A few joggers run on walkways underneath leafy arbors of tall oak trees. When I reach Navy Pier, I feel a sudden craving for shrimps like those I used to eat at a tiny restaurant on La Caleta Beach near my home. Bathed in cocktail sauce, these crustaceans look good in red, but I still don't have a taste for them. I'd rather eat them boiled in salty water or grilled. Every country enjoys its own gastronomy. So does my cousin, who is ready to surprise me with an idea that must have lingered in his mind all day. He excuses himself with his girlfriend and says,

"I have to go fishing with my cousin."

I don't know what he really means but I am sure it has nothing to do with any water sport because I don't see him taking a rod along. We head off toward an Irish pub a few blocks from our building. The place teems with groups of young women and men drinking and engaging in spirited conversation. My cousin and I jostle a place at the bar and sit next to a blonde with a coke-shaped body, a permanent tan, and a pair of gorgeously contoured thighs her short skirt has regaled our eyes with.

"Nice girl," he says. "You need one like this to sweeten your stay. Besides I have to work, you know. How do you like her?"

I tell him that I don't believe in casual friendship. One of these days I'll propose to someone in my hometown. I have my eyes on a couple of them and eventually I'll make a decision. For now, helping my father at his fishery in the Plaza de Abastos and playing chess are sufficient distractions. I watch him smile at her and talk to her as she requites his compliments, I guess, because I don't understand much except for 'paella', "Spain," and "dancing." My cousin turns as she smiles at me,

"You are a lucky son of a gun," he says. "She likes Spain and she has been in Seville where she took a course on flamenco dancing."

I smile back and feel great because here I am at an Irish pub in Chicago making an acquaintance with a sympathizer of Spain, which in my view is the closest thing to another Spaniard. Yet, she must be waiting for someone. I observe her fidgeting with her hands, and wonder whether my cousin has realized there are two glasses of wine in front of her. As I stretch out my hand to shake hers, a tall muscular blond, who might as well have come from the Mr. America contest, walks toward us and says something that must be funny. It has my cousin in stitches and the woman takes sidelong looks at them both. Amidst his convulsive guffaws, Mauricio manages to translate for me,

"I'm glad ... ha, ha! I only went to piss ... ha, ha, ha! If I have stayed for further business ... ha, ha, ha! You'd have stolen my girlfriend."

He explodes in laughter. I say to myself these Americans have a better sense of humor than I have ever anticipated. Now the girl raises her arms in a gesture of disgust and leaves, her boyfriend still laughing his head off and groping for something that will convince her to stay. I see her out and she looks at me as if I were a knight of the Round Table. Grabbing a napkin from one of the serviettes, and propping it against the wall, she writes something and sticks it into my shirt pocket. As she rushes away, I look at her note, which I think may contain her name and number. I read it to myself,

"All men are morons!"

I have to conclude women are as unpredictable in the U.S. as in my hometown. Why should they be different? We humans are what we are. Now that I am taking the time to observe these people's faces, I could swear I have seen them somewhere else before. Perhaps I met them in my hometown or nearby, for before this trip I did not travel beyond eighty miles. A man in a blue jacket bears resemblance to my uncle Antonio. I feel at ease. Searching around, I wonder whether I will come up with someone who looks like me. I have yet to find one. Come to think of it, detecting someone with your facial features among a crowd must be difficult or impossible, since your mind has only a mirror image or one-dimensional photograph of yourself. As I return to the bar, my cousin and Muscle Man continue their rampage.

"*Mira primo*," he says, winking his eye at me, "my new friend and I have been closely watching the parade of camel toes. You know what I mean."

I ask him what he is talking about and he looks at me with a big smile full of exulted sensuality and merriment. He gloats about his answer with as much voracity as a bulldog gorging on a piece of meat.

"Camel toes … you know! It's the new fashion. Women wear their pants so tight that the fabric splits their crotches and outlines the female anatomy like a camel toe."

His euphemism hasn't impressed me. My cousin has been away from my hometown beach so long that he doesn't remember the topless bikinis and the scanty bottoms that our young neighbors wear to freshen up in the water. There, one doesn't need to turn into a camel toe watcher. Here on the beach the women wear swimming suits or discreet two-piece bikinis. Puritanism still rages in this country. This is neither the time nor the place to bring this up. My cousin keeps talking, his eyes flashing like a little child admiring a toy train running in circles. I don't make any comment and suggest we call it a night, for I have fished long enough.

The next day we head out to a huge chess salon. The room has a dome and there are chessboards of every imaginable size on tables, floor, and screens hanging from the walls. Laser beams zero in on each. Computers loaded with special programs sit ready to take on any challenger. At all four corners, flat monitors display a mind-boggling game that has been going on at the center of the room for the past three days. The players' eyes are riveted to the giant board as if mesmerized by the huge wooden pieces twice or three times the size of a bowling pin. Every face in the crowded room contorts with concentration amidst a sepulchral silence. Overhead, the occasional scratching or tapping noise of a moving piece echoes in the cupola.

My cousin introduces me to the owner, a baldheaded Russian man. He ushers me in front of a computer and gives me some instructions, which I understand well since he shows me each one with as much swiftness and arrow-directed precision as those of the funny wizard in Microsoft Word. Soon it dawns upon me I am being tested. After a few moves, he enters my evaluation into a computer and draws up a list of players who match my skills. Immediately a schedule of games, which will keep me busy for the next week, flashes on the screen. Neat—really neat.

Playing chess in America is different than in my hometown. My opponents take the game too seriously. Their expression makes them look as if they were wearing Halloween masks. Scary. I feel like telling them, "Chill out!" No one jokes, takes a break for a soft drink, or kicks you in the leg when you make a move that has everyone scratching his or her head. All they say is, "Time out."

I see them go into the men's room to clear their thinking as they gaze down upon their streams. I wish it were that easy to find my fountain of inspiration. Chess is a serious business. So is life, but one shouldn't take it quite so hard because both chess and life are games we end up losing eventually.

After a tough game last evening, I sleep soundly until I hear my cousin pacing and stomping in the kitchen. The door closes behind him after he leaves for work. I get out of bed as Matilde arrives from her night shift. Her face is pale with fatigue, but in the center of subtle dark rings, her eyes wear the placid, reassured look of a woman who radiates goodness and tenderness. I can understand why my cousin loves her. She seldom talks. When she does, I don't understand her well either, for although she speaks Spanish—her parents are from Puerto Rico—my cousin has asked her to address me in English only. I serve my breakfast and she sits in front of me for her dinner. The expression in her eyes is that of someone who can never hold ill feelings. The dimples on her long pink cheeks cast a constant smile and she moves, talks, and even bites an omelet, a piece of bacon, or a forkful of scramble egg with such care that one would think she is apologizing to the food for the trauma she inflicts upon it. It's hard for me to get used to the smell of these comestibles early in the day. I have tried to enjoy them at this hour but to no avail. It seems that in my childhood not only have admonitions and warnings been wired into my brain but also a fondness for simple coffee and toast. My stomach revolts so much against the fragrant items featured in the American breakfast that I have to pinch my nose with a clothespin when I cook them for Matilde before she gets home. Otherwise, morning sickness overtakes me as if I were pregnant. This state would be more of a miracle than that of Our Lady's because besides being a male I have never known a woman affectionately. My virginity doesn't stem from my personal choice. Some days I could hump a table leg like a dog in heat, but I just haven't found the right woman to share those intimacies.

Today I haven't heard her come in. She has unlocked the front door and swept inside with more stealth than a cat on the prowl. Startled, I jump as she catches me with the red clothespin hanging from my nose. She cups her mouth to restrain her laughter. My hand scrambles to remove the ad hoc obstruction, recognizing I probably look like one of those tribal men from the heart of the Amazon.

"Oh, no, you can leave it on," she says, smiling. "You still look good."

I don't explain my clothespin and she thinks I am trying to prevent my sneezes, which explode with such full force that one can propel anyone before me all the way to Cancun free of charge.

After eight weeks of taciturnity, Matilde feels more talkative and appears comfortable discussing a wide variety of issues. If I don't understand something, she simply repeats it for me in Spanish. She talks about her family, taking extra time to extol her little niece's and nephew's cuteness, and her little brother Chico's kind-heartedness and artistic vein. She adores them. Her eyes look at me with a loving and wondering expression as an unexpected question pops up,

"Um ... if I may ask, are you gay?"

Before I can answer, she explains that she is as at ease with me as with Chico—that we both are sensitive people. After affirming my heterosexual orientation, I state my respect and understanding for those who choose same-sex partners.

Her own dreams revolve around saving enough money to open her own business—a florist shop. I haven't realized she has a knack for arranging artistic bouquets like the one gracing the kitchen counter.

"These gorgeous roses grew in Colombia," she says. "Touch their petals and feel how luscious and velvety they feel. Smell their fragrance."

I inhale the scent. The lingering odor of fried bacon assaults me and makes me feel nauseated, but I don't tell her anything because I'd break her heart. The red roses are mixed with lush yellow and white carnations and adorned with a rich assortment of wild flowers. The dazzling arrangement fires up my imagination and calls to mind Plaza Las Flores in my hometown. I used to sit at a little fountain boasting the Roman statute of Columela— an ancient local writer famous for his treaties on agriculture—and admired the stands awash with bouquets of roses, carnations of various colors, and daisies. Their scent competed with the odor of *churros* and coffee wafting from the outdoor tables of the cafes.

"What are you thinking about?" she asks.

"My mind drifted to a small plaza in Spain, which is full of flower-shops. Over there, people have time to smell the flowers and bask in the sunny weather and the beauty of the surroundings. They don't allow life to pass them by. Here, everything is so fast ... so business-like."

She expresses her wish to visit my hometown in the future. When I offer to serve as her guide, she smiles. She shows a genuine interest in my progress at chess. I relate some of the successes and innovative moves I have devised. When breakfast comes to an end, she excuses herself and goes to her bedroom with her arms hanging down, her slippers shuffling, and her gown floating around her like a ghost. As she disappears behind the door, I seize the opportunity to get rid of my dark-pink jeans and light green jersey, fashionable items in Spain, but more a source of confusion here.

Upon my return from the chess center later on that day, I find my cousin winding down a fight with Matilde. They must have engaged in an important dispute because she bears traces of crying. Relationships involve a lot of effort and sometimes misunderstandings crop up. But when they result in a woman's tears, it breaks my heart. I realize lovers often quarrel almost as a subconscious means to afford themselves a sweet reconciliation. I am not nosy, but I haven't heard any moaning or other telltale sounds of lovemaking coming from their bedroom since I arrived from Spain. Young couples forge their love in their bed. The old ladies in my hometown repeat this axiom over and over. Obviously it isn't the only condition, but my aunt Pepa once told me,

"You might have a woman with a good character, charming personality, a religious and loving person ... but in bed if your bodies and minds don't click like a seat belt, the whole thing goes to hell."

I reckon she must have known what she was saying because she had married and been widowed three times. I don't know much about these things and probably wouldn't recognize that click from a cough or a sneeze. Now Matilde forces a grin at me and is civil with my cousin as she departs for work. He looks as refreshed as a green lettuce at the farmer's market. Nothing unsettles him.

The next morning his girlfriend has one of those days off that the government employees enjoy while everyone else in the country slaves away at their place of employment—Columbus Day. A couple weeks before, my cousin suggested that Matilde take me to watch the parade on Michigan Avenue and she agreed.

So now we ride the L to our destination. Ever since we left home I have been admiring how beautiful Matilde looks in her blue jeans, white blouse, and red jacket. Her scent wraps me in an enchanting world as if I were daydreaming at a botanic garden. She wears onyx jewelry: a large ring shaped like a snake, a bead necklace, and silver bracelets studded with small stones. Their glowing black splendor sets off her shoulder-length dark hair. The street teems with Italian flags, American banners, artistic floats, and awesome marching bands. America revels in its multiethnic heritage. The colors and music, done up as only Italians can, fascinate me. But I'm never sorry to inform them that they didn't discover America, we Spaniards did.   Anyway, Spaniards and Italians have similar personalities and we love and get along well with one another. Not long ago I kidded around with a few of my friends whose ancestry traces back to the boot-shaped peninsula. I told them I'd agree to accept their claim to the New World if they also took responsibility for all the screw-ups and hubbub we Spaniards had cooked up in this continent. They laughed and replied a middle finger salute.

After the parade Matilde decides to take me to Navy Pier. The sun shines in a clear sky. The crests of ripples of the lake ease toward the sandy beaches, edged with white lace foam, and the calm waters sparkle with brilliant lights as if sprinkled with diamonds. The glitter in Matilde's eyes enhances the spectacle. I try to avert my gaze lest she finds out something as inappropriate as what I have begun to feel for her. Her lusciously contoured lips part like a seashell, drawing my eyes downward. We ride a huge Ferris wheel that rises up twelve stories high. At the top she feels dizzy and rests her head upon my shoulder, her long dark hair falling over my chest. After she closes her eyes, almost inadvertently, my hand touches her locks. The soft, crispy feeling sends a wave of electricity down my spine. When she lifts her eyelids again, her lips are so close to mine that I feel as if iron chains were ratcheting mine toward hers. My eyes rove back and forth between her lips and her eyes until I have to shut them and pronounce the first thing that crosses my mind,

"This contraption would look nice on La Caleta Beach in my hometown as a waterwheel. People would go there and watch it go up and down. But there it is so windy that the water would spray down all daylong. They'd have to wear raincoats from head to toe like Marilyn Monroe in *Niagara Falls*."

She draws herself up and looks at me as if I have just landed from another planet. At lunch she opens the conversation in Spanish,

"Paco, *me marcho*, I'm leaving your cousin. I have waited until now because I promised to take you out today. I can't stay any longer. He doesn't love me. I'm only one on his long list of women."

I don't answer her. I just look at her and let her open up to me. I don't want her to see any expression of elation on my face. I should feel bad for my cousin. But I don't. My callousness disappoints me. I thought that I knew myself better, that I could never revel in my fellow man's misfortune. Maybe my regret has to do with human nature. Long ago, my father—and my mother—admonished and warned me,

"If under a woman's spell your Mister Weiner raises, your brain goes to hell."

As soon as we get home, I realize she has already packed her suitcases and written a farewell note to my cousin. Tears swell up in her eyes. I ask her to leave her new address and phone number with me, but she looks at me over her shoulder as she drags her two suitcases through the front door.

"*Llamame*—call us when you settle in!" I say.

She lowers her head and keeps going. I feel like running after her, clutching her in my arms and never releasing her, but my sense of duty toward my cousin, my entire notion of propriety, holds me back like ropes mooring a ship.

When my cousin reads her note, he fumes.

"No woman leaves me!" he screams. "I get rid of them. They don't dump me. How dare she?"

He mutters an obscenity and I try to calm him down, pointing out she is a good woman and, perhaps, if he feels so bad about it, he should go and patch things up with her. He lets his tongue run.

"I'm not going to do that. She isn't worth it. I can have a hundred women more beautiful than she is. And what is she to you, anyway?" he snarls. "Did you go to bed with her? You did, didn't you?"

"You're crazy."

"You, S.O.B."

"If you don't trust people who care for you," I say, shaking my head, "then you don't deserve our love and respect. Perhaps that's the reason why she left you. Maybe you should reassess your principles and goals in life."

"You're a clodhopper! You think you can give me advice?"

I rifle through my drawers and throw all my clothes in my suitcases as my cousin stands at my doorway still screaming. I keep quiet, which infuriates him even more. I don't know what else to do short of punching him. I am not a violent man and, after all, he is my cousin. At seeing me leave, he calms down and asks me to reconsider. He hasn't apologized. I keep going and fall silent when he asks me to let him know the address and phone number at my new place. His mood changes again and he screams,

"Are you going with her?"

I find a little studio, not far from his neighborhood. I miss Matilde terribly. The weeks rush by and soon orange lamps and the huge pumpkins of Halloween grace home façades. At first I have a hard time understanding this very American festivity. I have never laughed at death. But, after a careful and logical analysis, I have concluded it's healthy and makes a lot of sense. One mustn't take this dream we call life too seriously. While in Cadiz everyone goes to the cemetery to dust off their late relatives' tombs and attend the Mass of the Departed, here in America, adults indulge in an extravaganza of parties, spirited larks, and a myriad of weird disguises. I have seen some of the homes decked with the most macabre adornments and even headstones with epitaphs such as,

"I TOLD YOU I WAS SICK!"

This is great humor. Soon after, the orange decorations give way to multicolored lights and Santa's reindeers announcing upcoming Thanksgiving and Christmas. Americans like to display their happiness by illuminating everything. Even the used car dealers fill their yards with a multitude of ornamental bulbs, as if every day were the Fourth of July. What's so exciting and exhilarating about dumping a big lemon from Detroit on you? Those guys should get real and flash a warning sign:

"Don't judge a book by its cover."

Perhaps I am getting bitter because time trots by and I haven't heard a word from Matilde. Chess absorbs me. I expend hours in the Chicago Library downtown reading book after book on the subject. There are probably more manuals written about chess than about any other game. I am so fired up that I keep a board on my nightstand to put into practice any move my mind concocts in my dreams. My days wear on at the Chess Salon. My eyes keep a close watch for any new tactic that might advance my games. After a while I sit ready to beat the computer that has been programmed using the approach of Kaspárov, the world champion. The machine unsettles me. It doesn't have a mouth to discourage or trick an opponent. Nor has it a face where I can read an expression or an attempt to hide enthusiasm as I sensed a few days ago when I played with Jose. A well-seasoned Argentinean, he bore a smug smile as he tried to upset my concentration with his remarks.

"Where is your mind, *Che*?" he asked. "Watch what I'm doing, *adios*, goodbye! I capture your knight."

"You didn't capture any knight," I replied. "You missed the day. Here comes the bishop and he kisses your queen off."

Jose went berserk. A smart riposte can surpass a clever move and inject a good dose of excitement into a game. A computer can beat you out of plain boredom. This time it doesn't. After five hours I checkmate my opponent. I qualify for the Illinois State Championship.

After five weeks, my mind still does not stay focused on the games because I have not been able to forget Matilde. Breakfast is my worst time. I usually skip it to avoid dealing with my memories. The smell of bacon and scrambled eggs claims control of my senses and brings back her perfume as if these victuals had turned into opium and taken hold of my mind. I have been inquiring at the local post office branches in hopes of an affirmative answer about her whereabouts—but to no avail. I figure her coworkers don't know those who work different shifts. At the huge downtown post office, a different Matilde comes out to meet me. This corpulent African-American woman asks me whether I will settle for her, since she knows of no other employee who goes by her name. She tries to embrace me with her big hands and squeeze my 140 lbs, 5'7" body against her huge pendulous breasts. I shake her hand and rush off as a chorus of guffaws echoes in my ears.

A dream surprises me tonight. It is early evening and I am flying hand in hand with Matilde over the promenade along Victoria Beach in my hometown. The place bustles with people lounging along the seashore or sitting at the outdoor tables of the restaurants flanking the two-mile boardwalk. African peddlers display their merchandise on small wooden counters—watches, jewelry, belts, neckerchiefs, hats. A few tenacious beachgoers are still swimming. I can smell the scent of *pescado frito*—fried fish— potatoes with calamari, shrimp tortillas. The flavor of lager beer floods my senses. People chat and smile and the happy murmur of conversation fuses with the whispers of rippling sea waves. Spellbound by the beauty of the surroundings, Matilde kisses me. The warmth of her lips sends my heart pounding and changes the course of my dream. We now walk by Navy Pier: rippling waters, flocks of seagulls, restaurants, shops, theater, boats, happy crowds, Ferris wheel. Matilde stands about a hundred yards away, facing me. To impress her, I skip faster and faster along the edge of the pier toward her. Opening my outstretched arms I perform a superb dive toward my precious reward. Instead of a soft hug, a terrible racket wakes me. The board and chess pieces atop my nightstand have crashed onto the floor where I now lie with a bunch of wooden figurines poking into my ribs.

Later, as if the dream has portended a shift in the wind, my cousin and his new girlfriend knock on my door. Tall, blond, with gorgeous blue eyes, Carol walks up and looks at me as if she were the Queen of Sheba. Men have spoiled her. I can see that. The way she inspects her nails and flings her hair over her tiny ears must have been learned in some charm school. Even her sugary voice takes after Bob Derek's. I'd rather stick with Matilde. At least she behaves normally, much like the girls I have known in my hometown.

"You like her?" Mauricio says. "Do you like her? She is beautiful, isn't she?"

I assent while the young woman's fake smile flashes before my eyes.

"Anyway, I came to apologize. We are cousins, you and me, with the same blood. Do you remember when you hit me on the head with a hammer? Did I hold a grudge against you? No, I didn't."

"You made me swallow a small lizard alive! Anyway, we were only five years old ..."

"It doesn't matter."

I shrug as he gives me a hug. A guilty feeling overcomes me because I haven't answered any of his calls. I have been upset with him. Now I seize the opportunity and ask him whether he knows Matilde's whereabouts. His new girlfriend is out of earshot, gawking at a couple of small silvery trophies, one shaped like a pawn and the other like a tower, which I have won in recent local competitions.

"Carol responds better. She's smooth and drivable in bed like a Cadillac on the road," he says, his eyes gloating and his mouth boasting a big smile. "Anyway Matilde is staying with her family at 334 N. Wabansia in Humbold Park, the Puerto Rican section of town. Melendez is her family's name. I don't advise you to go—"

I do not allow him to finish before I am on my way to find her. It's cold outside and the autumn wind chases the leaves off the few old oaks lining the small street. Traces of old graffiti and brand new paintings populate walls and trash bins. The three-story redbrick building where she lives has a front walk made of broken brown tiles set in concrete, an entrance stoop with ragged worn-down steps, and a façade scarred with holes left by fallen bricks. A neighbor who happens to come out of the house pauses for a moment, but lets me go in after I mention Matilde's name. The steep, narrow stairs lead to a wooden door that displays her family name, Melendez. Someone's eye peers at me through the peephole. I identify myself. A woman in her middle fifties opens the door. She resembles Matilde though she has large baggy eyes, heavy legs, and a big belly draped by a blue cotton dress stamped with yellow flowers. An unshaven young man in a short-sleeved undershirt and jeans sits at a table over a can of beer watching television. A little girl with large vivid eyes in a pink dress stands next to a playpen while her male counterpart trifles with a toy train on the floor. The whole house smells of *arroz con pollo*. My father's words ring in my ears,

"Remember my son, you don't marry a woman … you marry a family. Before you get serious with a girl, make sure to check what her mother looks like, because that's the way she'll look after a number of years. You'll be married to her mother."

At first the mere thought gives me the creeps. Later it dawns on me that by then I'll look like him—with white hair and more folds on my face than those of a walnut shell. Matilde looks radiant but surprised as she rushes out and recognizes me. She must have done her hair in a hurry and thrown on the nice white dress fringed with lace.

"Tell Mauricio," she says in angry tone, "I don't want anything to do with him."

After I have explained my visit has nothing to do with my cousin, she calms down. My nervousness gets to me, because every single line I have prepared for this moment goes blank. I end up inviting her to come over to the chess center and watch the semifinals of the Illinois Championship this coming Saturday, which will pit me against a tough Russian opponent. She seems restless.

"I don't know," she says. "I started seeing someone a couple weeks ago."

"I see. It's okay. You can bring him."

"I don't think I want to get involved with any Spaniard. They have a streak of wildness in their blood. Sooner or later it shows. It's like you have been born to run bulls or bullfight. I already had a bad experience."

I don't harbor that kind of wildness. I have never stampeded bulls through streets nor fought them. I know better than that. Nevertheless, I have heard my mother saying over and over,

"*Para muestra basta un boton*"—one example is enough."

I understand Matilde's hesitation. Now I realize she has never requited my feelings for her.

I don't care about what my family says or what her family looks like. Matilde represents a flower in the midst of barren fields, an oasis in a desert. But she never shows up. After twelve hours my cousin witnesses my defeat by the superior Russian player.

"You are among the four best players in the State," he reminds me to help cheer me up. "I'm proud of you."

I decide to visit Matilde again. My heart races with emotion, but she never comes to the door to greet me. Her mother and her brother-in-law behave civilly and even feel sorry for me. I can hear their voices trying to convince her to at least acknowledge my presence. She doesn't budge. The following week my attempt to hand her a bouquet of roses fails. No explanation is given. Days loom tough before me. Her rejections are hard to swallow. After a few nights without one wink of sleep, my urge to see Matilde surges again. I stand at her door with dark circles around my eyes and a face paler than a nun's rear end. A young man opens the door. He is tall and thin, wears tight blue jeans and his upper eyelids are tinged with subtle blue.

"I'm Chico, Matilde's brother. Come in," he says as he lifts the bouquet of roses from my hand. "Don't stand at the door like a preaching Mormon."

I observe him walking in front of me. His slick black hair is plastered down on his scalp, his steps are swaggering and light, and his leather-soled shoes tap the wooden floor like a flamenco dancer. She comes out with her arms folded across her chest, wearing blue jeans and a Cubs sweater. Even now, when her expression is one of annoyance, her red lips bear such a luscious semblance that it makes me shake inside.

"Please, leave me alone. I have a new boyfriend," she says in an imploring voice. "Let's just stay good friends."

This does it for me, I guess, at least for the time being.

It is hard to accept my defeat, but I manage to limit the damage inflicted on my self-confidence. Dunking my head into a full tub proves to be as valuable as gargling salt water. Both calm me down. Christmas lies around the corner and my visa is up. Snow and ice transform the landscape into a fantasyland. Trees turn into chandeliers, bare bushes into ice statues, and ponds into giant mirrors. The weather grows so bitter in Chicago that the cold freezes my breath as it hovers over me. It's hard to leave a country I have fallen in love with. Tears welling in my cousin's eyes tell the same story—half of his heart wants to fly with me back to Cadiz and half wants to stay. As I line up to get into the airport terminal, I turn to bid farewell. He jumps up and hollers,

"Don't forget to strip naked before you pass security!"

This is my cousin Mauricio, madder than a hatter.

LA ALAMEDA

VICTORIA BEACH

"Stop playing with my father's life," I screamed at God. "He has been a good man. He doesn't deserve to suffer. Stop it! Return him to his family or take him with You."

It was Friday morning December 12, 2008, and I was hurrying by the deserted promenade flanking Victoria Beach. The walk was close to the hospital where my eighty-nine-year-old father had been in a coma teetering between life and death for the past two days. Gray sea waves ruffled by cold winds pounded the sand as if angered by the sadness of the moment. Far on the horizon a thick white cloud stood still with sunrays fanning out from under the silver lining, the same way God is depicted in Biblical scenes. There were three small gaps in the big cumulus forming two eyes and a mouth. God stood there—I was certain—presiding over everything that went on, pulling the strings as if we all were marionettes.

When I arrived at the hospital, the coma had deepened, for my father's pneumonia had worsened. I stood next to him while I observed his ashen complexion under a breathing mask. His eyelids rested on his sunken orbits but no longer reacted with a blink to light touch. His heart rate was 160 per minute as if he were running a marathon, and his respirations had risen to thirty-two per minute, almost three times the normal rate. A monitor shaped like a large TV remote control and a short cord with a clothes-pin-like electrode was attached to his right index finger. Except for the pulse and breathing, the other vital signs were normal, including the oxygen in his blood. I stared at the monitor. In the two-bed hospital room, the contraption cried like a rotten brat.

The other bed, which was empty, was covered with my relatives' coats, for everyone—my mother, four of my siblings, their spouses, four of their children, two cousins—sat in the lobby in silence or chatting about events in my father's life. Great sorrow hovered over them. Across from me sat my brother Miguel, his chin on his chest and his eyes heavy with the hours of witnessing my father's fight for air. His face bore great tiredness as he kept pushing his glasses up his nose. It was probably the same way I looked at this moment because people confused us all the time. Thirty years earlier, he had been making his living selling books door to door in a city two hundred miles away from Cadiz when the brother of one of my colleagues, whom he had never met, answered his knock and asked him without hesitation whether he was my brother.

I had a few of my father's facial features, but I took after my mother. My dad was handsome and taller than I was. Until five years ago, my father had been able to do everything he had done as a young man short of playing soccer. He walked, swam, had a good time with friends, and danced the evenings away. He and my mother, who was six years his junior, won a tango contest. The old man could hold his body straight with his erect head turned away from my mother, step in time to the music, and pivot on one foot with more elegance than a matador sweeps his red cape in front of a bull.

But infirmity caught up with him. His mouth sank and his voice weakened. Every part of his body went to the dogs but his mind. It took him a couple of minutes to get up from a chair. He leaned his trunk over, shifted his body forward, tucked his legs under his knees, pushed his hands against the armrests, and after repeated trials propelled himself upward. He then pulled his pants up and shuffled one foot barely ahead of the other, his figure slouching forty-five degrees. His body had grown so thin and feeble that he looked like a fishing pole bent by the might of a big catch. Yet there was not any big fish, just the strong gravity of aging, which acted as if the earth called him down and he resisted the order with his fragile bones. Flights of stairs did not deter him from venturing out of the house alone. He held on to the rail and descended them step-by-step, then set off down the streets. Curbs grew into big walls to clear and climb. Every step he took turned into a feat. Neighbors saw him teetering on his feet and warned my mother about his impending fall. He did not listen to anyone. He had been in command all his life and was not going to give in without a fight. As time went by his balance deteriorated. A cane helped but this device was something almost offensive to him. After a while, he could not walk downstairs anymore, so he relented. Once on the street he dragged it at his side along pavements as if it were a dog, using it only to prop himself to stand up from a bench, negotiate uneven sidewalks and curbs, or hurry through pedestrian crossings. Last spring he stumbled as a gust of wind threw him off balance and made him pitch headlong to the ground. Three passersby picked him up and brought him home where he was found to have a few bruises on his elbows and hips. Later I warned him about fractures.

"*Hijo mio*," he said, "if one gets frightened, one can't live."

Unfortunately, my premonition became a reality. On December 3rd 2008, my father bent over to pick up some shoes from a closet, lost his balance, and fell to the floor. The emergency room physician diagnosed him with a fracture of the middle of the left femur and admitted him to the hospital. He was operated on three days later. He had been taking blood thinners for a venous thrombosis in his right leg three years earlier and his abnormal clotting precluded an earlier intervention. After the surgery restlessness took hold and kept him awake all night. An X-ray showed pneumonia. As a doctor, I knew the dismal prognosis of such a finding. As soon as my sister told me, I hung up the phone, rushed to the airport, and caught the next flight for Spain.

Aboard the plane my thoughts drifted to a conversation my father and I shared a year and a half earlier. He had always avoided discussing death, but that day he asked me,

"Do you think I have to suffer in order to die?"

"I don't think so, but that is God's decision," I said in a reassuring tone.

My father already knew what my answer would be. He just needed to put his mind at ease. A long pause ensued and then he said,

"Years ago, you said I would live to see my nineties."

"I think so. Your brother and your sister made it to their nineties. You can live another ten years ... you are healthy."

At that moment, on the plane, when my soul was as agitated as the ocean below, my father was three months short of ninety.

It had been a complicated, tortuous trip, but I arrived in the hospital on December 8, twenty-one hours after leaving Chicago. The previous night, my father had been so sick that no one had expected him to pull through. When he saw me, his exhausted face shone with happiness. Even the gray veil of death that hung over him could not dampen his expression.

" ... *por alli?*— ... over there?" he managed to say, raising his eyebrows in his characteristic gesture.

He was asking about my family whom I had left behind in America, but I only understood the last two words of his sentence. His shortness of breath made his speech almost unintelligible. I fought back my tears and showed him the pictures of his great-grandchildren on the screen of my i-phone. His face bore several days of white stubble and the tender expression in his eyes aroused a memory: the last time I shaved him. It happened last summer before we went out to dine. Chopping his sparse gray hair, I steered the electric razor through a mesh of fine wrinkles, little veins, and dark spots. His face boasted a graceful silhouette and venerable features like those of an old portrait. His lips had sharpened, and although his eyes radiated love, they had sunken and lost their sparkle. In the past they had shone with the happy sadness of the orphan who had overcome dire poverty, for he had been born a few months after his father's death. They also bore his resolve to bring up six children on a meager security guard's salary and his tenacity to assure a better future for his family. He singed his eyelashes while he studied under candlelight in the loneliness of the night, in whichever inhospitable places his job as a security guard required. And there always was the sudden drop of his eyelids, which tinted his eyes with the honey glimmer of goodness, and the grooves next to his mouth, which sketched an incipient smile ready to bloom. That day he stayed still as the razor ploughed deep into his folds, and, with my hands resting upon his face, I wished I could transfuse into him half of my vitality.

On Tuesday December 9, 2008 my father woke up tired but tried to keep an upbeat mood. I opened the blinds. A few large clouds peeked into his hospital room from a sunny sky and, since he wanted to watch the bustle on the street, I positioned his bed facing the window. Christmas decorations were already up. I observed peacefulness on his face. The constant fever caused him terrible thirst and made his breathing worse. Flanked on either side by a narrow groove, his ribs were reined in as if their overlying skin had gotten stuck to the surface of his lungs. With every respiration his belly barely raised, his chest ratcheted out, and the woman's face tattooed over his heart grimaced.

Since I was a child, this tattoo had piqued my curiosity, but it had not been until last summer that I had learned its origin. That day I took him to Victoria Beach, which was about two hundred yards away from my parents' home. My father could walk everywhere but it took him forever. As we approached our destination, we could hear the sea sounding like the hollow hiss of a seashell placed up to our ears. Only the distant playful voices of children trilled over the noise. A mint-like fragrance of algae wafted toward us on a salty breeze. Victoria Beach burst into our view with the stone wall of Cortadura Fort abutting on the seashore like the bow of a schooner. Beyond this point the coastline of golden sand extended southeastward farther than the eye could see. On our right the old silhouette of Cadiz's oceanfront raised proudly, the cathedral's yellow cupola glittering like a topaz ring in a bride's hand, and on either side, twin East and West Towers stood straight and high like two sentinels. His eyes drifted toward the sight and then flitted through the three- and four-story houses painted in various colors–blue, turquoise blue, yellow, orange, white, brown, pink– so that fishermen could recognize their homes from afar when they returned from the high seas. His survey lingered on the jetty where the lighthouse towered over the San Sebastian Castle, the sea waves breaking and climbing its fortified walls. He had looked at this scenery so many times. Yet it now brought him so much emotion that a veil of moisture coated his eyes. I remembered that a few months before I had debated what present to give him for his eighty-ninth birthday. It was a hard choice because I had exhausted my list of little tokens and gadgets. I decided on a book with a large collection of post-cards of Cadiz dating back to the time that he was born. I wrote a small poem on the first page,

You love your Cadiz so much
That there is no Cadiz without you,
Nor watchtowers to overlook
Its eternal waters and salty blue–

A soft wind from the west swept the sea. Overhead in a tur-quoise sky, the midday sun warmed the azure-blue sea as long stretches of white foam rode over the tops of the waves. Lights trembled on the surf. The low tide exposed an expanse of wet sand. A large crowd had gathered this day. My father liked it that way. He loved people. Next to us two topless young women played volleyball.

"*Los ojos siempre son niños,*" he said, smiling. "Our eyes are always young like those of children."

He took his shirt off. His chest rested upon a flabby abdomen so sunken that it barely held in place his swim trunks. His deformed spine had spread the ribs wide apart, stretching the woman tattooed over his heart. Her features bore resemblance to Isadora Duncan's: her short waving hair parted in the middle, her nonchalant eyes, her grave straight lips. The drawing never failed to evoke in my mind images of women dancing the Charleston. I asked him again.

"I had the tattoo done at the battlefront during the Spanish Civil War," he said, "on one of those rare quiet days when we weren't shooting at one another. I got her picture from a magazine."

I held his hand and escorted him to the seashore. He had not been in the water for the past four years. His face lighted up with the excitement of those who are about to meet an old friend. We walked a few steps into the water. A fizzling coldness caressed our feet. We blended into the never-ending blue of the ocean, fluffy white clouds sweetening the horizon like cotton candy as we waded farther into the sea. The waves hit our bellies. Feeling his frail elderly body, I placed myself behind him, wrapped my hands around his waist, and held him tight. He bent forward and let the waves roll over him again and again as he stretched his arms out to hug the water.

"*El agua está buena*—the water feels wonderful. I made it," he said as he laughed with his hands upon his face, his hair ruffled like the feathers of a victorious fighting cock.

On Wednesday December 10, 2008, my father fell into a coma. Initially it was superficial because he still blinked when I touched his eyelids. His nose became sharper and his mouth thinner, and his eyes and cheeks sank. With each breath the bed shook and the monitor bleeped. I noticed breathing pauses. My heart jumped, afraid that each was his last. His battle against death raged on. Outside, the sky joined my tears and wept downpours of rain. My father loved life so much, that I knew he would still put up a strong fight to survive. Giving up was something he had never done lightly. The last time he conceded defeat was four years earlier when he got rid of his ten-year-old car.

He used to park it on the street in front of his balcony where he could always keep an eye on it. Every week, he washed it with a special cleaner, dried it, and waxed the red body. It shone resplendent. Even the tires and hubcaps looked brand-new. He went down and dusted it every day. The car sat idle most of the time, except when it took him and my mother for their weekly grocery shopping, and once in a while, on short trips to nearby villages. They enjoyed country cuisine and walking around quiet parks. Insidiously his reflexes slowed down, and he had a few incidents where he cut in on approaching vehicles. The near misses did away with his driving. He kept the car parked, but the weekly wash, wax, and engine idling went on for a year, because he could not find in his heart the strength to sell it.

On Thursday December 11, the coma continued to deepen. His pneumonia did not respond to antibiotics. He had feared these turns of the events. He had felt the forebodings. He did not want to go to the emergency room after his fall. He felt safe at home, as if death were not able to find him in his hideout. Despite the intense pain, he waited for four hours before he checked into the hospital. He was afraid of not returning home. He expressed this fear over and over.

My parents lived in a five-story building on the outskirts of my hometown since I was a child. It was a cozy, three-bedroom condominium. My father sat in the northwest corner of the living room, and my mother across from him on the opposite side, next to a tall lamp with an oak barrel keg and a small shade that my parents had bought in Chicago on one of their trips to visit me. It had a small sunny balcony, where I used to watch as a child the trains rattling by a few yards away. Back then eucalyptus trees, prickly pears, and marshes with tall reeds filled the fields around the building. Now the trains ran underground and a concrete city of high-rises had mushroomed along with roads, plazas, shops, restaurants, and a soccer stadium. The room's walls were graced with pictures of his six children, thirteen grandchildren, and three great-grandchildren.

"When your mother and I got married, we moved to the Pyrenees to begin our life together," my father once said. "It took us five days to travel a thousand miles on a rickety steam train. I never dreamed that such a slow engine would lead us here to this large family."

The next day, the morning of Friday, December 12, I reached the hospital shortly after my diatribe against God. I found my father in a deep coma. His death was imminent. A painful silence hovered over his room except for the hisses of the oxygen, the ticks of the intravenous pump, and the howls of the monitor. Outside, life continued as if nothing were happening. Visitors filled the ward with their chatter and laughter, and some family members pushed the wheelchairs of lucky patients who were being discharged. Across his room, an old woman had lain immobile in a coma for over a month. Her eyes had been wide open as if staring at the ceiling, her mouth agape like the crater of a volcano. I sat with my relatives out in the hall. They were exhausted from the ten-day vigil. Overcome by sleep, my brother Antonio lay down on a wooden bench. My mother sat on a chair with one of my sisters-in-law next to an elevator, hugging her chest with her own arms each time the exit door to the stairs opened and the cold air rushed in. Her face bore great anguish. The rest of my relatives sat in silence on another bench, looking into emptiness. I was tired too. I had not left the hospital since I came in from the airport except for a few hours of sleep at home.

Amidst the sadness surrounding me, I thought how badly I was going to miss my father. We shared so many passions. When I was a youngster, we watched countless soccer games from the flat roof of my parents' building. The parapet overlooked the entire playing area of the stadium, except for a narrow strip across the middle of the field, where the view was obstructed by the tall score tower. Years later, separated by an ocean, we still followed the important matches on TV, calling each other on the phone at halftime and at the conclusion of the game to praise the good plays, celebrate our favorite team's victory, or lament the loss. We loved bullfighting—with some reservations about its cruelty toward the animals—and admired the matadors' courage, their elegant dexterity at fooling the bulls, their flirtations with death. Flamenco occupied a special place in our hearts, an art that on special occasion he rendered with style and in good taste. How am I supposed to plow through this life, I thought, without his comments, his observations, and his insights?

As if hypnotized by these thoughts, I sat in a trance, fretting over this acute sense of loneliness, with my eyes gazing into the void of the hall that led to my father's hospital room. I saw my nephew Antonio Jaime walking toward me as if he were floating inside a cloud of fog. His voice startled me.

"Grandpa is moving his arms."

At first I thought it was a figment of his imagination. My father's illness affected him so much that his mother forbade him to stay with his grandpa longer than an hour. The youngster missed his frequent walks with him, had not slept for several days, and had woken up early every morning to go to school. Shortly after, my niece Patricia came over to me, her face illuminated by excitement.

"Grandpa is moving his lips. I think he might be mumbling something."

That early afternoon a gradual awakening took place and, in the early evening, my father sat up in bed fully alert. His face shone as resplendent as Moses' might have looked when he came down from Mount Sinai after seeing God. His eyes were wide open and his newly grown white beard made him look more handsome and younger. He smiled, recognizing everyone. Happiness radiated from his countenance as his grandchildren pampered him,

"*Abuelo*—Grandpa—you have beautiful feet," Patricia said as she kissed them.

He did not speak a word. He laughed, assenting with his head and raising his eyebrows. A soft cinnamon-like scent emanated from his skin. His feet were indeed beautiful: the nails clear like nacre, his toes perfectly shaped like a baby's. Not a single callus or deformity. So were his hands—soft and spotless.

"They sent you back," I said to him, joking. "They did not want you up there yet."

He raised his eyebrows and smiled. My mother and everyone in the family greeted him and rejoiced in this turn for the better. As relatives surrounded his bed, his loving eyes scanned each of us one by one. His respiratory rate calmed down to 24 per minute, and the rest of his vital signs held firm. After a while we let him rest.

I was jubilant. My father had proved me wrong. The pneumonia was not lethal after all. All my knowledge of medicine had been flushed down the toilet. Early on Friday evening, I left for my apartment. I walked toward the promenade next to the waters, and heard the murmur of the waves. Victoria Beach came into view, immense and lonely. The wind had formed numerous white dunes and the coastline deserted by the reins of man seemed to regain its virginity. The sea waves played with the sandpipers, which darted around picking at the shore, and several seagulls flew overhead, squawking in the salty breeze, while flocks of them alighted or walked on dry sand. Only a sailboat bobbed in the distance. Overhead, the sun shone midway down the horizon. Mountains and valleys of clouds collided against one another or ripped asunder as if a new world was being created before my very eyes. Ashamed of my rebukes of God, I was relieved that His presence, the mask under which He had hidden earlier, was nowhere to be seen. I looked at the cityscape of Cadiz and saw it more resplendent than ever. It was as if I expected the bells from the now glittering cathedral and all the churches around to ring with happiness for my father's miraculous improvement. The breeze seemed to breathe life into the fragrance of the sea, the green carpet of moss on the rocks, and the golden color of dry sand. I stopped at a nice restaurant. The place was packed with hungry revelers who were just beginning their weekend spree. My appetite returned. After expounding on the reason for my celebration to one of the waiters, I sat alone at a table near the bar. He served me *salmorejo*—a delicious soup similar to gazpacho—topped with diced Iberian ham, and baked corvine a la olive oil. I washed the delicious food down with a glass of Rioja, my father's favorite. I left no room for dessert.

The next morning, Saturday the 13th, dawned with heavy rains and gusts of winds that tore up umbrellas and left their skeletons dotting the streets. The city, which usually enjoyed good public transportation, collapsed: long lines formed for buses, no taxi cabs were available, traffic crawled. At night my father had again drifted into deep unconsciousness. His breathing became fast, his pulse weakened, his blood pressure dropped, and his fever rose. The pneumonia invaded both lungs and all attempts to stop the progression failed.

He passed away the next morning. I felt the forlornness of the orphan. Yet I realized that God in His immense compassion had granted me both of my requests—He had returned my father back to me fully awake for a final goodbye and then taken him under His loving care. My father's ashes rode the crests of the sea waves on Victoria Beach, not far from where he and I had waded into the waters.

PLAZA DE TOROS

On Corpus Christi Day the Plaza de Toros de Cadiz, the local bullring, stands filled to capacity. It is the main *corrida*—bullfight—of the year in the town, and even the provincial governor is in attendance. Manolo and I sit in the bleachers next to the steps separating the galleries, waiting for the moment of truth. He has talked of jumping into the ring, of dodging and outrunning the policemen and bullfighters who will try to detain him, of fighting a bull and giving a masterful performance.

"There's no other way," he has repeated over and over. "This is a cut-throat business. No one is ever going to give me the chance to prove myself otherwise."

I disagree that he will not have the opportunity to find an agent who will promote him as a *novillero*—a novice bullfighter. Manolo is young—seventeen—though the odds are against him. One out of a hundred makes it to matador, the highest rank in the profession, but I believe he has the talent, skills, and guts to succeed. I pray that he doesn't go through with his plans. It's simply too dangerous. Handling the bull requires his undivided concentration. Any minor distraction can end his life. The featured outstanding matadors and their entourages will use any means to restrain him before reaching the center of the ring to face the bull. He will have to set his eye not only on the beast but also on his pursuers. If he survives, the punishment for his audacity will be harsh: incarceration for several months and a five-year prohibition of stepping back into the *ruedo*, the arena or yellow-sand ring.

As minutes go by I watch him. He stares into emptiness, deep in thought, his teeth clenched, his eyes full of determination, his arms folded on his chest. My mind goes back to the time in our early childhood when we dreamed of becoming famous bull-fighters. There had been no role models among my relatives. But Manolo had grown up in a family where three generations, his great-grandfather, grandfather, father, and two of his uncles had labored with no success at this passion. His father came close to achieving his goal, but he was called up and had to endure three years of fratricidal civil war. When the peace finally arrived, his career never took off again.   Frustrated, he ended up reminisc-ing about bullfights and bulls all day while working alongside my father, who listened patiently to his nostalgia and sorrow. Manolo, his six younger brothers, and three sisters have been my neighbors since he and I were in the third grade at the Salesian School. I was at the top of the class, but he never cared too much about any subject, reading being the only exception.

"I need to read about bulls and the art of bullfighting," he would tell me, putting aside any math or science homework. "There must be a better way to deceive an animal, get closer, and avoid been gored."

For me school was easy. Every month the teacher gave me a rubber soccer ball as a prize for being number one in the class. If the reward had been a bullfighter's cape, Manolo would have beaten me.

My friend was a child of few words. When he talked the theme revolved around bulls and bullfighters. He could name and iden-tify all the different *castas*—castes— of brave bulls. Castilian had a light brown color and a fur band of lighter color along the entire dorsal spine; Jijona had intense red fur and more height at the withers; Navarra was short in height and had a big head. He could go on and on describing the rest of the varieties. On one occasion I asked him who had been the best matador of all time. He went back to the early nineteenth century and mentioned names that I had never heard before, such as Paquito and El Chiclanero. He settled for Manolete.

"I have observed him fighting a bull in a movie," he said. "He stretched his cape out and lured the animal to charge at him close to his body. I watched in constant suspense as the horns were about to thread him through like a needle does a button."

From then on I realized that he was trying to mimic him all day, his lineaments frozen in a solemn expression. Manolete's big aquiline nose and thin cheeks accentuated his serious air. But Manolo's small nose and rounded face made him look as if he were about to sneeze. I reminded him that Manolete was killed by a bull in 1947, two years after we were born, and advised him to follow in the footsteps of those successful bullfighters who had retired alive and well. A sour-grape face would not win him any friends, I added.

"Why should I smile?" he replied, his mouth twisting into a grimace. "I haven't even come close to a bull."

He had the bullfighter's body: tall and lean, erect shoulders, and a graceful strut as if he were showing off at a *paseillo*—the initial bullfighters' entry and parade into a ring at the start of a bullfight. One might have thought that he tried to impress our neighborhood girls, but he did not. It was me who at nine years already thought of the fairer sex as the cream of the earth. He paid no attention to them.

Manolo often came over to my place and asked me if I would go upstairs and practice bullfighting with him. I had not yet made up my mind whether I would become a soccer player or a bullfighter. So I agreed to join him and practice a few *pases*—passes—namely, the sweeping movements of a cape or a *muleta*—a folded cloth draped over a wooden stick—to deceive a bull into charging past a bullfighter's body. A flat roof served as our arena. The place was so hot that the sun had bleached and cracked the bricks. It was quiet, though, as no other building stood for half a mile around and neighbors slept their afternoon siestas. Only the blue sky watched over us. Armed with a faded red towel as a cape, he stood erect and firm, pivoted on his feet and in slow motion swung the outstretched cloth. His silhouette and the outline of his cape blended into a profile that reminded me of a dancing flamenco couple –the man, posing straight and solemn, and the woman waving her long ruffled skirt to the rhythm of a guitar. After his *veronica*, as this *pase* was called, he practiced *chicuelinas* spinning and wrapping his body around the cape as he lured and feinted at an imaginary bull. I mimicked the bull by placing my hands up against my forehead as if they were horns. I hunched over and lunged against his cape over and over. When his time came to reciprocate, he balked.

"I don't know if I should be the bull," he said. "I don't want to get too familiar with an animal I'm supposed to kill."

When I complained, he relented.

Before the rapid growth that came with our early teens, we managed to slip into the bullring to watch the most important *corridas*. Like most parents, ours believed that their children were going to play soccer table all afternoon. But our plans were bigger. The first time we got in I thought it was going to be tougher than it was. In our Sunday best, we walked to the bullring. The Plaza de Toros stood next to the blue seawaters, a mile from the ancient walled-in downtown. Circular like a coliseum, it had been built with a skeleton of stone pillars. The lower two-thirds of these pillars were embedded in a brick wall and the open upper third was crowned by a white ornate entablature. Beneath large geometrical blue-tiled panels, high arched doors were opened to the public who stood waiting in long lines. The sun shone in full force. For a few cents, scores of children offered long swigs of water from earthenware pitchers. The environs bustled with onlookers and peddlers who hawked their wares over the hubbub of voices. The smell of toasted hazelnuts, almond pralines, and dry sand wafted through the surroundings.

After reaching the bullring, we scanned the area. A well-dressed, serious-looking gentleman served as our unsuspecting accomplice. We saw one and jumped the queue in front of him. Cunningly, Manolo held a couple of old tickets and waved them at him.

"My father is waiting for us inside," he said, grinning at the man.

When we reached the door, I looked ahead, lifted my right hand, and pointed with my thumb over my shoulder, indicating that someone behind me had my ticket. Manolo followed suit. Amid the doormen's screams, we hunched over and ran in between the legs of the people climbing the tiers. We split, put our visors on and sat among the spectators.

Rows were overcrowded all the way up to the covered galleries and boxes. Below us a few young beautiful women sat in the first row. Their colorful shawls hung over the railing before them, enticing the matadors to dedicate a bull to their attractive owners. Farther down was the *callejon* or runway. In this trench the bullfighters waited for their turn with their hands on the wooden fence, or *barrera*, and their pensive eyes looking out into the sand ring. Overhead, a circular row of waving red-and-yellow Spanish flags towered over the venue. The municipal band began to liven up the event by playing a bullfight *pasodoble*. Emotions surfaced in the crowd and even the stoic expression softened. Tears welled up in my eyes. Those songs exalted people's valor, life's defiance of death, and triumph's challenge. A statement made by Antonio Ordoñez—one of the best matadors of all time—illustrated the spirit of bullfighting:

"There are some afternoons when bullfighting is so important that even life is not important."

Under the spell of the music, the fiesta began when the three matadors dressed in silk suits with gold and silver sequins and black-velvet hats marched into the ring with their entourages of subaltern bullfighters and picadors filing behind. As soon as the parade and the music ended, a trumpet called for the first bull to be released. I always looked forward to one of the matadors weaving a most graceful and masterful *faena*—an array of passes—for it prompted the band to play a *pasodoble*, brightening up his performance. At that magic moment, the man, the bull, and the music fused in the arena like a toy ballerina in a jewelry box. A rush of emotion rose inside me. Unfortunately, such scenes were infrequent. This would be so on this occasion, for this *corrida* proceeded perfunctorily. There were three matadors with two bulls apiece. Each bull went through the thirds or three acts of the fight: lance, *banderillas*, and death. In the first third, a matador swung his pink cape with yellow underside to execute artistic *veronicas*. He steered the bull to charge against a picador, who waited on his steel-armored horse with the metal point of his wooden pole aiming at the animal. The lance inflicted a one-inch-deep wound in the withers and drew rivulets of shining blood which slid down the black fur. After the bull had been weakened with two or three punctures, the trumpet announced the end of this act. In the second third, without a cape or any other protection, a subaltern stood near the center of the ring shouting gutturals to rouse the bull to action from afar. The animal took off and lunged at him. He made a feint. The distraction drove the animal brushing against his body as he raised his arms and sank into the flesh the harpoon-shaped steel tips of a pair of *banderillas*. The colorful wooden sticks dangled over the flanks as the *banderillero*—as these specialized assistants were called—ran for his life jumping over the fence to safety, the enraged bull tramping close on his heels. After this maneuver was repeated thrice, the last third followed. The matador grabbed a *muleta* and a sword and composed a repertoire of statuesque passes which wore the bull down. The bull's charges turned into steps and head tosses. The matador performed half passes and steered the bull to a standstill position with his forelegs and hind limbs close together and head slightly bent forward. The animal was ready for the kill. The matador stood straight before the bull with his right foot a short step ahead. With his tiptoes fixed on the ground, he raised his sword and sighted along the blade at the target area between the bull's shoulders. The sand-brushing lower edge of the *muleta* came closer and closer to his muzzle to egg him on. Then the matador flung his body forward and sank the sword into the bull's flesh. Two bulls died after staggering for a few seconds; one hemorrhaged profusely and collapsed; the rest received several misplaced stabs and ended up executed with a dagger sunk into their nape. One of the bulls received the public's applause in recognition of his bravery and nobleness as a team of mules adorned with little bells, ribbons, pompons, and flags dragged him away from the arena. None of the bullfighters was granted bull ears or tails as trophies. At the end of the event, I met Manolo outside the ring. On our way home he commented on the incidents at the *corrida,*

"The second bull was not brave enough. He kept digging sand with his legs, and the fifth couldn't see well out of his left eye. Didn't you notice how he had a harder time charging on that side? I don't think Bienvenida understood the animal. He kept insisting on fighting him with his right hand."

With the coming of adolescence, our free access to the bull-ring ended, but not my penchant and my friend's passion for the bullfight. We attended a few *corridas.* It required a great deal of sacrifice on our part. We collected stale bread from our homes and our neighbors' and salvaged small scraps of yard metal to sell. A month's worth of work paid only for one ticket. By that time, we also began to frequent the Matadero Municipal —a slaughter-house—which lay half a mile away from our building. We made up the excuse of visiting the manager's son, who was a *maletilla*—an apprentice bullfighter. This youngster practiced with real bulls every week and flaunted his superior training over us. The slaughterhouse received those animals that had been rejected for *corridas* by choosy matadors and breeders. A bull was considered fit to fight if he was over four years of age, at least 950 pounds, brave and *limpio*—clean of any defect such as a broken horn or a blind eye.

We hoped El Niño del Matadero—the Slaughterhouse Kid as he called himself— would take pity on us and let us fight a bull. It never happened. His father forbade us to hone our skills at his facilities. It was plain jealousy. Short and coarse, his son handled the cape and *muleta* with less finesse than a man hanging laundry out on a wash line. Manolo decided to use the shadow of the night to hone his bullfighting skills and correct this gross inequality. He convinced me to join him. I asked whether the security guard at the slaughterhouse would catch us.

"Don't worry," Manolo said. "Earlier this evening I handed him some money and a bottle of wine. He's a good old man. He'll turn a blind eye. He likes me, you know. I understand his predicament. He had some bad experiences. A few weeks ago a few guys gagged him and tied him down until they finished fighting the bulls. He knows I would never do that to him ... that I'll always ask for his permission."

With the help of a full moon, we climbed the brick fence-wall and stood atop of it. An eerie silence fell upon us. Now and then, lows of cows and chirps of crickets broke a stillness laden with the stench of manure. Below us lay a large square courtyard.

"We'll bring a bull down there," Manolo said. "The floor isn't made of sand like at a real *ruedo*. It's concrete. If a bull tosses you high in the air and you hit your head against this hard surface, you are through."

The full moon had risen behind us and illuminated our way casting our tilted shadows on the ground. In the courtyard, two corrals were separated by a door, each with eight bulls waiting for their death the next day. We teetered along the edge of the fence toward the corral walls. The animals were lying down and as we drew closer they began to puff and grunt. A big bull that kept away from the rest of the herd raised his head and pointed his two long and wide horns at us, his eyes aglow like a pair of embers in the dark. The animal stood up, burred, and shook his head. Manolo jumped inside one of the corrals, opened the door, and pushed the bulls with his hands, goading and steering them into the adjacent enclosure.

"Bulls don't attack men when they are together," he explained as he was doing it.

He allowed one bull to move back into the empty corral and closed the door. I opened another door that led the isolated animal into the courtyard, where my friend was already waiting. I climbed back to safety. The bull trotted out across the expanse and stopped next to a few troughs attached to the wall opposite the corrals. Manolo extended his cape and stood in the center of the improvised *ruedo* with his shoulders arched backwards and his chest stuck out. He flapped the cape once. The bull charged toward him, his tromps resonating in the sepulchral silence of the night. Rotating slowly, his cape swung in front of the animal like a mainsail caught by sea winds. He looked at me and smiled. After a repertoire of passes he invited me to come down. I declined. He wielded his *muleta*. The moonlight silvered his silhouette and the bull's, as he anchored his feet on the floor to pivot. He lured the animal back and forth without moving an inch. Suddenly, passing behind the cape, the bull stopped halfway, jerked his head up and to the side and tossed my friend down to the ground. I jumped down with my cape, but before I could intervene Manolo had rolled out of the way of the bull's horns. He sprang back on his feet and signaled me to stay away. I could sense his anger. He challenged the bull again and again until he imposed his dominance.

After a while we managed to return the bull to the corral. When we were about to call it a night, the manager—who had paid an unexpected visit to the facilities— burst into the courtyard. I took to my heels but he grabbed Manolo before he could clear the fence. From afar I heard swearwords mixed with screams.

"I'll speak to your father tomorrow. If I catch you again, I'll drown you! Do you hear me?"

I did not see Manolo for a month. He had been grounded, but he never admitted this to me when he finally came out of the house. He did say something about the manager dunking and holding his head into the troughs over and over until he almost drowned him.

"I reminded my father of what he had told me many times ... that bullfighting requires a lot of sacrifice, that you have to sweat ink before you can call yourself a bullfighter," Manolo said. "I did what I had to do. He ranted and raved, but I knew that deep inside he was proud of me."

Nothing dissuaded Manolo. No sooner had his wounds healed than he fell back into his old ways. He would go to the slaughterhouse in the middle of the night and tell me all about his escapades the next day. As for me, I decided to hang up my cape. A soccer stadium was built in front of our building and this sport captured all my attention. It was only then that I began to question bullfighting. I had always seen the blood and death of a bull with some reservation. In the past my mind avoided dwelling on those issues. Now when I mentioned my qualms to Manolo, he looked me straight in the eye and said,

"Have you ever witnessed the killing of bulls and cows at a slaughterhouse?"

I shook my head and he went on to describe the horrors.

"When animals are herded to be slaughtered, they're aware of what's taking place in front of them. Often bulls have to be forced to go into the killing station by hitting or electrocuting their genitals. Once in the line, they flail around and moo in terror at the smell of blood and bovine corpses during their one-long-minute stay in death row. Butchers lock them inside a narrow cage, immobilize their limbs and neck with chains, and cut their jugulars open with a knife. Animals are kept alive for about eight minutes, so that their hearts can pump all their blood out of the hemorrhaging veins. Otherwise, their meat loses value.

"There must be a better way of doing it, isn't there?" I said.

"Well ... yes. At some advanced facilities abroad, bulls are zapped unconscious with electroshock before their throats are sliced, except those sacrificed by the Jewish kosher rite. They must remain conscious throughout the bloodletting. In this country, butchers sometimes use a pointed knife to sever the medulla and paralyze bulls completely or hammer their heads open. Some animals convulse for a while before passing out. Do you think these methods are more humane than bullfighting?"

"I know," I said. "There isn't any humane way of killing. But you're missing the point. The problem is that bullfighting takes place in public, before men, women, and children."

"There're worse public spectacles. Some people who turn a blind eye to boxing condemn bullfighting as immoral. It's pure hypocrisy."

"Granted, but it doesn't justify it."

"Put yourself in a bull's place. Would you rather die inside the arena fighting or at a slaughterhouse with your feet and hands tied up? I mean, both ways take about the same amount of time."

"That isn't the point. It is the public exposure to violence that counts, the bull's blood and death, the bullfighters' injuries or death."

"Violence? Don't people go to movies to watch violence? Death is part of our daily life. There are deaths in sports such as boxing or car racing. Bullfighting is like a tragicomedy. It's the representation of life and death. It's an art, a beautiful and dangerous art."

"If only the bull's life were spared as it is in Portugal."

"In Portugal, bulls are killed right after the *corrida*. Besides, the last third, the death of the bull, is the most important part of bullfighting. You know that. A bullfighter can do a beautiful *faena*, but if he doesn't kill the bull on the first stab, his work is worthless. Good matadors distinguish themselves from the less skillful by the way they kill."

"Manolo, that's today's concept. It can be changed. Maybe there are ways to make bullfighting more acceptable."

"Well, let me tell you something. It wouldn't change the position taken by animal lovers' groups. Nothing will stop those people until they turn us all into vegetarians."

For the next three years I met Manolo every now and then. He was often away busy with his bullfighting. Then, one day I was called to visit him at Residencia Zamacola. He had gone to a *tientas*—a testing of brave calves at a bull breeder's ranch—and had been gored in his right groin. The horn had injured the femoral vein, but by the skin of a nail, it had spared the femoral artery and the internal organs. Otherwise, I would have been at his funeral. A surgeon sutured his wound with forty stitches. He looked pale because of the loss of blood. Yet his happiness was evident in his radiant smile. He could barely talk because it aggravated his pain. He mentioned he had enough *cojones*—balls—anyway, even if he would have lost the right scrotum, which the surgeon had reattached. A week in the hospital and a month of rehabilitation led to his recovery. Back on his feet, he was back to his old habits.

A few days later he asked me to accompany him to pay a visit to an *apoderado*, a bullfighters' agent, Don Francisco Aranda. The obese businessman bore a red baby-like complexion, a smug smile, and a brown-haired wig that stuck out from the nape of his neck. Hanging on the wall behind his mahogany desk were pictures of him, one shaking Generalissimo Franco's hand and another kneeling before the late Pope John XXIII. He sat smoking a big cigar which he plucked from his lips with his right fingers every few seconds after exhaling big puffs of smoke.

"Don Francisco, this is Pepe. We have been friends through fair and foul, so I have asked him to join me for this important moment in my life. Last month at Don Jose Cabernero's *capea* you asked me to pay you a visit in a few weeks. You said you might have a place for me at a *novillada*—bullfights of young bulls. You remember, don't you?"

"*Sí, sí*, I remember. You handle the cape well. Maybe I can do something for you. I have launched quite a few good bullfighters: Rafael de Paula, Jose Fuentes. But this is an expensive business."

"You won't be disappointed, Don Francisco."

"You must understand. There are a lot of expenses. The tickets only pay for the bulls and the facility. Someone has to pay for your *cuadrilla* ... three *banderilleros*, two picadors, and one *mozo de espada* ... you know, everyone who has to assist the bullfighter inside the arena."

"We all risk something. I risk my life. If I triumph, as I will, you'll make up for your losses and reap good returns."

The businessman sized Manolo up from head to toe, nodding in a condescending gesture. This character made my friend grow more and more disappointed as he tried to dissuade him. I could smell a rat.

"No, that isn't the way it's done nowadays," the businessman said. "You must pay part of those expenses or there won't be any *novillada*."

"How much?"

I couldn't hold my tongue anymore.

"Manolo, if he doesn't value your life, why should you do business with him?"

"Oh, a know-it-all ... I thought your friend was just a witness, not an adviser,"

"It's okay, Pepe, let him set the conditions."

"Ten thousand pesetas. That's all you'll need."

There wasn't any answer. That was a lot of money, more than three months of a worker's salary. My friend shook his hand and signaled me with his head that we were departing. I took my leave with a nod. One should make enemies only when it is absolutely necessary. In this business, Manolo already had enough stumbling blocks. The disappointing experience did not discourage him. One evening he walked into the Cafeteria La Camelia on San Juan de Dios Plaza, where I was drinking a cup of coffee with a couple of friends. The place bustled with beautiful girls in miniskirts and male university students who tried to seduce them. Through the thick mist of smoke, I saw Manolo dressed in *campero* attire—suits worn by bullfighters between *corridas*—a gray tight short jacket, close-fitted pants, black Cordoba hat, and brown ankle boots. The girls noticed him. He came over, ordered a cup of warm chocolate, and called me aside.

"I came to ask you a favor," he said. "Would you accompany me to tomorrow's *corrida*? I need a friend next to me when I jump into the arena."

I accepted. I knew I could not change his mind. The next day he kept to himself on our way to the bullring. He wore a gray cap, white shirt, ironed jeans, shining black shoes, and carried on his back a small faded-green backpack with a couple of ripped pockets, greasy leather straps, and a rusty clasp. I did most of the talking and now and them he stared at me. He wasn't listening. I asked him whether anyone in his family knew of his intentions and he looked past me.

Right at this moment, we sit at the Plaza de Toros. This is one of the most important *corridas* of the year. In the presidential box, I can see the president of the event and the provincial governor of Cadiz. Manolo has his head bent forward as if looking into his heart. He holds a sweaty scapular in his fist and his lips are pursed. A soft prayer escapes from them. The bullfighters must be following suit at the small chapel in the *plaza de toros* before getting into the *ruedo*. It is customary. Yet, my friend's devotion surprises me. He has never been religious. In our school days, the Salesian priests forced us to go to daily Mass every morning, but he paid no attention. When I asked him later, he would confess that he had been picturing himself facing a bull, devising in his mind new passes to deceive the animal or techniques to improve his skills. He didn't waste his time with priest's stuff.

Now, after he finished his conversation with God, he looks intent. The crowd is loud and the heavy hubbub around us doesn't distract him. He smiles. It's five o'clock and the moment of truth has arrived. He pulls out a rolled-up red cape and asks me to hold the empty backpack for him. The crowd's bustle dies down as a trumpet announces the release of the first bull. He stands up, makes the sign of the cross, and rushes down the gallery. He jumps into the barricaded passage, up over the wooden fence, and down into the ring. A group of spectators cheers him as a subaltern tries unsuccessfully to grab him. A great murmur rises in the bullring. Policemen stand impotent behind the fence, watching how the black bull erupts stampeding into the ring, his front legs up, his muzzle closed, fuming, blinded by the sunlight, charging forward at Manolo's blurry figure. He kneels in the center of the ring right in front of the pen with his cape hanging from his hands, barely shading his belly, the red cloth spread before him as his only protection. I can hear his voice and the heavy bull's footsteps echoing in the midst of the silence, which has fallen upon the plaza.

"Huh, *toro*! Huh!"

The bull tramps toward Manolo and as he approaches, the cape rises up, swirls in the air and lures the animal to pass by. The bull's large heaving body brushes against Manolo's shoulder. The crowd erupts in *oles*, cheering him on. Manolo stands up with his feet fixed on the ground, strikes an elegant profile pose, and tempts the bull with the cape from afar. The bull lunges against the cape and Manolo spins, rolling it around his body to deceive the bull. The animal races by him so close that not even a sheet of paper could fit between the man and the beast. He repeats the same pass again and again. The people reward him with a standing ovation. I can see enthusiasm in their faces and those sitting nearby smile at me. He is in command. Their voices rouse excited through the gaps left in between their lips by cigars and cigarettes tipping out of their mouths. Smoke clouds billow over them. Some look at each other and nod their heads in agreement. He now performs a group of *veronicas* with his masterful elegance. I note restlessness down in the barricaded runway. Policemen move from side to side. The bullring president makes angry gestures at them. Wielding their capes, three subalterns go into the ring to lure the bull away from my friend and put an end to his *faena*. The spectators boo them. The bull stops, raises his horns, and breaks into an unexpected charge against Manolo, who stands looking at his pursuers. A cloud of sand rises behind the bull.

"Watch it!" I cry out, my shout drowned by the crowd's screams.

Manolo reacts by stretching his cape out before him and jumping backwards, but the left horn punctures the cape and sinks into Manolo's body. The bull pushes him up and tosses him down onto the floor as if Manolo were a rag doll. People scream,

"He's killing him! He's killing the boy!"

Instinctively I stand up and run down the tiers. Two men hold me tightly. The three subalterns, which by now have reached the tragic scene, cover the bull's face with their cape, harness the animal, and lead him away from the victim. Manolo kneels, put his hands together as if in prayer and sets his eyes on the provincial governor. He begs his pardon and drops on the ground headlong. People are dead silent. A couple of subalterns pick him up by his arms and legs. His blood stains the *ruedo* and his blue face and bloody shirt bounce up and down as his rescuers rush him to the edge of the ring on their way to the infirmary. Everything turns calm in the bullring.

As I walk out of the grades to check on my friend's condition, one of the matadors is fighting the beast as if nothing has happened. I walk into the first-aid area. The door accessing the room looms ahead of me jammed with policemen and personnel. Inside, a strong chloroform odor feels as offensive as a slap on my face. Next to a wooden desk and a couple of rickety chairs, a couple of male nurses and a doctor in blood-stained white gowns stand talking with a middle-aged stout subaltern dressed in an worn-out, opaque attire. I ask them about my friend. The subaltern's leonine face turns red and his bushy eyebrows knit an angry expression.

"You stupid boys!" he lashes at me. "Why do you want to get killed? This is not a game!"

He doesn't let me speak. The two male nurses grab hold of him before he can reach out and punch me in the face. I raise my fists to defend myself.

"You put us at risk too!" he shouted, trying to free himself. "If you want to kill yourselves, jump in front of a train! But not on our watch!"

"Get the hell out of here, Montero!" the doctor says with a hoarse voice, his right hand fussing with his plastic black-framed glasses, his left holding a lit cigarette. "I don't want any fight. This young man hasn't done anything wrong."

I again inquire about my friend's state.

"He's badly wounded," the bullfight surgeon says. "The horn penetrated his lung. An ambulance has taken him to Residencia Zamacola. I couldn't do anything for him here."

I am afraid to ask him whether he thinks Manolo will make it. I go out of the bullring. I can hear the spectators' applause and cheers for the matadors from several blocks away. I press ahead. The main street is almost deserted. A couple of ladies in black wait for a tram. The sun swelters overhead while the sea breeze has died down as if grieving over the tragedy. I think of how some people have short memories, of how expendable a young life might be in their view. Right at this moment everyone enjoys the *corrida* while my friend hovers near death or maybe he is already dead. Tomorrow, on the last page of the local newspaper, lost among advertisements, there will be a small note mentioning his untimely death. The governor's granting of his posthumous pardon will be also printed in small letters, since I saw from the corner of my eye how he held out a white handkerchief at the crowd's insistence, vouchsafing their request. It's still hard for me to understand why someone would bounce into a ring and risk his life. I know bullfighters seek more than fame and money. To them, bullfighting is like a cult, a way of life, a feeling stronger than any other attachment. But the public considers it just entertainment. I can see putting my life on the line for a worthy cause, but not for that. I guess one must be born a bullfighter to do so.

Deep in thought, I find myself before the flaking whitewashed structure of Residencia Zamacola. The security men let me in. They must have noticed the shakiness of my hands and the paleness of my face. I inquire about my friend, fearful that I may be directed to the morgue, but he is in surgery. On the third floor, where the surgical suites are, the waiting room reeks of smoke. The off-colored white tiles and stale yellow walls frame the eerie silence. A couple of smokers stand at the door entrance and two women sit across from one another with pensive looks. I ask them about my friend. One waits for news of her daughter who has had an attack of appendicitis and has no idea about Manolo's condition and the other looks at me with teary eyes and shrugs as if I have spoken to her in a foreign language. I am nervous and fiddle with Manolo's backpack. In one of the side pockets there is a clean white comb inscribed with the name of an inn, La Hacienda de Aragon. Most bullfighters are vain and try to keep their hair in order all the time even when they are before a bull. My friend is not. He commented to me about this little inn in Boquiñeni where he had stayed overnight after fighting wild cows in a makeshift *ruedo* at the village's main square. I find a pair of railroad ticket stubs from this trip and a newspaper cutout from El Periódico de Aragon, which reads as follows,

"Yesterday the wild cow contest in Boquiñeni was a great suc-cess in public attendance and enjoyment. Among the aspirant bullfighters, Manolo Hernandez stood out as a valiant and prom-ising figure. His handling of the animals ..."

It goes on to describe how his performance surpassed by far those of the rest of the *maletillas* who had flocked to the little town.   In another pocket inside the backpack is a picture of his family. It must have been taken four or five years ago for their large-family document, which allowed his father to get a monthly supplement of a few pesetas for each of his children.   His par-ents sit smiling and holding his youngest brother Lorenzo and his baby sister Maria in their arms. Next to them stand his two middle brothers, Cipriano and Javier, and before them are the six older children, Marta, Rosa, Salvador, Gonzalo, Pedro, and Manolo, who stands first from the right. All his siblings, even the baby, exhibit stoic expressions, as if they had been promised a marionette performance but were taken to a piano concerto. I guess they all realized that they were not celebrating anything. Manolo wears a jacket, short pants, and a wide tie that stops at the lower border of his ribcage. His eyes shine with the determi-nation and certainty that suggests nothing can stop him from reaching his goal.

Just when I think I have emptied the backpack completely, I find a folded envelope crammed into a small inner pocket. It is folded, sealed, and smeared with a few dirty fingerprints. It bears my name: "*Para Pepe Pastrana Lopez.*" Inside, there is a folded note, three one-thousand-peseta bills, and his national identifica-tion card. The handwriting reflects his painstaking penmanship.

Dear Pepe,

I'm sorry that I have to put you through this mess. But we have been together for many years and you know that my life belongs to the bull. I have hidden my national identification card so that no one can find out who I am until you identify my body—I hope the bull has left my face intact. Otherwise, please make sure my mother doesn't have to see me dead.

I am bothered now by the fact that I have inadvertently over-looked a note written on the lower part of the envelope. It reads as follows,

"Please, open this envelope only in case that the bull kills me."

It is too late now, and of no real consequence because the chances for my friend's survival seem dismal. I continue reading it.

"The three thousand pesetas should help with my funeral expenses. I have picked a lot of grapes and strawberries in France to save this money. My family cannot afford more financial strain. My poor father has a hard time making ends meet with so many children. I wish I could have become a good matador and freed them from poverty. Tell my mother that my last thoughts were of her and that I loved her as much as she loved me. She made me happy, but bullfighting is in my blood, and no one could have stopped me. I was determined to suc-ceed or die. Please, hand my identification card to Marieta. She likes me and I like her too, but I never told her. I wanted to be a man with a future before I asked her to be my girlfriend. At the very least she should know that I was not indifferent. You can have my "campero" suit. You will be able to hit on girls with improved success, I can assure you—even if you are not a bullfighter. I am kidding. You know I never joke, but this time I have to. I hate saying goodbye. Think of me doing a "veronica" because I will keep practicing up there until your time comes. We will meet again, though I hope after quite some time, since I wish you a long happy life.

> *Your friend,*
> *Manolo*

I didn't know about Marieta, the slaughterhouse manager's youngest daughter. He always said that women were a distrac-tion for men who wanted to make it; that you should not get involved or even think of women until you had progressed in your career. Her father must have pardoned him for his trans-gression, or he might have seen her on the sly.

The automatic door yawns open to let out a male surgical nurse in green attire with a mask under his chin and platform sandals. I ask him about my friend,

"*Oh, sí, el espontaneo,*"—a young aspirant bullfighter who jumps into the arena—"Doctor Marquez is operating on him. A bad gore. We have been transfusing blood like crazy. What blood type are you?"

"Type A."

"Good. Let's go down to the blood bank."

On our way down, he informs me that the horn didn't penetrate deeply, but the fractured ribs did, causing as many deep wounds as if he had been stabbed several times. His heart is holding. The surgeon is almost sure he will make it. A nurse asks me a few questions while she punctures a vein in my elbow. My blood flows inside a bag. I wish my blood would infuse Manolo not only with my strong desire for his recovery but also with a steadfast determination to abandon bullfighting. The latter will be highly unlikely.

I go back to the waiting room. His family is here. His father and brothers appear composed and solemnly proud, his sisters resigned, and his mother devastated, her head sunk into her lap sobbing. She now lifts her head and I wonder how many times in the future, those eyes, which look so much like her son's, will bear the same expression of despair.

FACADE OF THE CATHEDRAL OF CADIZ

CARNAVAL

The boy was alone, right in front of the carnival float where I stood with my fellow choristers. He must have been about five or six years old. His brown eyes stared ahead with an expression of joyful impatience for the music. He wore gray shorts, a white shirt under a blue V-neck jersey, a red cone hat, a red-and-blue garland that hung around his neck, and a pair of shining black leather shoes. A jubilant crowd packed San Juan de Dios Plaza. Guitars, lutes, and mandolins burst into melody and the tango *carnavalesco* came to life:

"Cadiz, *no sé que encierras dentro de tus murallas...*"
I do not know what Cadiz keeps within its walls,
That infuses calm and serenity into me.
Perhaps it is magic or some kind of spell
Or it's because I am in paradise..."

Mesmerized, the child mumbled the song between his lips. I noted his emotions rising: his face reddened, his jaw clenched, his eyes sparkled with excitement, and his breathing rushed as if driven by a heart, which had unleashed all the contained love and admiration for this celebration. I could sense his yearning to grow up and become a man, so that he could fulfill his dream: to dress in costume and lift a voice from a carnival float. When the tango ended, he broke into applause. I turned to the side to shake a hand proffered to me by a spectator, and when I looked back to the area where the little child had been, I could not see him anymore. I heard someone shouting,

"Pepe! Pepe! *Dónde se ha metido este niño?*—Where has my child gone ?"

It was a woman's shout that brimmed with concern and fear. I could not see her, for a thick wall of people stood in the way. I felt guilty that I had not acted right away when I realized the child was alone. I had not paid proper attention to him. My ego ran away with me at seeing him admiring the costumes of the forty members of my group, the Leprechauns: green attire, pointy ears, red beard, a pilgrim green hat, two large green butterfly wings with large black dots, and black leather shoes. We were a proud coterie and had spent several evenings every week for six months, rehearsing and preparing our yearly repertoire. Last year we had been dressed as Bedouins and people had loved our songs. This year our costumes and songs were even better. I felt great. I had the impression that I had lived the entire year just for the sake of standing here today, singing to the crowd.

"Pepe! Pepe! Answer me, my child."

There was no answer. Then I heard her describing him to the people around her.

"Have you seen my little boy? He is four and wears a red cone hat, a red and blue garland, and a large mustache."

No one seemed to pay any attention to her. No one answered her request. Or there were too many people for me to make out their comments. Yet I could hear her clearly as if she were on the other side of a tall brick fence in front of me.

"Is anyone going to help me? Please, if you see a police officer, let him know. Maybe I can call my child on the loudspeaker."

I cried out that I had seen her child and that he was fine, though he had lost his fake mustache. No one acknowledged my words. I looked around for a police officer, but I saw none. The place was jammed with people. I decided to look for him. The poor woman was in so much distress. Now and then young children had gotten lost during these celebrations, but had usually freaked out and bawled until their parents had found them. This boy was different. He had shown no fear. Spellbound, he mingled with the crowd, listening to songs, guitars, and mandolins.

His eyes shone with enthusiasm as if he could hardly wait to grow up and become a chorister. While singing, I watched him mimic my hand gestures, which, like those of a conductor, accompanied my baritone. A tilted fringe of hair reached the child's right eyebrow and swept his forehead back and forth, as if driven by the excitement in his voice.

I got down off my float. I heard his mother's screams but I still could not see her. I stood on my toes, craned my neck, but to no avail. I could not see her.

!Pepe, Pepe! ... *dónde estas, hijo mío?"*

Her voice became higher pitched and tinged with anxiety. I heard a man's voice. I figured it was the child's father,

"Calm down, we'll find him. How could he get away from you?" He sounded confident and said it in a loving tone.

"I don't know ... he just scurried away between the people's legs."

"That boy is so naughty. He is probably watching one of the choruses so engrossed that he does not even hear us."

"It's your mother's fault."

"My mother's fault?"

"Yes, your mother, she teaches him all sorts of old carnival songs."

I envisioned them: the man smiling at his child's devotion to Mardi Gras, thinking that it was probably his doing as he lifted his eyebrows, dropped his eyes, and scratched his forehead in an expression that belied his apparent calmness, and the woman blinking repeatedly as she tried to fight back tears and shaking her head in disbelief. I screamed after them that I had seen their boy. They could not hear me. I tried to reach them and followed the path of their voices, but somehow I lost track of them. There was no time to waste. I looked around for the missing child. Four other choruses stood atop their own floats in the plaza, each wearing different costumes to match the name of the group: Freedom Battalion, Nightmare Phantoms, Tango Men, and Coliseum Romans. Large crowds surrounded them.

Smaller groups of about twelve singers—*chirigotas and comparsas*—attracted their own smaller audiences. One group was dressed in Star Wars costumes. Among them were Darth Vader with his black mask and dark attire, Luke Skywalker with the *jedi's* robe and light saber, Princess Lea with her long white gown and a bun on either side of her head; Yoda with the face of a Chihuahua crossed with a frog and three-fingered claws, and C3-PO with his golden face and robotic limbs. I could not hear their song but they had their crowd bursting their sides with laughter. At the edges of the plaza, fortunate customers sat at outside restaurants and cafes enjoying food and music. An appetizing scent of fried fish and wine wafted around the area. People were having a good time. Some dressed in their best, some casually, some wore simple costume items— red hats, big cones, large mustaches, masks, wigs, whistles, flutes—and others flaunted elaborate costumes: pirate, fairy, Zorro, geisha, Roman emperor, transvestite. Confetti and streamers carpeted the streets.

It was getting dark and the strings of lamps shone above the plaza, as if the entire place were under a giant cobweb of multi-colored twinkling lights. A monumental terrace in the City Hall building displayed large banners and flags. Several dignitaries watched the enjoyment of their constituents. Among them were the president of Spain, Rodriguez Zapatero, or someone disguised as him, and the leader of the opposition, Mariano Rajoy or his impersonator. A truce from their constant wrangling must have taken place, I thought, for each had an arm over the other's shoulder. Anything was possible at Mardi Gras.

I had to jostle through the crowd to find my way. Revelers greeted me with flutes and whistles, threw confetti and streamers at me, or removed them with colorful dusters. Laughter and smiles erupted from everywhere. I could not hear the child's parents. They must have been looking for him in another area of the plaza. After a while, their voices reached me again.

"He might be in front of one of those choruses," the father said.

"Why does he do this to me?" The mother said. "He is going to kill me with worry."

"Let's go over there ... he likes that choir."

"He likes all of them."

I caught a glimpse of their backsides as they walked farther away from me, jostling their way through the crowd. The woman had a graceful figure. She was a little short, wore her wavy brown hair bobbed, a long white skirt adorned with large light blue flowers, a white blouse, and high-heeled black shoes. Her husband, who was tall and thin, had an aristocratic bearing, well-trimmed brown hair, and wore light-blue pants and a white *guayabera* cotton shirt. The upper parts of his ankles looked as smooth and dainty as those of a ceramic figurine, for he did not wear any socks under his blue canvas shoes. Both had their hair full of confetti and tried to make their way by pouring through a jungle of streamers, as revelers threw the colorful ribbons at one another.

Out of the corner of my eye, I saw the child. He held on to the doctor's gown of a tall lanky man, who sported a surgical mask, and large plastic framed glasses. Man and child plodded along with the crowd, the child in front of him. Carrying a large syringe in his hand, the man guffawed as he faked injecting the passersby. The syringe was the size of an air pump for a bike, and the needle was a piece of plastic pipe. Most people approached by the fake doctor avoided him or laughed at their own fear, but some went after him with colorful dusters and hollowed plastic hammers. The impact of the hammers made musical notes similar to those of a xylophone. The child's laughter rang out like peals of little bells. I tried to reach them through a narrow gap between the crowds but a large column of Teutonic looking tourists got in the way, marching five abreast.

The Germans were dressed in their customary garb: men, in black shorts, long white socks, red vests, and green suspenders, and women in long blue skirts, white shirt with lace collar, and red vest. A tall beautiful blonde in her twenties broke through the ranks for a moment and offered me a bag of peanuts. She spoke a pidgin Spanish and said they had come from Hamburg, pointing to two large buses parked next to the harbor. She invited me to join the group, but I courteously declined and kept an eye in the direction of my target. Hunger came upon me. I rolled a soft peanut shell between my fingers and peeled one, enjoying their roasted scent. On cue, their leader played a trumpet and the members of the line put their hands on top of the shoulders of the one in front of them. They then all moved forward in unison, dancing, laughing, and singing in Spanish,

"La comba de Jalisco ...
Comes and goes,
goes and comes ..."

When the group of fake Germans passed me, I saw the tall man with the syringe in the midst of a crowd, but the child was nowhere to be seen. I approached him and asked him about the boy's whereabouts.

"I don't know, man ... he wasn't with me. I did not pay any attention. There are so many people around. I wish I could help you. He probably went home."

I plodded out of the plaza onto Pelota Street and saw him again near El Populo Arch—the door into the medieval quarters. There was a thick crowd around a man dressed in a black tuxedo and a topper, who held a tripod with a poster nailed to it. The boy had managed to creep into the audience and reached a position next to the elegant *romancero*. The *romancero* held a baton in his hand and pointed to the poster where a colorful comic strip filled the entire display: bulls running on the streets, ladies dressed in white mantillas, bullfighters with swords, children with red capes, policemen running from the bulls. On top of all these drawings was a headline in big letters:

LA CORRIDA DE TOMAS CRUCERO,"— that is, "Tom Cruise's bullfight."

I listened to the beginning of his monologue as I jostled my way through. His voice resonated warm and hilarious. He recounted his own version of an incident that had occurred in Cadiz in November 2009, when bulls escaped from the movie set of *Knight and Day*, featuring Tom Cruise. Unfamiliar with running bulls in the streets, the city of Cadiz was in for a surprise. The story started as follows:

"Tom Cruise fell in love with a dame from Cadiz.
Since she did not give a damn about him,
He let the bulls run loose on the streets"

As I was getting closer to the child, I saw the *romancero* aiming his pointer to the second comic strip.

"Old women ran away from the bulls,
young wives ran amok after his balls,
—excuse me, I meant to say bulls—
Tom Cruise gave them the slip;
husbands ran after him angrier than the bulls;
sword in hand, toreros ran close to his bulls,
Tom Cruise took to his heels ..."

Mimicking the audience, the boy laughed when the people laughed and applauded when the people applauded as if he had a keen understanding of the double meaning of every word the *romancero* had said. I was sure that he did not. When I finally reached the first row of the audience, I looked at him and tried to catch his eye to put him at ease. He never glanced at me. When I was only a few yards away, I saw him leaving. He held his cone hat with his left hand, and jostled his way out of the crowd between the legs of the spectators. I yelled to him,

"Pepe, wait! Your parents are looking for you. Let me take you to them."

Everyone looked at me laughing as if my screams were part of the comics. No one attempted to stop the child.

"Couldn't you people see that the little child is alone... for goodness's sake!"

"What child?" asked the *romancero*. "Be cool, man ... it's Mardi Gras."

I roamed the streets looking for the boy. Crowds had petered out. I no longer heard the anxious calls from the child's parents. It was a splendorous night with the moon hovering in the center of a starry sky, and a restful silence fell upon the city like a white veil on the face of a bride. The murmur of the seawater was everywhere. A refreshing breeze had set in and only an occasional distant song from tireless revelers laced the stillness. Spotlights were on the City Hall building. It boasted an arcade made of oyster stones, which supported a façade with four portentous white marble pillars arising from a large terrace, and four solemn balconies that flanked the structure on either side. The stillness of the night enhanced the cozy beauty of the building. Its white splendor dazzled me and filled me with relief. It made it hard to conceive that anything bad could occur in this town. The thought comforted me. It made me envision the child at home: the boy asleep resting in a little bed, a light-blue blanket covering him, the mother tucking him in, the father watching him with loving eyes, the warm marks of their kisses on his forehead, the parents' grateful prayers to God.

My reverie was broken by the sight of the child and an overweight police officer, who had a large mustache, plastic-framed glasses, and a subtle limp in his left leg. They came down from Pelota Street and stepped into the plaza, the child jumping over the granite cobblestone separating the asphalt from the sidewalk at the foot of the City Hall's arcade. He almost tripped and fell. The ground already lay slippery with the early dew and salty sprinkle from the nearby seawaters. Pepe still wore his red-and-blue garland and his red cone hat and held a chocolate bar in his right hand. They passed by me in a hurry, the officer pulling the boy along by the left hand. I overheard them talking, their words interrupted by their attempts to catch their breath.

"Your grandma ... also lives ... there?"

"Yes ... my two grandmas ... and five aunts ... four uncles ... and fifteen cousins."

"How in the heck ... did you get lost ... with so many people ... around you?"

The child's voice rang like a peal of little bells and contrasted the coarseness and firmness of his companion's. I was tempted to stop the officer and asked him where he had found the child, but he had not even acknowledged my presence, nor had the boy. The child seemed happy and showed no trace of crying on his face. They rushed into Santa Maria Quarters by Sopranis Street, their heavy and lame tread and quick and light footsteps faded in the distance.

I sat down on one of the benches in the plaza, to smoke a cigarette. I had enough excitement for one day. The place was deserted. The tall palm trees barely swung in the wind, and a few sleepy parakeets chirped on their tops. The branches of the four-story-high leafy acacias almost touched the balconies and windows of the small buildings flanking the plaza. The clock on the small tower of the City Hall building showed 1:10 in the morning. A few rings of smoke spiraled from my cigarette upwards, to melt into the quiet darkness of the morning. Deep in thought, I stared at the pavement in the center of the plaza, which years ago had been turned into a pedestrian promenade, as it used to be centuries earlier. Under the multicolor net of lamps, narrow stripes of little black pebbles sparkled, as they alternated with square-shaped white marble tiles streaked with delicate brown, gray, and pink capricious drawings. The rectangular area was encircled with small trees, which had been recently planted. My eyes gazed up along Pelota Street to the Cathedral Plaza and set on the East Tower, now silvered by the moonlight.

I turned my eyes toward the east side, where the majestic Puerta del Mar—Gate to the Sea—led to the harbor. In the middle of the restful night, the majestic outlines of the main door of the city stood out in the outside world and seemed to proclaim, more than ever, Cadiz's maritime calling. My thoughts went to the many expeditions that sailed off Cadiz and changed the map of our world. I saw the statues of jumping dolphins flanking both sides of the gate and the two tall columns with the inscription of Non Plus Ultra—meaning that the ancient world ended here—the left crowned with Spain's emblem and the right with Cadiz's emblem. A large cruise ship put out late and passengers leaned against the rails on deck and enjoyed the peacefulness of the bay and the dormant city after a hectic day of revelry. A few employees of the bars and restaurants on San Juan de Dios Plaza piled up the outdoor chairs and tables, ready to call it a day. Their fatigue made them silent and only the clangs and thuds broke the stillness. Far off, towering above the square in the northeast corner was the Trocadero Building, where the lights of the Burger King on the first floor were off. A few yard away, almost at the foot of the same building a taxi stand stood. Now and then I could hear the laughter of two taxi drivers, who chatted and smoked next to their cabs. I could hear their laughter now and then. A couple of customers came, and off they went. I sat for a while, basking in the joy of the certainty that the child now slept in the safety of his own home.

Five minutes later, I heard someone approaching. I looked over my shoulder and saw the lame police officer with the big mustache and glasses. He looked flabbergasted: his face red, his eyes bewildered, and his voice tremulous.

"Have you seen a little boy alone with a blue-and-red garland?"

Puzzled, I responded no. I asked what had happened, since I had seen him with the child earlier.

"When we got to where he said his parents lived ... he panicked. He could not find the house ... he began screaming, 'No, no, this is not my house! Well, well, it is ... but it is not. It has changed. Papa! Mama!' and he darted off before I could get hold of him."

"Where did he say he lived?"

"*La casa de la posada.*"

"That house does not exist anymore ... it was demolished at least ten years ago ... I used to live there as a child."

"I know ... two new buildings and a café have replaced it."

"An old neighbor said that she remembered a family with his last name, but they moved away many years ago before the building was leveled to the ground."

The officer rushed away toward the cathedral where he had first found the child. I kept wondering about the child's last name, but I had forgotten to ask him and I did not want to shout at this early hour of the morning. Suddenly an eerie sensation overcame me. The east side of San Juan de Dios Plaza, which led into the harbor, appeared enveloped in a mist, as if I were looking at it through a steamed-up glass. There were a few cabs in the foggy center of the plaza. It was weird. Over a decade ago, this taxi stand had been dismantled and moved to the eastern outskirts of the plaza. The ghost taxi stand lay on asphalt. I could not make out the black pebbles and marble tiles of the rectangular promenade or the encircling little trees, which had replaced the resurrected blacktop a long time ago. Late 1970s and early 1980s model cars sat waiting, painted with a distinctive long red stripe on either side of the body. The acacias and palm trees were dwarfed, and the Puerta del Mar—Gate to the Sea—along with a railing, which separated the eastern border of the plaza from the harbor, appeared to have been moved nearer to where I was. On the northeast corner, at the Trocadero building, the Burger King Restaurant was not there. A little closer the defunct Samuel Restaurant had come back to life and now loomed in the background. Fixed to one of the doors was an old red poster announcing the Carnival of Cadiz. I could not distinguish the date but I saw that it depicted a large emblem of the city covered by an enormous red mask. The restaurant was closed for the day but the lighted red neon sign blinked off and on in the mist.

In contrast, on the west side of San Juan de Dios Plaza, where I stood, it was sharp and clear. It looked as if it had burst into view by lightning: the blue-and-white lottery stand with an octagonal shape and a pyramid-shaped roof, the swinging tall palm trees, the sidewalks paved with circular and sinusoidal stripes of little white and black pebbles, the pay phone booth. I reassured myself of my sound mind when I observed the white Picasso-like poster of the Carnival 2010—abstract revelers sang in the foreground of tall palm trees bent by the wind and a looming deformed cathedral with a large yellow cupola—on the window of a lottery stand.

Suddenly, in the midst of the hazy plaza, I saw the child's parents. They stood next to Samuel Restaurant. With each red flicker of the sign, their faces came into focus as clear as in daylight, and then sunk back into gloom a moment later when the neon faded. The woman cried and wiped her tear away with a handkerchief.

"Don't cry ... we'll find him. Maybe he is at one of your sisters'."

I then saw them rushing toward the area where I had seen the child the previous evening for the first time. The child sat on the floor asleep, leaning against a four-branch lamppost near the middle of the plaza. The gloomy area became sharp and the clear became fuzzy, as eeriness disappeared and wonder took over. I watched in awe. The parents stood in front of the child. The multicolored reflections of the strip lighting illuminated the child. He had his soft eyelids shut and a joyful smile graced his face. The red cone hat rested on his forehead. His right hand lay flaccid over the ground full of confetti, barely holding the red-and-blue garland. A few dark smears around his little mouth revealed a recent feast on the chocolate bar.

"Wake up, Pepe, my son," I heard the mother say softly. "Let's go home."

The parents kneeled in front of him. For the first time, I took a good look at them. She was young and beautiful, in her middle twenties, and he was handsome and in his late twenties. Her small contoured hand caressed her youngster's forehead, removing the hat and moving the fringe of his hair aside. She bore a loving expression as she attempted to wake the child without startling him. I could see her rosy cheeks, which contrasted with her white and spotless complexion, her brown bobbed hair hovering over her wondrous eyes populated with long eyelashes, and her rosebud mouth rendering a feeling of tenderness in her smile. Their faces seemed familiar to me, as if I had seen them before. Yet, I thought that people from the same neighborhood or town share similar physiognomies.

I kept watching them. About to hold him in his arms, the father passed his right hand under the child's shoulders and his left under the thighs, for the child had not awakened. His fingers were long and slender. Upon lifting the child, his face contracted and formed a long dimple along the side of either cheek, as if the effort caused him to smile. His nose was straight and elegant and his brown eyes shone with a honey hue when he looked at his son. The parents rushed home, the father carrying the child in his arms, the mother taking hold of the boy's left hand. His little arms rested on his chest, and his legs dangled flaccid. They hurried by me so closely that I could have touched the boy. With the woman's flowery perfume still lingering, I turned around to greet the couple,

"Good night, I'm glad you found your son."

They ignored me. For a moment, I thought they were afraid of strangers. Then something caught my eye. The boy had a birthmark on his left thigh. It was reddish, the size of a quarter, and shaped like a strawberry. Oh, God! That is the same birthmark I have on my thigh, I thought. That child ... is me!

"Papá! Mamá!"

With open arms, I ran toward them. But my embrace found only the void space of their shadows. I stood with my arms hugging my own chest, while I suddenly saw the mist lifting around me. The ghost plaza transformed before my very eyes. It rose and disappeared into thin air by the might of a silent force. From all sides of the plaza, big pieces of cityscape akin to the parts of a puzzle burst forth. I watched in awe, how the pieces seamlessly, began to fill in the emptiness and, quickly and noiselessly, reversed the transfigured area. The entire plaza recovered its original appearance, and the serenity of the night enshrouded everything as if nothing had happened.

THE ACCORDION MAN

Another day broke in Cadiz as a twilight sky shone with a sprinkling of stars and a gibbous moon stood still above the lighthouse. As soon as he opened his eyes, Dominick asked himself whether he would be able to eat today, put a roof over his head, and be able to send a few euros to his family in Romania. The walls of his tiny guest room seemed to be closing in on him. He rubbed his slanted blue eyes and smoothed his shoulder-length blond hair, now messed up from a long restful sleep. He sat up on the couch. The mattress sunk and the spring whined like an injured dog. He swallowed saliva, which tasted drier and more bitter than his life. He grabbed a cigarette, lit it, and after a deep inhalation, exhaled unhurriedly. A few sunrays had managed to slip through a crack between a worn-down windowsill and a sun-faded mini-blind, illuminating a puff of smoke that hovered before him. A coughing attack blew away the dancing cloud. He looked at the only piece of furniture in his room besides his couch: a small rusty table next to the window on which sat an accordion. The instrument was coated with a resplendent layer of nacre-like red, and its bellows, also red, contrasted the dazzling ivory-white of the air buttons and the black-and-white keyboard. Its front was graced with a couple of waving black snakes and its borders decorated with golden arabesques. Only the dark worn-out leather of the shoulder and wrist straps bore the marks of heavy use. There was nothing in this world he enjoyed more than his accordion. His eyes, his lips, even his expressions played to the rhythm of his music, for every note, every cadence moved him as deeply as the soft feeling of his fingers caressing his faraway wife and two children.

Next to the accordion were a few one-euro, half-euro, and five-cent coins, which reminded him of his good fortune the day before. A big smile beamed across his face. As today was Sunday, the prospect for takings seemed good. At noontime patrons liked to sit at the cafés and little restaurants flanking the large plaza, which was presided over by an impressive marble and jasper cathedral looking out to sea. Its bells now peeled nine times. Moments later, languid calls echoed from neighboring churches summoning the faithful to morning Masses. The jingles reminded him of his duties toward God. His lips quivered with thanks to the Almighty for his granting of another day of life and for the graces bestowed upon him. As he prayed he pictured the startled pigeons and seagulls that had nestled on the cathedral flying off into the sky, their wings glittering in the tepid morning sun around the marble columns and white domes of the east and west belfries and the yellow-tiled cupola. Most of these birds fluttered back to perch on the huge ornamented pillars of the main door and the two statues of the patron saints of the city, which stood atop them. Some behaved with deference and lighted on the tall palm trees gracing the plaza. Others, however, insisted on their desecrating behavior and landed on the low belfry and windows of Santiago Church, a small baroque jewel sheltered under the lee of the cathedral.

The area was familiar to him. There, he had collected most of his money for the past year, his music fitting in the plaza like Schubert's Ave Maria inside the temple. From his improvised stage he watched people's faces, and observed how their smiles bloomed when the notes of his accordion burst into life. Most walked by him without even acknowledging his presence and seldom did someone thank him or deposit a coin on the jacket lying in front of him. Yet, there were also the problem-ridden wives or husbands who paused to admire sentimental tunes as their minds unloaded their heavy burden for a while. Or parents stopped to listen to the sweet sounds, and place a few coins in their children's hands to teach them an appreciation for music. On one occasion, an act of utmost kindness rallied Dominick's hopes for mankind. After a long coinless stretch, his plaintive voice and accordion music clamored in a romantic tango. Impervious to his entreaties, onlookers and passersby held tightly to their wallets until an old lady strolled by and joined him singing, she in Spanish and he in Romanian. When their duet was over, she gingerly bent down and emptied her purse on the jacket lying before him.

His reminiscence brought a smile to his face, but did not dissipate the incrusted smell of cigarette smoke and the overnight stale stench of humanity, which tainted the air of his guest room. He stood up, opened the window, and let a gush of fresh air rush in. A large brick wall loomed so close in front of him that he could have touched it with his fingertips. It was painted with whitewash that had flaked off leaving patches of capricious shapes. The one right across his window caught his attention, because it bore the outline of the Romanian map. The Transylvanian Alps, the Carpathian Mountains, the Danube River, the Black Sea Coast, even major cities like Bucharest, Cluj-Napoca, and Craiova flashed before him, every single place where he had tried to make a living and failed. Leaving his country had been a tough decision. He had a wife and two children to sustain, not enough food, and no money for the rent. After being evicted, he and his family ended up as squatters in a rundown single-room studio in the infamous Ferentari sector of Bucharest, where drugs, crime, and prostitution abounded. Like most of their neighbors, they had no access to electricity, water, or sewage. Dominick stole power and water and even secured an illegal connection to discharge their waste. The situation distressed him. No jobs were available and his accordion did not bring in any cash. Others issues weighed heavily upon him. His parents were getting on in age and his three brothers and two sisters were close.

"My son," his father had said, "it's hard to see you go but I understand your decision. I grew up in a Communist regime. I have always been poor and hunger has dogged me since I was a child. Now with this new democratic government things are even worse. I am an old man. I need less and less food, but you are still young and have a family to take care of. Go and do what you have to do and let God provide for the rest. He's merciful and will grant us that we meet again."

Dominick interpreted the vision of the map as a good omen for the day to come. Before venturing down to the street, he wiped every single speck of dust off his accordion and, after wetting a little handkerchief with his saliva, polished off one by one each of the buttons and keys. It was too early to try the new songs he had heard on the radio. He got dressed and walked down a narrow stairs covered with worn-down, ragged marble stones. At the inner courtyard, next to a well, he came across Señora Petra, the landlady. Her big nose, thin hunchback body, and black mourning attire reminded him of an old eagle.

"*Buenos dias, señor* Lavidaki," she responded to his greeting, her lentil-sized black mole swinging off the right side of her lips.

"Lavidikus, Señora Petra, Lavidikus. *Mi nombre primero ser* Dominick," he said in pidgin Spanish.

"I'm sorry but I don't use first names when I deal with my guests. Anyway, remember that if you want to keep your room, you must bring ten euros by four PM. Otherwise, it will be available to the first person who walks in with the money."

"*Sí, señora, ya lo sé,* why repeat that every day?"

For the past few months he had been a fortunate man. He had met his quota—enough money to survive, to afford his family a modest life, and to put away a few euros for his return to Romania. His wife and children now resided in a well-kept, three-room apartment in Rahova, a resurging working class neighborhood. His dream was to save enough money to open a small restaurant, where his wife could excel preparing *ciuperci umplute*—stuffed mushrooms—or *gusita sao drob de mile*—lamb pudding. In his opinion, no one could cook like her. He envisioned himself entertaining patrons with his accordion while they feasted on the best food in Bucharest. A small notebook tucked in his pocket kept track of the extra euros he had sent to his wife. When he was alone in the evening, he calculated the Romanian *lei* held in their bank account and concluded that at the present rate his goal would be achieved in ten years. Last Sunday he earned fifty euros for three hours of music at a First Communion. If only more people hired him to make their private parties more pleasant, he could then meet his target in three or four years. He didn't skimp on any efforts. Lately his only indulgence was the indoor lodgings, which he could afford on account of his good collections. This had not always been so. In the past he had slept outdoors with his accordion propped on his chest and a worn-out gray blanket enwrapping his instrument and his body from head to toe. Summer did not pose any problem. He lay on the dry sand on La Caleta or Victoria Beach, watching the stars wheeling overhead until he fell asleep. Winter was tough. He sought refuge in the entrance halls of the banks on the upscale Ramon and Carranza Avenue, his blanket spread out next to the ATM machines. His ears focused on the money-shedding slit hoping for a miracle. He once dreamed that a string of fifty-euro bills were spewed out, coating him with a thick layer of money. His hands thrashed around searching for the cash, but found only the cold tile. He could have sworn he had heard the bills pouring out and landing on him, but the only noises and taps that woke him up were those of a policeman ordering him to vacate the area. He ended up wandering through cold streets in the early hours of the morning and settling at the stoop of a store, with his legs bent, and his feet and head pressed against the doorway frame for the rest of the night. Despite the inclemency of weather, he always kept a smile on his face. Now and then he could not help it and fell into the doldrums.

"I'm sorry but I'm a human being and nothing is perfect about humans. You know that. You know everything," he reasoned with God aloud.

Today, however, was a special day. Once every two weeks, he talked with his family in Bucharest. He walked out of the inn, which was located in El Populo Barrio, and went down a narrow alley that ended on the winding Calle El Meson, the main street of the medieval quarters. Behind him lay the recently unburied Roman Theater, breathing the sea breezes after a two-thousand-year interment. A friendly silence engulfed him. People were asleep or waking up, their television sets and radios sitting idle. Housewives were not singing as they hung their wet laundry on their clotheslines on balconies or flat roof terraces. He always enjoyed their melodies and wondered how many could have become famous divas had they been given a chance or ever followed music as a calling. It was a difficult career. A realist, he considered himself a professional musician who lacked any ambition of being famous. His enjoyment of music and a few euros were enough compensation. He wished he could make a better living, but things were as they were.

He kept on walking in the old nutshell-shaped quarters and directed his steps to Las Rosas Arch, a medieval gate that had been part of the stone wall which had encircled the ancient neighborhood. Higher up on his left side, he saw Santa Cruz Church, which had been built over an old mosque. Next to the church, the square brown-stoned Sagrario Tower stood on the base of an ancient minaret. Its Arabic arched doors were sealed as if hiding the secrets left by Muslims after five and a half centuries of civilization.

When he arrived at Plaza Las Flores, a pang of hunger assaulted his stomach, for he had not taken anything to his mouth since he dined early evening the day before. He sat over a cup of coffee with *churros* at an outdoor café next to the Municipal Food Market. The breakfast was cheap and supplied him with enough calories to keep going until he collected money for his dinner. The warm odor of espresso and the crispy pastry sent a wave of comfort from his stomach down to his feet and up to his heart. He felt revitalized. The sun was out and a blue cloudless sky covered the town despite the forecasted rain. Rain would have been a most unusual occurrence lately because of global warming. Bulky gray clouds passed over the fields without dumping a single drop of precipitation. Nearby, a few stalls stood proudly graced with colorful flowers as water rippled from a white fountain presided

over by the marble Roman statue of a famous local writer—
Lucio Junio Moderato Columela. The fragrance of flowers, the
warm odor of coffee, and the scent of fresh baked pastries wafted
around the environs. Housewives began their daily pilgrimage to
the Plaza de Abastos to fill their shopping bags with fresh food
for the day. No one was in a hurry. Some stopped, chatted for
a few minutes, and went on to complete their errands. Others
stood observing the shop-windows. Men sat at the outside cafés
pretending to read the daily newspaper *Diario de Cadiz*, while out
of the corner of their eyes they watched the good-looking women
parading by, brunettes, blondes, young, not so young, tall, short,
long hair, short hair, big eyes, small eyes, tight pants, long skirts,
swinging hips, soft perfume. All moved their contoured bodies
with a graceful rhythm aware of the attention paid to them. A
contagious joy hovered over the plaza. Dominick admired the
passersby as if they were part of a beautiful painting, for his heart
belonged to his wife Rumilla.

"My beautiful wife, with dark innocent eyes like a fawn's, a
body lean and curved, and a walk with the musical cadence of a
violin," he said to himself, his mind drifting toward his family.

He lighted a cigarette. Ten o'clock was getting close, and the
time in Romania was two hours later. He envisioned the sun
in his hometown well above the plains with the shadows of
spruce, pine, and oak trees reflecting on the placid waters of the
Dambovita River at the Piata Eroilor as the morning breeze rustled their green leaves. His mind regaled him with images of his
wife and his two children walking toward Lazar Internet café near
University Plaza.   His wife took them downtown to enjoy the
afternoon after their telephone conversation. He envisioned his
family crossing one of the bridges and walking by Lake Cismigiu
and its spacious gardens, the cool spring filling their breaths with
a mint-like fragrance. Last month when he talked to them, he had
been able to see them on a computer screen. His wife, who had
just turned thirty-five, looked older and more tired and even the
blurriness of her image on the screen failed to hide the glimmers
of sadness. Her eyelids drooped as if attempting to conceal the

importune revelation. She wanted to fake a happy face, but only a forced smile materialized. It had been so long since they had curled against each other, whispered in each other's ears, made love. But there she was, wearing the red dress and the black kerchief that he had sent her for Christmas. Her fleshy lips opened like the bellows of his accordion, arousing in him an uncontrollable desire to kiss them as his fingers slid across the computer to caress their softness. All he felt was the screech of cold plastic.

His thoughts drifted to his children. Nine-year-old Lora and eight-year-old Pietro, were growing up well. Lora was svelte and nervous like her mother. In his previous month's phone call, she kept tossing her long brown hair and fluttering her eyelashes over her hazel-green eyes, her voice so sweet and beautiful that it moved her father almost to tears. For no obvious reason her expression often changed from laughing to sternness in the blink of one eye. That day she carried on about the Spanish doll in a red dress with polka dots he had mailed her last Christmas. He had bought it at a flea market at a good price, restored the dislocated right arm into the right shoulder socket, sewn part of the dress, and attached a couple of missing tiny buttons. His son took after him, his long blond hair, dimpled chin, and blue eyes set wide underneath an ample forehead. The child gave the impression of clear thinking and fierce determination. Even his small pudgy hands, which had then held his latest gift—a toy fire truck with a siren and a rotating red light—had a strong resemblance to his. On that occasion for the first time, his children had not asked him when he was coming back home. He thought they were getting used to an absent father. For them, he had turned into a ghost image on a screen, a promised deliverer who had so far failed to set foot on holy ground and bring forth their fountain of happiness.

Today his children's voices sounded happy and their laughter and excitement filled the booth. As usual the minutes of conversation would run quickly. There were so many things to tell, so much love to share, so long a distance to bridge.

"Dominick, my love, how do you feel?" Rumilla asked. "I see tiredness in your face."

"No, it's frustration that I can't see you and the children on the screen. The video camera is not working. I'm fine. Things are going well. People like my music and I'm getting more engagements for weddings and first communions. You'd flip out if you saw how Spaniards celebrate first communions. It's like a wedding."

"This month we haven't deposited much money in our saving account."

"I know, sweetheart. Spain is expensive."

"Are you sure you are taking care of yourself? You look thinner. Are you eating well? Do you wrap your scarf around your throat? You get colds so easily. Don't forget to put a teaspoon of salt in a glass of water and gargle before you go to bed. Stop smoking, Dominick, please, I need you back healthy. We are counting the days until you come back."

"Yes, yes, I'm not smoking that much, anyway. Did Lora stop wheezing when she runs? Did you take her to the pediatrician?"

"She can tell you. She is doing fine. Here, talk to your dad again."

"I'm well, daddy, the pills are working."

"Oh, my little princess, you are growing so fast. I don't even know what size of dress to get you anymore."

"Pietro, speak to your father again. We don't have much time left. This phone call is going to cost him too much money. Dominick, Pietro got excellent grades. His teacher said that he can become anything he wants. Wouldn't it be nice if he could study to be a doctor?"

"Dad, did you send me the video games I asked you to get?"

"I love you, Pietro, keep studying and obey your mother. I love you all."

Dominick's face reflected the happiness of his family in Bucharest. There was some sadness too. Deep in thought he walked toward his inn. Again he thanked God for all his blessings. His family's good health and his own welfare burst forth from his lips as his only entreaties. He would be able to sustain them for as long as he could work. Hard toil didn't frighten him. Today would be a good day. A cruise liner would soon put in at the harbor. Looking for little tokens and souvenirs, tourists would flock to downtown Cadiz and stroll by narrow streets protected from the winds and warm sun. They would drift toward the Cathedral Plaza, sit outside at the small cafés and restaurants, and admire the grandiosity of the temple, dawdling the lazy afternoon hours away over paella, fried fish, and Jerez wine. These foreigners tipped him well. Maybe he would get lucky and catch up with his savings.

With the accordion on his chest, hanging from shoulder straps, he walked into the busy plaza and took a seat on the steps leading to the main door of the cathedral. The sun was out in full force and his audience kept themselves comfortable under the palm trees and canopies. He crossed himself, laid his jacket in front, and opened his accordion. A note, sharp like a lament, pierced the quiet drone in the plaza. A new workday began. Patrons continued their conversations as unstirred by his music as by the sound of sea waves pounding against the nearby stone wall, or the breeze rustling the fronds and leaves. With his voice vibrant with emotions, he raised his eyes to heavens and sang.

LA CALETA BEACH

THE ARCHANGEL'S TORN WING

"Escóndete! The falangistas are rounding up people. You'd better hide!" my cousin Juan shouts to me from the seashore as I anchor the little boat I borrowed from him at La Caleta Beach—a small cove on the most northwest coast in the city of Cadiz.

"Why?"

"Haven't you heard? General Franco has risen against the central government. He's bringing his regiments from Morocco and the *falangistas* have joined the rebel troops."

"What have I done to those fascists?"

"No importa—that isn't important. If you aren't one of them you're their enemy. They're detaining all leftists … anarchists, communists, and socialists, all of us," he says as he darts away.

Flanking the seashell shaped beach lie the stone forts of Santa Catalina and San Sebastian, which over the years have protected the city from pirates and enemy fleets. I observe groups of soldiers marching by the battlements and looking out of the loopholes. The cannons have been aimed out toward the sea and the Spanish banners don't wave from the flagpoles. Everything else seems quiet. The sun dips down into the dark-blue waters by the lighthouse at the very tip of the jetty, which guides the entrance into the Bay of Cadiz from the Atlantic Ocean. The sky and the earth turn purple-red and the golden sand is coated with a fine crimson veil.

"*Deprisa*—hurry up, Paco, hide!" my cousin shouts as he runs out of sight onto a side street.

I can't hide. I must go home and make sure my mother, my younger brother, and my girlfriend are safe. I walk faster on the promenade that flanks the coastline and leads to Campo del Sur Road. The esplanade where people sit to watch the sunset and chat now stretches before me absolutely empty and noiseless. The silence can freeze the still air of this warm 18th of July 1936. I can hear my own steps. Farther down the road, the sea waves pound the high stone wall that nearly encircles the entire city. And a few blocks away, the cathedral stands high. The sunset has painted its large yellow cupola purple-pink like the color of shell nacre.

My cousin's warnings have unnerved me. To calm myself, I caress the steel-blue mackerels and the silvery snappers, which swing their tails and jump inside my half-full basket. No one has the right to jail law-abiding citizens for their political views, regardless of their beliefs. I'm a leftist who believes in people electing their own government. As a socialist or a social democrat, I stand for a fair distribution of wealth among everyone. But I disagree with the views of anarchism and communism. They seek a society where people own nothing and share everything. For them the ends justify all means, including revolution. Anarchists want to achieve this by abolishing any form of government, and communists by imposing their own dictatorship. This is utopia. I'm against all anti-democratic ideas including those of the extreme-right political parties like the Spanish *Falange*.

Falangistas can be fanatics. My coworker Manuel, who is one of them, fails to understand that people can disagree and still live together. When I talk to him, he turns his back and walks away. He says that in my family we're just a bunch of anarchists and communists, except for my brother Gabriel who never talks but at least can listen. I tell him that I'm not a communist or an anarchist, and my brother doesn't pay attention to anyone who talks politics, anyway. But he'll also become a good socialist when he matures a little more. I have no idea why two neighbors and former classmates, like Manuel and I, can grow up to hold such different views. He thinks that duty to our homeland comes before our own families or anything else in this life. I agree. But the way he says it in his stonyhearted voice, it's like he doesn't care about his parents, his siblings, or any of his loved ones. When he argues with me, his face turns red as he speaks of a free Spain where Catholicism will reign, of going back to our time of greatness, of getting rid of all the political parties, which he blames for all the ills, of doing away with the people's vote—and of dying for what he believes. But I tell him I am free. When I row my fishing boat under the blue sky, rocked by the waters, and I admire the little towns encircling the bay of Cadiz like pearls around my girlfriend's neck, I am free. When I cast my line far away with my fishing rod and wait sitting for the fish to bite, my hands behind my head, my hair ruffled by the fresh breeze, and I daydream of her black onyx eyes, I am free.

I can't believe a war has broken out now that my girlfriend Carmela and I have planned to get married next year. We have waited for so long. We have known each other since our births and shared the same building. She lives on the first floor and I on the second. Saving for our wedding has commanded our attention for the past five years. I have scraped a few *reales*—pennies—selling candies in every plaza where children play on Sundays. That's the only day I don't work at the foundry. Today is my first Saturday off in a long time. For years Carmela has been filling her dowry chest with carefully ironed linens, towels embroidered with our names, dishcloths, aprons, and a knitted black blanket with red, white, and yellow flowers to cover our legs and cuddle each other underneath in cold winters. The few times she has unlocked the brass clasp and lifted the wooden lid to let me peek inside, a cloud of white lily scent has risen and carried me to a promised land full of joy.

But now my earthly paradise is farther than ever. I hear a clatter of gunshots. It comes from somewhere deep in the city. The noise sends a shiver down my spine. Far down Campo del Sur Road a military convoy rolls toward me. I instinctively jump and lie stretched behind a bench. Five jeeps and five trucks bristling with troops and guns pass by me.

"*Váyase!* Out of the streets!" a soldier hollers as he aims his rifle at me.

I'm glad he hasn't pulled the trigger. I hear more shots. Columns of dark smoke billow from the heart of the city. Militant leftists must be setting fire to some of the stores and churches.

I witnessed similar acts of violence five years ago when I was a teenager. I remember running down Botica Street and seeing how they had just burned down Santo Domingo Church, a block away from my house. Flames rose above the east side of the building where priests and monks had their dormitories. At the plaza in front of the church a crowd of riotous leftists paraded a prostitute atop the float used for holy processions. Her breasts exposed, she held a golden monstrance in her right hand and wore a green velvet mantle with silver brocades of Our Lady of the Rosary. The people were laughing, screaming, and uttering one blasphemy after another.

"*Viva nuestra Virgen!* You're our Virgin now! Death to the priests and nuns!"

She drank red wine from the monstrance and spilled it all over her body. She rolled her eyes and imparted mock benedictions with her left hand.

"Come up and have Communion. Lick the wine from my teats," she cried out amidst roaring guffaws.

Amidst that chaos, pieces of saints' statues lay scattered on the stairs leading to the terrace in front of the church. One had been an archangel because I saw a large uprooted golden wing with a white stump of ragged borders. Saint Francis's head rolled downstairs and rested on the pavement. In front of the main door was a priest who lay unconscious. He was naked, his face covered in blood, his eyes swollen shut, and his hands tied behind his back with his rope belt. A crucifix had been crammed into his left ear and a rosary encircled his neck tightly. His body and lower limbs bore the blue bruises of the beating. A few women from my barrio and I lifted him up and rushed him to San Juan de Dios

Hospital, only a block away. A few rioters, led by a tall redheaded man with fiery eyes, tried to stop us. I said that the priest was a human being. I wasn't going to let him die. When the rioter raised his hand to hit me, I positioned my arms to parry his blow, then my cousin Lolo came to my aid because he's much older than I.

"*Déjalo*—leave him alone. He isn't a *falangista*; he's a socialist. He's my cousin," he yelled.

As I left I saw how he joined the other rioters and resumed writing graffiti over the façade of the building, which read:

'*LA JUSTICIA DEL PUEBLO, POR LADRONES* ... '—'the people's justice for all your robberies ...'

We left the priest in the hospital where the doctors revived him. After a few weeks I would learn that he survived and left town. After the riot my cousin came over to my house and we sat down outside.

"You shouldn't have done what you did," Lolo said. "You could have been killed, you know?"

"Well, I have to do what I have to do," I said. "Thank you for helping me."

"You either participate with all of us or stay away from trouble like your brother Gabriel. I don't like him and he doesn't like me. He's a strange bird, though ... never talks, but at least he doesn't put me in a tight spot."

"You have no right to talk about my brother that way. He's a good man. He just doesn't care about politics ... and what have you done for him to like you or be proud of you?"

"Sorry, but I don't trust him."

After reprimanding me, Lolo went on to state that this country would never change unless a Bolshevik revolution rose up. Otherwise the fascists would take over as they had done in Italy.

"I don't condone killing priests and nuns," he added. "The guys got carried away because the priest wouldn't budge."

"That doesn't justify what they did."

"People are suffering. We don't have the basic rights. We should be able to eat and take care of our families."

"But that is not the way."

"What else can we do? Haven't you seen the flocks of labor-ers, waiting at San Juan de Dios Plaza every day? Have you seen what they wear? They are dressed in rope sandals, frayed shirts, and pants full of patches."

"I know ... there are a lot of poor workers ..."

"They are not poor workers ... they are beggars. They're beg-ging for a job. When a capitalist throws a one-day job at him like a bone to a dog, that day he and his family will eat. Otherwise they will go to bed hungry."

"Blood feeds on blood," I said, "for he who sows the wind shall reap the whirlwind."

"You and your altruistic ideals ... peaceful means have not gotten us anywhere."

"Where has all this violence led us? What happened in Casas Viejas?"

I did not have to explain it to him. The incidents at this village, which was a few miles from Cadiz, had been reported in length by the national and local press: A group of peasants rebelled against their living and working conditions, took over the village, and in the process killed a sergeant. The police went in and massacred every one of them. The captain ordered his troops to "shoot to kill and aim at their bellies."

"We need to get rid of this government," Lolo said. "It isn't protecting the poor. These elected officials are so weak that they can't control their own army or the police."

"At least the government made the captain accountable for the slaughter. But some of you anarchists and communists aren't using your heads anymore."

"What do you mean?"

"There are rumors circulating that all banks in the city are to going to be held up and the spoils distributed among the citizenry."

"What's wrong with helping the poor?"

"It is not the correct way. And what the heck does a labor dis-pute have to do assaulting banks, raping nuns, killing priests, or burning down churches?"

"*Tienes que enterderlo*—you must understand that the clergy have aligned themselves with the rich. You have a poor memory. Don't you remember what you saw at Santa Maria Church in Arcos when we visited our grandparents?"

"Nothing can justify what is going on."

"Of course, it does. What kind of treasure did the church boast for anyone to see? Coffers full of gold, diamonds, rubies, emeralds ... and where did the bell-ringer reside with his wife and four children? Up in the belfry in a single room as small as a kitchenette."

"Everything is relative, Lolo. A lot of people in that little town lived in terrible misery. We never saw the priest's quarter. Maybe he lived worse than they did."

"You missed the point. One shouldn't flaunt so much wealth amidst so much poverty and hunger."

"Those are treasures that the church has accumulated for centuries. In the past the poor parishioners were the ones who offered to their saints what few pennies they eked out over the years."

"So what? Give the money back to the people who now need it."

"That is not the solution. What people need is education and training. A few pesetas will go only so far. We should all support democracy and peaceful evolution rather than revolution."

"I hear you! You say you're a socialist. Well, let me tell you something that you're too young and naïve to know. The *falangistas* consider you as *rojo*—as red—as I am, even if you are not a communist or an anarchist. Don't ever forget that."

The trumpets of this revolution that my cousin Lolo talked about have been blaring for a while. Impatient and disappointed with the elected officials, large numbers of members in my own party have joined the ranks of those calling for an uprising. Socialists who believe in democracy, as I do, have become a minority. Extremist ideas have been brewing. I remember a poem written by Alejo Hernandez that appeared in an April,

1929 issue of *El Socialista*. In a few words the author framed the
growing trend. The verse read as follows:

> Neither wheat, nor work,
> Nor paid by the piece,
> We should be resigned to.
> Each must farm his land,
> Or else let the fields burn
> In a total war like hell.

Back then it made me realize that Spain was heading for chaos
unless the views of the few moderate politicians in power would
prevail. So far this year has been terrible. The country swarms with
radical rightists and leftists who want to get rid of the Spanish
Republic and install their own dictatorship. Ever since the leftists won the elections last February, the anger has run high. A
few days ago, four radical rightists opened fire and murdered a
prominent leftist lieutenant in downtown Madrid before the very
eyes of his newlywed bride. The same night, after his wake, a few
of his comrades went to the home of an opposition Member of
Parliament and arrested him. As soon as the detainee got into
their military vehicle, they shot him in the back of the head, and
dumped his body at a local cemetery.

Lolo shouldn't have lectured me about poverty. I live on
Mirador Street, the poorest area of my hometown. It's paved with
cobblestones and flanked by three- or four-story buildings with
flaking whitewashed façades. The tenements have an interior
courtyard covered with bricks around which lie eight to ten family quarters. Inside, it has a big deep cistern that collects rain. The
neighbors use it to lift buckets of water for washing, and now
and then to jump inside and commit suicide when life has grown
too tough to handle. About fifty people live on every floor. If
you walk in there during the day, you can always hear someone
singing. It's usually a sad song, for everyone sings to forget or to
cry. All members of a family are crammed into one or two rooms
crawling with cockroaches and mice, regardless of how much
you try to keep them clean. If you're fortunate enough to own
a kitchenette, like I am, you also have to battle white-and-black

rats as big as cats that steal your food. If you dare them, they turn around and confront you. The tenants sleep on hay mattresses or on planks of wood. On each floor everyone shares the same toilet bowl and in some of the houses the same kitchen too. And when you cook there you have to watch the pot closely. Otherwise, a hungry neighbor may come over and steal your food. Once a week you can take a full bath from a glazed earthenware bowl in the washing place on the flat-roof. But your brother or your mother must watch out to keep anyone from walking in on you and finding you stark naked.

Living in poverty doesn't justify violence. Why doesn't reason rule the mind of men? When I talk with my brother Gabriel about these issues, he doesn't agree or disagree and merely shrugs. He's a couple of years younger than me but I wish he had grown into as good a socialist as I am. That's why I talk to him frequently, explaining my strong belief that extreme leftist or rightist views are equally bad for the future of this country. He doesn't acknowledge what I say and looks at me like I'm crazy. The other day I walked into his small alcove where he lay in bed with his hands folded under his head staring at the ceiling. The images of Our Lady of the Pillar, Saint James the Apostle, patron saint of Spain, and the Sacred Heart of Jesus hung on his wall as if looking down at me. For a while I thought that he was going to become a priest. But it dawned on me that I had never seen him going to church. I sat on the edge of his bed with a copy of *Diario de Cádiz* in my hand. I was about to tell him the accounts of the meeting held at the Socialist Party headquarters. He twisted his mouth and turned his back on me.

"*No me hables*—don't talk to me about your political non-sense," he said. "Just read to me how the critics extol Chicuelo's triumph at the Monumental Bullring in Barcelona."

"No, listen to me. Spain is going through bad times. The country is in need of good socialists, good people who will support democracy or we'll sink into another military dictatorship. We need you."

"You don't need me. Leave me alone. It's easy for you. You're happy. You have Carmela who loves you … and mother too."

"I love you. Mother loves you as much as she loves me. She may even love you more, because you're the baby. And Carmela has a sister. Have you ever thought of asking her out?"

"I hear you."

"Wouldn't it be nice? We could be brothers and brothers-in-law at the same time."

"Stop making fun of me. I don't like her. She isn't like Carmela."

"Promise me that you'll think about joining me as a member of the Socialist Party—like our late father used to be."

"Father was Father. I am someone else."

"Are you saying that you aren't going to join?"

"I haven't said anything. You're the one making all the statements for me."

I don't know why he thinks that my mother loves me more. She has always cared for both of us. As kids we squabbled all the time. I remember fighting about sharing our rubber soccer ball. When I took hold of it tightly, he yanked it from me, and we ended up wrestling on the floor. As usual my mother came and reprimanded us, pleading with us to embrace each other and make up.

"You shouldn't quarrel," my mother said. "There are times that brothers will have a disagreement or even a fight. It happens in all families. But you should always make up with a big hug so you never go to bed angry with each other."

We hugged and grew up trusting each other. When we played rough games, grappling on the floor, throwing cushions, giving each other a dunking on the beach, we walked away laughing with our arms around each other's shoulders. Neither he nor I ever conceived that one could hurt the other on purpose.

As my thoughts quiet down, I keep moving faster. Bursts of gunshot can be heard coming from the heart of the city and more columns of smoke are rising. As I pass by the slope next to the cathedral, I come across two women. The older, with a long blank veil over her head, has pleading eyes as she carries long rolls of dress materials in her arms. The younger, in a long polka-dot skirt, wears flashing eyes like those of an angry dog, and carries a big foreleg of ham and long strings of chorizo on her shoulders. I want to smile at her but only a frozen grin crosses my mouth. I watch other people rush by me with their hands full of shirts, shoeboxes, suits, food. They don't look at me or utter a single word. A few hundred feet away, the Royal Prison overlooks the deep and now dark waters of the ocean. Civil guards keep vigilance wearing dark green uniforms, which look more ominous than ever. As I rush to the other side of the road, their black three-cornered hats sparkle in the evening twilight like the eyes of an owl.

It's getting darker. The sea waves lap against the rocks and they sound like lashes against my bare skin. I'm not afraid of dying. Well, maybe a little, but I'm mainly concerned about putting my loved ones through such a terrible ordeal. I have nothing to repent. I have led my life as if my girlfriend Carmela were always watching me. When my friends and I played in the interior courtyard and they tossed their spinning tops and then my turn came to throw mine, I felt her eyes on me even if she was nowhere to be seen. I stretched the cord tight around my top so the loops touched one another, and with a quick flick, my wrist cast it across the floor. I proudly watched it spin longer and more gracefully than my friends' tops. My conscience is clear. I have always done my best at school, at work, and everywhere else so that she would be proud of me.

A voice interrupts my thoughts:

"*Rindanse!* Surrender or die!" a loudspeaker booms from a side street perpendicular to the road where I'm now standing, the threat coming from the environs of San Juan de Dios Plaza where City Hall lies.

"We shall overcome! *Viva la República!*" someone shouts from inside City Hall as a burst of shots follows.

Hunched over, I scurry toward the wall flanking the yard of Mirandilla School where I used to attend classes as a child.

Several stray bullets whiz by me. One hits me in the left arm. I'm so pumped up that I barely feel it. A group of soldiers must have surrounded the mayor and aimed their guns at the windows and balconies. He and his aldermen are resisting the military coup. I wish that I could help them. What rights do these soldiers have to fire at our elected officials? Why do they forget their pledged support of the constitution? My arm feels wet. I take my shirt off and tear a piece to bandage my wound. It's bleeding. I need to get home and reunite with my brother so that we can join the loyal troops. I wonder how he feels about this war. Indifference is no longer a choice. He has been born of good stock, so I'm sure that he'll make the right decision and agree to come with me.

Blood dribbling down my arm, I head toward a small alley that leads to my street. As I pass by Santa Maria Convent, I observe its façade charred by the fire set by militant leftists a few months ago. A thick cloud of smoke covers the center of the town, and the wind blows it toward me. The dark smell of destruction permeates everywhere. The bleeding has stopped, yet I feel a little faint. My arm hurts and I can barely move it. The rattle of shots intensifies. I enter Mirador Street where I see some neighbors rushing into their houses and yelling,

"*La guerra! La guerra!* The war! The war!"

I still hear the staccato sound of machine guns followed by an explosion coming from the heart of town, maybe from City Hall. The black clouds of smoke are turning purple in the twilight and their unraveled edges are tinged in red as if dripping blood. Down the street I can make out my girlfriend waiting at the steps of our building. A black veil covers her hair, for she must have just returned from church. Her arms are folded across her chest and her eyes shine with fear. Even on a day such as this she feels like a fresh breeze on a muggy summer night to me.

"Paco, you're wounded."

"*No es nada*—it's nothing. It's just a scratch."

"Scratch? Your shirt is sopping with blood. Let me clean it up. You look pale."

"Let me go and see about my mother and my brother."

"No, wait ... let me get a piece of cloth," she says, hurrying inside the house.

She cleans the wound. I can see two small irregular holes, one a little bigger than the other, on each side of the belly of the bicep. Black clots and small pieces of red flesh and skin still hang from their ragged borders as blood keeps oozing out.

"You almost got killed. Your mother is okay and your brother stopped by a while ago and left. He said he was looking for you ... his face—"

"What was it?"

"*No sé* ... some odd expression."

"He's scared, I'm sure. I have to find him."

"No, he said if you show up, you should wait for him over here. That he was coming back soon."

"He should have stayed."

"Paco, let's get married now. Our parish is open," she says, with entreating eyes. "Before you leave town, I want to be your wife."

I'm wonderstruck. Even now, under these horrendous circumstances, the idea of marrying Carmela reaches my heart as deeply as the honey glow of her eyes when she bills and coos over me. What right has anyone to cut off our future and our happiness?

"Now?" I ask.

"*Sí.*"

"Let me go upstairs to leave the fish, get dressed, and tell my mother. I need a shirt and my pants are all patched up. Look at my feet. I'm in rope sandals."

"No, *por favor, no*, we have no time to waste. Leave the fish here in my house and let's go. My sister will give them to your mother. I'll get a clean shirt for you," she says as she rushes inside her house.

She returns in less than a minute.

"Here's my father's long-sleeve white shirt. I heard that the city is falling into the hands of the rebels. Tomorrow morning the war ship Churruca will arrive with three thousand troops, legionnaires and moors, to reinforce them."

I have a few hours left to say goodbye to my bride and my mother, since I don't know when I'll see them again. My brother and I should be on our way long before dawn. Once we join our troops, we'll be expected to endure whatever sacrifice is required from us, even if it means death. In a war human life is worthless, anyway. If I die I'll be just a number, one casualty. Officers may even fail to register the loss and my name may not appear anywhere. At best my wife and my mother will get my body inside a plain wooden casket and they'll never know whether it's mine or someone else's. Or my brother might be killed and it would be terrible if I had to be the one to tell my mother. I'd rather die than go through that calamity.

Two blocks from our house La Merced Church is guarded by a group of parishioners to prevent any looting. Carmela and I walk into the main nave. It's almost empty. Only two old ladies dressed in black kneel on the first pew with their heads bent forward and their fingers caressing the beads of rosaries in reverie. Outside, gunshots break the silence. The image of Our Lady of La Merced graces the center of the altar with her big dark eyes, a soft smile, and her skin as dark olive as that of a gypsy woman. Padre Manrique sits alone at the confession box. He's tall and thin with a long nose and a head full of silvery hair. Since I was a child we have called him Padre Quixote, for he resembles the illustrious knight. He never smiles, but he always has a kind word and a piece of bread for the hungry.

"Padre, can we talk to you for a minute?" Carmela says.

"Yes, do you need confession?"

"No."

"Okay, let me take my stole off."

"*Queremos casarnos*–Paco and I want to get married now."

"*Ahora?* I can't do that. You know I have to announce your marriage at the Masses for three consecutive Sundays. Besides, I don't think I've seen Paco in church in a long time."

"*Es verdad,*" I break in, "but I believe in God and I pray to Jesus and Our Lady every day. Padre, we have no time for the banns. These are difficult hours, you know. There is a war going on outside."

"*Lo sé*, my children, but those are the rules."

"There must be a way," Carmela says. "I mean ... in an emergency. How do you call it? Dispensation. If a child is dying I can baptize him, can't I?"

"That's different."

"Padre, you don't want us to commit mortal sin," she says. "Things are bad outside. If we die, where will we go?"

"*Vayan*—go to the altar. Take this paper and write down your full names."

Padre Manrique goes into the sacristy and fetches a black Bible. As he stands before us he sketches a smile and reads a passage from the Holy Gospel,

"... A man shall leave his father and mother and be joined to his wife, and the two shall become one flesh ..."

I look at Carmela. Her eyes are riveted on mine. My mind goes back ten years when I held her hand for the first time. My fingertips still remember the texture of her skin as velvety soft as the moss growing on sea rocks. Now Padre asks us to pretend that we have rings to place on each other's fingers and from deep in my heart I repeat the words of my wedding vows.

"I, Paco ... take you Carmela ... to be my wife ... I promise to be true to you ... in good times and bad ... in sickness and health ... I will love and honor you ... all the days of my life."

Carmela blinks and smiles and her mouth quivers. I wish I were a seaman sailing through the dimples of her cheeks, for there is nothing more beautiful than my Carmela's face. Her turn comes and I hear her sweet voice.

"I, Carmela … take you Paco … to be my husband …"

Her words bring me great happiness but leave an aftertaste of terrible sadness. Only God knows whether our life together will be years, days, or hours. The mere thought of leaving her alone on this earth hurts me. Her eyes shine with love and her teeth sparkle in her open mouth like the tears of a weeping Madonna. But nothing comes out because emotions trap her words in her throat. Yet, I know what she wants to say, what she thinks, and what her soul treasures. My heart jumps at the touch of her hand. And as we kiss before God and the warmth of her lips sticks to mine, I wish this feeling would stay with me forever.

After the ceremony we head for my house, where my mother, after having lighted a candle to Our Lady of the Carmelo, kneels praying. The candlelight flickers when she turns around. Her eyes are red with deep dark circles under them. She wears her black dress and a black veil for my father's death two years ago. Although her face has no wrinkles, she looks much older than forty-seven. With my departure looming so near and terrible, I don't know whether I'll return to see her again. When Carmela tells her about our wedding, tears run down my mother's cheeks.

"I'd have wanted so much to be there with you. I love you, Carmela, like the daughter that I never had."

"Mother, we had no time and—"

"*Hijo mio*, I understand. You look pale. You must be very tired. You both stay here with me and go to bed. I'll be up waiting for your brother. It's your wedding night."

The night has set in. Everything falls in silence, a hair-raising silence that resounds more than the weapons. The poster commemorating the Spanish Republic hangs on the wall by my bed. It boasts a laurel-crowned lady dressed in a white tunic and a red cape that holds the scale of justice in one hand and a spear in the other. A lion stands next to her and the flag of the Spanish Republic waves in the background. I close the flower-stamped curtain of my alcove. I enter a new universe where only Carmela exists. I forget about my wound, my pain, my weakness. Her eyes turn into shining stars, her lips into crescent moons, her bosom into a heaving sun, and eternity is the time it takes for her petticoat to drop to the floor. There is joy in our hearts as we flutter like two little leaves in the wind.

"Paco, do you remember when you sold candies at the door of San Martin School. I'd come out and you'd sing your wares? '*Caramelos de menta, y limon*, girls, buy them from me.' You hawked the candies with such elegance."

"You had such a crush on me. I like singing flamenco."

"*Cantame*—sing it to me now ... low ... low ... whispering."

I kiss her once more. My lips are so warm from fever that hers feel tepid to my touch. Just then we hear a knock on the door that makes us jump. Rosario, our neighbor, talks to my mother and I can distinguish her words.

"The *falangistas* are rounding up leftists and taking them to the coal cargo ship Miraflores, which is anchored in the middle of the bay. My husband works there. He says that they are ordering the detainees to strip bare. They crop their hair and then push them inside the hold. Their entire bodies get smudged with soot as if they were giant pieces of coal with eyes."

"Why are they doing that?" my mother asks. "Are they crazy?"

"They're thirsty for blood. I don't know but my husband says that he is sure the poor detainees wish they were pieces of coal. Many are crying and calling out to their mothers and God. They are forced to swallow bottles of castor oil."

"Are you sure of what you are saying?"

"Yes, when my husband asked one of the captors on the ship, he spit on the deck and squashed the saliva with his boot and said, 'Why do you care about these *rojos*? We have orders from Franco's military command not to leave a single *rojo* alive in Cadiz.'"

"*Cálmese*—calm down. How can the *falangistas* tell who are and who aren't militant leftists?"

"They don't care if they're militant or not. The *falangistas* have broken into the local offices of the anarchist, communist, and socialist parties and gotten the lists of members before the clerks could destroy them. Tell Paco and Gabriel to go into hiding before it's too late."

I hear my mother's steps approaching my alcove.

"*Vete* Paco, you have to leave, my son," she says with a tremulous voice.

I can barely stand up. Now I can hear shouts outside and more gunfire too. Outside, the street must be crawling with *falangistas*. I can make out their screams,

"*Apaguen las luces!*—turn the lights off! Stay away from the windows, roofs, and balconies or we'll shoot to kill."

"Señora Maria," Carmela says, "Paco was wounded and he has fever. He can't run. He'll be caught."

"Quickly, hide under my skirt like when you were a child," my mother says.

"Mother, I'm too big for that."

"*Haz lo que digo!* You have to!"

My mother sits on a wooden chair against a wall, her long black skirt reaching the floor. I sit on the floor and bend my head forward as far as I can. With my two hands I force my legs to bend until my heels touch my buttocks and my knees press against my chin. My mother's thighs squeeze my head. Darkness and warmth envelope me like her womb did when I was a baby. I feel safe in here. As my eyes adjust to the penumbra, I can see the big veins in her legs swollen like a river of mud. Her calves and thighs are strong and thick like the roots of a dragon tree. My mother has worked hard. She cleaned houses and offices until the bones stuck out of her knees and feet, and she sewed linen and dresses made to order until her vision grew tired and blurred. Some nights she turned in starving, but she never allowed my brother and me to go to bed hungry. Lying next to her brings back my childhood days. She used to relieve my stomachaches by massaging around the navel over and over, and my earaches by placing small pieces of cotton dipped in warm oil inside my ears. I wish she could now soothe my body. I'm in terrible pain. My ankles, knees, and groin seem to have stretched out far beyond return, and my toes clasp the floor. I don't know if I'll be able to hold much longer. Outside, I can hear the *falangistas* ordering people around,

"*Afuera todos los hombres!* —All men are to come out with their arms up and line up against this wall! Don't bother getting dressed. Come out as you are or we'll come in and get you. Go! Go! C'mon!"

Menacing shouts get closer and closer, and are now coming from my building.

"*Abra la puerta!* Open the door!" their screams boom from the first floor and are followed by a flurry of shots ... pop, pop, pop, pop, pop, pop.

"No!" a woman cries out, "*Está sordo!* The old man lives alone and he's deaf like a wall! Oh, no! My God! Why do you have to shoot a poor old man and kill him in his own bed?"

There is a loud banging on our door. Carmela opens it.

"Gabriel!" Carmela exclaims.

"What are you doing here dressed like that?" my mother says. "Since when do you dress in a blue shirt with the blazon of the *Falange?*"

"*No se meta en esto,* Mother. Where is my brother hiding?"

"*No está aquí* ... he left. Go away. You don't need to wield a gun before your mother. Are you going to betray your own brother? Look at me!"

"He's a *rojo!*"

"*Por favor,* Gabriel, for whatever you love most in this world. Leave us alone," Carmela says.

"What do you know about what or whom I love or don't love? Have you ever even looked at me? Stay away! This has nothing to do with you. You should be at home with your family!"

"*Tu madre tenía miedo.* Your mother was alone. She was afraid."

I hear his frenzied steps stomping through every corner of the house—my own blood, my little brother. How many times did I come to his aid when other children bullied him? And what did I do for him when he was out of work? I gave him a small weekly allowance so he could go out with his friends. I let him have my own shirts, my pants, even my only jacket whenever he needed it. I did everything for him. My mother's thighs squeeze me, closing in on my shudders. I can hear him approaching her and blood rushes into my head.

"*No me toques!* Don't you dare touch me!" my mother says. "If you believe in God, you should know there is a hell waiting for you."

I'm sure he knows that I'm under my mother's lap. But no one is going to hurt her in my presence. I gather all my strength and, spreading my mother's legs, I charge at him like a bull rushing out of a pen. After pushing his pistol aside and holding his arms tight against his body, I try to wrestle his gun away. He keeps his fist clenched over it.

"*Cobarde*—you, coward, do ... you ... want ... your ... brother?" my voice booms out.

My mother has stood up and I can hear her shouting at us.

"Stop it, stop fighting," she screams, burrowing her hands between our bodies. "Behave like brothers. Gabriel, go away and leave Paco alone."

"Mother, don't meddle!" Gabriel cries out. "I am taking ... this *rojo* with me. *Viva España!*"

"Shut up," I say. "You ... crazy ... fascist!"

My strength is about to leave me and I pull hard to pluck the pistol out of his hand. Then I hear the popping sound of an ammunition discharge followed by a cry and a solid thump.

Carmela screams, "You killed your mother!"

Speechless, my brother and I kneel next to her body. Her eyes are opened wide in terror, a tiny hole in her forehead and a pool of blood rippling around her head. A fine tremor overtakes her legs for a few seconds and it's over. He puts the gun down and, with our arms around each other's shoulders, we cry like children. A flurry of steps rushes upstairs. I see four *falangistas* armed with pistols standing in my doorway.

"*Camarada*, are you okay?

Grabbing the gun again, my brother wipes the tears out of his eyes and looks at me. As if a mask has fallen off, his face experiences a sudden change because as he releases the embrace, his expression of sadness grows into a grimace of hatred.

"Take this *rojo* away!" Gabriel says, pointing at me, his eyes aflame.

"No! No!" Carmela cries out, tears running down her cheeks.

My mother's eyes are closed and her face is as peaceful and beautiful as when she fell asleep in her chair. My heart breaks into a thousand pieces. I wish I could turn the clock back to my childhood. I remember when she would walk into my alcove and place her soft hand over my forehead to check for fever and say,

"You're fine, Paco."

Life can be sweet and life can be cruel. Now that pain and sorrow ravage my body and soul, I feel only pity for my brother. My captors clasp my arms to shove me out of the room. I see my bride crying and shaking, her arms outstretched toward me. And in this instant devoid of farewells and future, I look into her eyes. Beneath the terror, I perceive such love that it makes me believe in heaven. But I am afraid. I am afraid of tomorrow when the sun will come out winking at the sea, and the surf will undulate like Carmela's hair, regaling the beach with a long gown of white lace—and I won't be there to witness that moment ever again.

THE POPPY FLOWER

I was lying in bed alone when I glimpsed a cloud-like figure shaped like a woman scurrying from left to right across the wall before me, grazing the ceiling. A pair of eyes hovered for a moment in the upper right corner staring at me as the vapory body seeped through the bricks out of sight as if sucked by a powerful vacuum. For a moment I had the impression that something had cast a shadow over the wall, but my nightstand lamp was the only light on and its dark outline remained fixed on the ceiling.

I thought that it might have been an illusion or a brief dream. I was poring over the 2003 edition of *La sombra del viento*—the *Shadow of the Wind*—by Juan Ruiz Zafón, but I supposed that I might have fallen asleep. I was a little nervous, because this was my first night in a refurbished apartment on the second floor, which I had just rented in the Barrio del Populo. This neighborhood of little streets with the haphazard distribution of a Moorish medina had endured the passage of different civilizations: Romans, Visigoths, Muslims, and Castilians. My bedroom had a small window that overlooked the tiny Plaza de San Martin. Here, the seventeenth-century baroque palace the House of the Almirante stood with a beautiful façade of smooth pink marble columns, upon which rested a large balcony framed with spiral columns of the same material.

My uneasiness was not caused by unfamiliarity with the place. In the evening, this area bustled with young people like me, who frequented numerous little bars and restaurants. As a child I had visited the House of the Almirante on several occasions. One of my cousins married a lady who lived there and celebrated their wedding in its colonnaded inner courtyard. By then the palace had deteriorated and had been used as a tenement for a dozen poor families. Now it was empty and in ruins, and plans were underway to restore it as a luxury hotel.

I blamed tiredness for the vision because I had had a rough day at work. My boss kept watching me like a hawk as if I were not doing my job. There was no reason for his distrust. I was a good shoe salesman. This job was not my cup of tea. I had graduated in philosophy and literature three years ago but, as my father had warned me when I picked this career, I was still looking for employment in my field. In the meantime, customers could count on my advice to get a good pair of Spanish-made leather shoes. I did not lure them into buying more expensive Italian merchandise of lower quality.

When I was about to conclude that everything had been a figment of my imagination, I saw her again out of the corner of my eye. Like a scared mouse, she dashed before me in the opposite direction. She had green eyes, as green as an emerald, the face of a porcelain doll, a chalk-white complexion, dimpled cheeks, fleshy lips, and long black hair down to her waist. Her ruffled white silk gown silently grazed the wall. At first she scared the wits out of me, but her facial expression was so sad and wistful that it rattled my insides like the noise of sharpening a knife on a whetstone. I wanted to ask her to stay, but my voice was stifled in my throat. The only trace left of her brief presence was a flowery scent, which lingered in my room for a while.

Unable to sleep, I waited for her reappearance. When I finally dozed off, restlessness took over. I got up and made myself a cup of chamomile tea, but it did not work. My pricked-up ears stood ready to listen for any unusual noise. I heard the racket and laughter of revelers who walked near my window, the rumbles of motorcycles, occasional distant horns blown by rude drivers, the repeated meows of a cat. My room was silent. When my alarm clock went off at seven, I had not gotten a wink of sleep. At work, day after day my mind conjured up her image whenever my concentration faltered. Back at home in the evening, I stared at the wall in my bedroom for hours. In the past when I did not go out with my friends, I enjoyed reading the daily paper, surfing the web, and watching soccer matches on TV. Now even those activities failed to catch my interest.

I was afraid to discuss my experience with my friends or relatives for fear they would think I had gone crazy. After three months of vigil and doubting my mental sanity, I again joined my group of friends—Antonio, Vicente, Pepa, Loli, and Luisa. As usual I found them amidst a large crowd of young people at San Felipe Pier chatting over a *botellon*—a large bottle of beer purchased at a supermarket. Under a starry sky, a fresh breeze rippled the waters. A crystalline full moon and the distant twinkling lights from small towns girdling the Bay of Cadiz flickered on the waves like the scattered stars trailing a magic wand. The peacefulness of the sea contrasted with the revelers' hubbub. Everyone made conversation by raising their voices over the neighboring groups.

My friends were surprised to see me. They had tried to contact me on numerous occasions and finally given up. Luisa was happier than the rest to see me. Tall and thin, she looked sexy in her high heels, tight jeans, and a short navy blue jacket well fitted to her waist. Yet she failed to stimulate my fancy. She was too modern for me. My friends believed I belonged to the days of yore and my ideas were too old-fashioned. There were certain expectations a man should not compromise and the major one was your better half. I expected my woman to be loving, loyal, trustworthy, sincere, sensitive, demur, and to exude strong motherly instincts. She should be my soul mate. Her passion in life should be to make our children and me happy.

Luisa got upset with me, because my mind drifted away and my eyes stared past her. The phantom lady had overtaken my thoughts. When I least expected, stimuli from the surroundings evoked details of her image I had seemingly missed: the bobbing of nearby little boats by the sea waves was reminiscent of the delicate batting of her eyelids; the drops of dew clutching to the fronds of the palm trees made me think of the pearly tears sliding down her face; the timid rouge on the distant horizon reminded me of the pastel pink color of her cheeks. I could hardly wait to go back home and stare at the wall, hoping to catch a glimpse of her. I spent the weekends at home like a hermit. I avoided calls from anyone including my mother and my sister Teresa. They would come by and knock on my door and I would peek through the peephole and stay put in silence. My mother decided to wait for me outside the store when I had ended my workday.

"What's wrong with you? Why don't you answer my calls? Look at your eyes. You have dark circles... you look terrible ... are you on drugs?"

"No, Mother, I'm fine."

"No, you are not fine. Are you involved with some crazy woman, a married woman?

"No, Mother, I'll see you on Sunday ... I'll have dinner with you. Now, please, leave me alone. I need to rest."

The following Sunday, I headed for Santa Cruz Church—the former Cathedral of Cadiz until 1830— to talk with one of the parish priests, Father Pedro Aranzabal. A block away from my apartment, the thirteenth-century temple was at the top of a steep slope, where it sat like a white chicken in a coop. Its two cupolas resembled two giant Easter eggs decorated with rectangular white and blue ceramic tiles, and its belfry looked like a huge lollipop covered with ceramic tiles of various colors. Father Aranzabal was kneeling at the main altar in front of the impressive, gilded baroque retable. Tall and muscular, he had the broad shoulders and square jaw of a boxer with dark eyes that expressed the mix of piety and skepticism of a recalcitrant theologian. I regarded the ancient stone columns separating the three naves and wondered what secrets and confessions these structures might have heard. I felt as if my impending inquiry would make them turn around and stare at me in awe.

"What has brought you here today?" the priest asked, approaching me. "You only come to church during Holy Week."

"Father, you know I'm a brother of the Jesus of Medinaceli Confraternity and my father was also a member until he passed away two years ago."

"Yes, he was a good Catholic. He and your mother attended Mass every Sunday. She still does. She doesn't miss a single novena. But you ... you come only once a year, dressed in penitent attire. You parade His image up and down the streets on Holy Thursday morning, and then never step into a church until the next Holy Week."

"Father, I haven't come to argue with you. I need your help."

As I explained my visions and obsession with the ghost, he frowned, scratched his head, and looked at me as if I were crazy.

"Have you seen a psychiatrist?"

"No, Father, I don't need a *shrink* ... I thought you might be acquainted with this issue. Can you help me? She is occupying all my thoughts and has changed my life completely."

"I have no experience handling something like this. Did she wear any religious article such as a medal with the image of Our Lady or a cross?"

"I don't know ... she disappears so fast."

"You should look for help somewhere else."

"I thought you dealt with spiritual things ... this is a spirit, isn't it?"

"Maybe yes, maybe no ... maybe your imagination."

"It is not my imagination ... do you think I would be talking to you if I wasn't sure?"

"I've known you since you were a child ... but this is weird."

"Fine ... I'm weird and my imagination has tricked me. Okay, forget what I've told you. Thank you."

"Wait, wait ... okay, I'll do my best. I mean your father was my friend, not just a parishioner. I'll bless you, so that you are free of this spirit."

"Father, I have no spirits inside me. She is in my apartment. She looks sad. She might need help ... special prayers, indulgences."

"Listen, don't fool yourself. She could be the Devil. He can adopt any form and can pander to any man's weakness."

"I don't think so. I don't sense any bad feeling. Maybe she is a lost soul."

"Lost soul? You should have studied more Catechism. There are no lost souls. Well, maybe God might allow a soul from Purgatory to revisit the place where they had lived, so that people can see them and pray for them. But most of the time it is the Devil. Go on home ... I'll be there in a while."

An hour later Father Aranzabal walked into my apartment with a leather briefcase in his hand. I ushered him in to my bedroom. He put on a white stole and placed a vessel or aspersorium on a small table. He then poured holy water into it from a tiny glass bottle, dipped a silvery brush or aspergillum inside, and began an invocation,

"In the Name of Jesus Christ, our Lord, strengthened by the intercession of the Immaculate Virgin Mary, Mother of our Savior, of Blessed Michael the Archangel, of the Blessed Apostles Peter and Paul and all the Saints, we confidently undertake to repulse the attacks and deceits of the Devil."

"No, no, Father, no devil stuff, just pray for her soul, so that she can return peacefully to her eternal rest. I know she isn't a demon."

We prayed three Paternosters and three Hail Marys and he dispensed the holy water over the entire room, repeating three times:

"May thy mercy, Lord, descend upon her, so that she may return to You in peace."

But she did not leave. That night I saw her again moving as fast as the two previous occasions. One of her tears moistened my pillow. I ran and touched it. It was cold like ice and stained the case for a couple of minutes. I made a few new observations: her dress had a red circular badge on the left side of the chest; her left hand held a red poppy flower, and a black-bead rosary with a silver cross hung from her right hand.

For a couple of days, I was in shock and did not know what o do next. Then luck struck. On one of my breaks, I opened the newspaper *Diario de Cadiz*, and I came across an advertisement: "*Rosa Ponce de Leon, médium. ¿Quiere saber su futuro, comunicarse con una persona querida en la otra vida? Le ofrezco profesionalidad y honestidad.*"

The psychic medium's place of business was in a modern apartment on Carranza Avenue. The thoroughfare flanked the harbor and exhibited an expansive brick tile walk in the middle, which led to a well-designed garden with a large fountain. On my way to my appointment, I could hear the restful murmurs of the waters. The elevator opened in a marbled lobby. I expected an old lady with a turban and a fancy sky-blue gown, but she looked more like a young executive, dark eyes, bobbed brown hair, gray suit, and black high-heeled shoes. She ushered me to a small room through a short hall where family pictures of her with her two children—boy and girl—and her husband hung from the wall. We sat at a small table facing each other.

"I don't think that I can help you that much ... my work usually involves contacting my customers' late relatives," she said. "The ghosts to whom you refer tend to populate the homes where they lived most of their lives. Some might have died there, although there are many exceptions to this rule. Others might have moved into a home that they coveted while alive. There are plenty of books about this subject. You might want to consult some of them."

Upon my insistence, she decided to accompany me home to try to contact my uninvited guest. Ever since she had begun her career as a medium she had been lending her voice to the spirits of the dead. Her customers had often attested to the authenticity of their departed's voices. We sat in my bedroom, lit a candle, and placed it on the small table. As soon as I turned the lights off, she heard footsteps in the wall, but I could not hear them, even though I pressed my ear against it. She concentrated and drifted into a trance in an attempt to get the interlocutor to use her voice to communicate with me. She suddenly jumped out of the chair and rushed out of my apartment, screaming,

"I'm leaving! I'm sorry ... I didn't mean to upset you. Forgive me! Forgive me!"

An eerie feeling rushed through my body as I ran after Rosa Ponce de Leon who had taken to her heels so fast that it took me a few hundred feet to catch up with her. I wanted to know what had occurred.

"Your ghost was friendly until I told her my name ... she went berserk. Sobbing, she threatened me if I did not leave her alone. She said that someone with my last name, Ponce de Leon, was the cause of her death. That's all I learned."

"Did she tell you her name?"

"No."

The next day I headed toward the municipal library, located near Plaza España, an expansive square full of flowers and palm trees. A huge stone monument lay on its center, which was dedicated to the first Spanish Constitution of March 19, 1812. It had served as the template for modern Spain. In the new legislation, the citizenry asserted their freedom, the right to control their own destiny, and the subordination of the monarchy to the will of the people. Bronze warriors on horses lent their arms to the new order, amidst the clamor of political figures etched on the stone and the divine protection of saints and goddesses sculpted in marble. Silence permeated the library where a few people sat reading. The clerk, an old lady with a tiny mouth, a black dress and a red silk scarf, frowned in perplexity as she handed me the 1857 edition of the Spirits' Book by Allan Kardec. I was apprehensive about what I could learn. It was as if I were reaching with my bare fingertips for a piece of bread inside a red-hot toaster. There was nothing peculiar about the appearance of the book and I did not notice any unusual feeling at touching the brown cover with the title in golden letters. A musty odor wafted off the first page, which at first deceived my senses with a reek of sulfur, an odor associated with witchcraft. The initial repulsion could not overpower my curiosity. Leafing through its pages yellowed by time, I was impressed by its comprehensiveness. A couple of sentences caught my attention:

Page 92: "The spirit is enveloped in a substance which appears to you as mere vapor ... it allows the spirit to float in the atmosphere and move through space at pleasure.... It can assume any form it may choose, so that, in dreams or in your waking state, a spirit can become visible to you and even palpable to your senses."

Page 232: "When a spirit attaches himself or herself to a living person, it is not always through affection only, for there may also be in that attachment a reminiscence of human passions."

The first sentence confirmed my suspicion that the spirit's adoption of her own physiognomy and facial expression had a definite purpose. Obviously, she wanted to incite me to investigate the reason for her sadness. Something must have bothered her to the extreme and had turned her eternal rest into a restless nightmare. Could this terrible fate be set aright? The information provided by Rosa Ponce de Leon had been quite helpful and provided some initial clue. The second sentence I selected might have some bearing on the reason why the ghost had picked me as the person who could help her. Was there any other reason? Do I resemble someone important in her life on earth? These questions kept racing through my mind.

I was not a Sherlock Holmes, but I decided to tackle these issues. I did not know the meaning of the poppy flower that the ghost had been holding; the cross was easy to interpret; and the red badge indicated that she was of Jewish ancestry. I confirmed this fact in the book *Judios en España*, by Adolfo de Castro, the famous historian. An initial inquiry to a librarian, a young man with courteous manners and dressed in a white gown like a doctor, yielded disappointing results. History books had failed to record anything about the Jewish presence in Cadiz. There were only a few articles about the ancient Jewish quarters in neighboring towns such as Jerez and Puerto Santa Maria.   If in the past there had been some Jews in the city, they must have resided in the Barrio del Populo where I was living, for it had housed the medieval quarters of Cadiz. I set out to visit the Historical Archives on Isabel La Catolica Street to identify the ancient owners of the apartment I had rented. The spring day was sunny and delightfully warm, and the blue waters of the bay had crests of foam riding on the waves. A couple of sailboats sliced through the surf as they ventured out to sea. For a minute I felt envious of the solitude and peacefulness of those aboard. My mind revisited the information I had gathered as I tried to break a code. The banishment of the Jews from Seville, Cordoba, and Cadiz was decreed in 1483 and carried out in 1485. Their final expulsion from the entire territory of Spain occurred in August 1492. The numbers were staggering for a country that had a total of eight million people: 50, 000 converted to Christianity to avoid exile, which engorged the ranks of the 200,000 who were already practicing the imposed faith; 20,000 died en route, and 175,000 emigrated.

By law, the exiles could not take their gold, silver, coins, arms, and horses. Their only alternative was the bills of exchange, which were often confiscated by the state. Most had no choice but to sell off all their belongings on the cheap. Their properties were abandoned or unfairly traded—a house for a dress, a vineyard for a donkey. Salomón Ben Verga described the exodus:

"And so everywhere they encounter afflictions, extensive and somber darkness, horrendous tribulations, rapacity, sadness, starvation, and plague. Some left by sea, looking in the waves for a path, but there the Hand of God disfavored them, confounding and exterminating them, because many of the banished were sold as slaves in every corner on earth and quite a few fell into the sea, ultimately sinking like lead."

My ethereal guest's life on earth must have occurred around those unholy dates.

The Archives were housed in an elegant old building with a large inner courtyard of marble floor, columns, and stairs leading to the second floor. A young woman with black eyes and even darker hair searched through a few bookshelves. Her lustrous white hands adorned with long red nails surfed across archives of dusty brown covers and frilled edges.

"No, I thought the archives went back to 1396 but there is nothing recorded before 1596," she said. "I remember those documents were part of all the ecclesiastic and civil archives burned by the English and the Dutch during their assault on Cadiz on June 30, 1596. Everything of value was ransacked. I have seen some of the stolen pieces of art in the British Museum in London."

Pedro de Abreu had described the desolation left by the attack: *"The streets filled with the corpses of horses, men, and dogs in putrefaction ... the best houses burned or torn down and those still standing could not be entered without great fear, for their destroyed walls bore huge holes, and their courtyards teemed with filth ... the plague of flies was so thick that no one could walk on the streets or stay in their houses ...."*

A couple of documents had survived this sacking because they had been kept in the neighboring city of Jerez: a census of the families living in Cadiz in 1467 and a list of neighbors who required bread supplies in 1468. Upon reviewing them, I failed to detect any obvious Jewish name. Nevertheless, Sephardic Jews—those Jews who were born in Spain and their descendants—shared most common Spanish names.

The search wore me out. I came back home and sat crestfallen on the edge of my bed. I noticed that a map, which I hung a few days ago, had dropped onto the floor. A cityscape of Venice had adorned the area above a small wooden table and chair when I moved in. It was darkened by time and depicted several gondolas and the tall campanile on the Piazza San Marcos in the background. It looked nice but I preferred to display something more to my liking in the bedroom. I took it down and hung it in the little living room. I replaced it with a world map engraved in copper, which I had found at a flea market. It showed the eastern and western hemispheres side-by-side, rivers, mountains and oceans in vivid colors, and the borders of all the countries in the late 1800s. Though about the same size, the map was heavier than the picture. I checked the old hook on the wall. It was rusty but it seemed strong and I felt confident that it would hold the map.

But it did not. Next to the map were the rusty nail and several pieces of mortar, for the detachment had damaged the wall surface. The resulting scar had ragged borders and a quarter-sized dark center. When I knocked on this area, I heard a hollow sound. I scratched around it with a small knife. White and reddish dust covered the lower edge of the wall and my face. An attack of sneezing almost threw me to the floor. It reminded me of the work paleontologists do when they find a dinosaur bone incrusted in a rock. I uncovered a small metallic container akin to a jewelry box. Measuring about ten finger-breaths, the rectangular side facing me was made of leather and was engraved with the figures of a Madonna breastfeeding Jesus. Their features looked graceless like those of medieval paintings. I dug until it was late, but unburied only half of it.

That night my sleep was restless. I dreamed that my ghostly guest was walking barefoot by La Caleta Beach. The moon covered the seascape with a silvery mantle and dozens of little fishing boats bobbed up and down on the waves as if riding a horse on a merry-go-round. The place was deserted, a mint scent of algae wafted about, and the waters murmured like a conch-shell. She looked beautiful. Her long black hair waved in the wind and a long white gauzy gown clung to her statuesque body. Her green eyes gleamed and a flirtatious smile beamed across her face. Her steps left a red-hot footprint on the wet sand and a plume of steam rose from each. As I ran towards her, the mist took on the shapes of huge seagulls. The birds came alive, clutched her by the arms, and lifted her far into the horizon. I woke up, gasping.

I did not stop to interpret my dream and continued with my task of unburying the hidden cache. After another hour of painstaking work, I managed to free it from the wall. It was a wrought-iron box covered with leather and shut with a clasp. It felt like the cover of an expensive encyclopedia and gave off an odor similar to that of sour wine. The lid boasted a picture of Christ's crucifixion. The bottom was decked with rhomboid geometrical figures painted in faded red and blue, and the sides were engraved with roses and two inscriptions:

On the right side, it read:

Recuerde el alma dormida	Beware of your soul's slumber,
avive el seso e despierte	Wake up and arouse your senses,
contemplando	To behold

On the left, the stanza continued:

cómo se passa la vida	How life passes by
cómo se viene la muerte,	How death arrives
tan callando ...	In silence ...

I recognized the poetry as one authored by Jorge Manrique, *Poems on the Death of his Father*. Written around 1476, the poem was one of the earliest written in Spanish. A strange feeling made me pause for a moment. My hands were cold and sweaty and a fine tremor overtook them. I opened the box. Its interior was painted red and held a rolled parchment. I wiped my hands on my pants. The paper was dry and I was afraid that it would disintegrate into small pieces, but it unrolled noiselessly, without any difficulties. It was well preserved except for a yellowish discoloration on the edges. I sat down to read it.   I felt as if I had been beamed back to ancient times and was about to learn a terrible secret. It was a written in old Castilian:

"*Martes veynte e dos dias del mes de mayo, año del Nasçimiento del Nuestro Salvador Ihesus Christo de mil e quadroçientos e ochenta e ocho años.*

En el nombre de Dios, amen ..." — "Tuesday twenty second of May, year of the birth of Our Savior Jesus Christ one thousand four hundred and eight. In the name of God, amen ..."

It was an affidavit signed by Beatris Sanches de Santa Maria, who identified herself as a nun at the Hermitage of Santa Maria. She went on to state:

"*Today Maria Spinola died at the stake, condemned by the Holy Inquisition for heresy and practicing Judaism. Her unidentified denouncers based their accusations on her possession of a crucifix with Jesus' feet amputated that was hidden inside a cupboard. Here I want to attest to her innocence, so that future generations exonerate her and*

wipe her name clean of all the sins and ignominies of which she wa
convicted."

The five-page manuscript was difficult to translate because
so many words and spellings differed from those of the modern
Spanish and the cramped calligraphic letters only compounded
the problem. Often I had to resort to a magnifying glass to focus
on a single word. But I kept reading, unable to stop,

*"It all began when the inquisitors, the Dominicans Frey Juan
Camacho and Frey Alfonso Sanches arrived in Cadiz. They bore spe
cific orders from the Tribunal of Seville to clean this city of heretics
and end up the 'judaizing' influence of false conversos* [Jews who
had converted to Christianity] *over Christians. The Sunday sermon
took place in the holy cathedral on January 7, 1488. The place was
filled to capacity. In attendance were all dignitaries, the Bishop Pedro
Fernandez Solis, the Alcaide of the Castle Pedro de Reyno, and the
Duke of Cadiz Rodrigo Ponce de Leon. It was the older friar, Juan
Camacho, who delivered the sermon of the Faith. He spoke of the ter
rible time Christians were facing because of the danger of heresy and
apostasy of the false conversos who, in the shadows of their home
and sometimes even openly in public places, proclaimed Moses' Law
to be the true ones, invalidated Jesus' doctrines, and condemned their
children to the eternal fire of hell because of their bad influence and
teachings."*

As I read it, I could envision where all the dignitaries sat on
the dais, the red carpet and golden chairs except for the preacher
who stood ahead of them. The solemnity of Gregorian music and
the swing of censers conferred on the place a deceitful feeling of
sanctity. God was not there. His holy name was uttered in pro
fane desecration amidst a forest of green crosses and Inquisition
banners. The standards displayed a crude cross made of heavy
knotted trunks, an olive branch that resembled a whip, and a
killing sword. Encircling the barbaric signs was a sacrilegious
quote from the Bible:

EXURGE DOMINE ET JUDICA CAUSAM TUAM. PSALM 73
Rise up Lord and Judge Your Cause.

I thought they had surely misspelled the first word and used it instead of the word EXURCE, which means to set fire, for that was what the inquisitors had in mind. I could see the Dominican preacher bearing a deceiving angel's face, his penetrating eyes, shaved head sparing a narrow crown of hair, long aquiline nose, and the white robe with black hood that gave him the appearance of a vulture. I could hear his voice. Fanaticisms erupted from his mouth as he pandered to the populace's jealousy of the Jews and *conversos*. Anger reddened the target audience's faces, and fear curdled the blood of the people of goodwill scattered in the temple. No one in the city dared dodge the service. Full of youth and beauty, Maria Spinola's green eyes must have taken on a frightful tinge as she stood in the crowd. Everyone was afraid. By then the Holy Office had already been responsible for death at the stake of at least 2,000 *conversos*; the mockery trials of their late relatives whose tombs were desecrated and their bones burned; the conviction in absence of myriads of fugitives, whose effigies were committed to the flames; and the heavy sentences— long incarceration, permanent banishment, the galleys—of a larger number. In all these cases their properties were confiscated and families subjected to destitution for two generations.

"At the end of the sermon, the Edict of Grace was read, which granted sinners thirty days to repent and come forward to confess their misdeeds. Everyone filed down the aisles to the main altar to take an oath, placing a hand upon the Cross and the Gospels as a sign of their loyalty to the Holy Office. Following suit, Maria and I walked together and then left the cathedral. Maria was the youngest daughter of Vicencio Spinola a Genovese Jew, who arrived in Cadiz in 1467. He engaged in the sale and transportation to Geneva of a good portion of the African gold that arrived to the harbor. Maria was born Jezebel Spinola the following year. She grew up a devoted Jew until the plague wreaked havoc in Cadiz in 1485. Along with other families, hers sought refuge in the Hermitage of San Sebastian, far from the city. There she met Diego Ponce de Leon, a nephew of Rodrigo Ponce de Leon, the duke and lord of Cadiz. Diego and Jezebel fell in love from the moment they met. Their relationship was an affront to society,

a liaison condemned by both Jewish and Christian courts. Diego had much to lose. He had a promising future, for the duke and his wife Beatris Pacheco had no children and he was considered a potential heir. I met Maria in the same place and it was through me that she learned of Jesus and the Gospels and the new message of hope and love Our Lord brought to mankind. On the sly she would come to me and eagerly learn about the Messiah. She became a devotee of the Virgin Mary. I helped Jezebel. It was dangerous, but I did it for her, because she loved Diego with all her heart. When the time came for her family to obey the banishment order of Isabel, the Catholic Queen, Jezebel decided to stay. She was baptized on December 1, 1485, and took the name of Maria."

I had read that many of these mixed relationships had ended with sentences that included the deaths of the lovers at the stake, disfigurement of the woman's face, castration of the male, and jail sentences. A woman's misdeed never went unpunished, but Christian men often got away with their infringement of the law. I was eager to continue the translation, but I had to go to work. I tucked the manuscript back into the box and placed it under my mattress. I did not know why I hid it; I guessed it was a sign of my obsessive-compulsive trait.

At the shoe store, my concentration lay somewhere else. My mind revisited the information I had learned. Over and over, the name of Maria resonated. Her name was simple and beautiful like she was. I could see her eyes sparkling with love for her man, Diego Ponce de Leon. He probably did not resemble me at all. I was medium height, a little overweight with hair receded at the temples. The nun had not provided a description of him but he must have been tall and muscular with fair skin, hair halfway down his shoulders, and warm eyes gracing a virile face. Did he cause her demise? I could hardly wait to get home. From the very beginning she must have known how dangerous, their relationship was. The vigor and fervor of her love stunned me. I wished I could find a woman who would love me as much as she had loved him.

Entertaining these thoughts, I arrived home in the evening. The sun was barely above the horizon. The dwindling daylight sneaked through the small window and filled my room with a weak flare akin to the glow of a dying candle. I turned the lights on. Before taking up the translation of the manuscript, I was grabbed by the apprehension of what I was about to unveil. I thought it might be too painful for me to endure. But my curiosity and sense of duty prevailed.

"*On February 9, 1488 after the grace period had ended, the Bailiff Pedro de Reyno knocked on Maria's door and detained her. She was taken into the castle before the inquisitors, Frey Juan Camacho and Frey Alfonso Sanches and the Prosecutor Alfonso Lopes. The Clerk of the Court Anton Benites recorded her interrogation. A couple of guards stayed behind, went into her home, and rummaged through her things. A desecrated crucifix—without feet— was found in a closet. Rumors spread through the city and I learned of this by way of one of my neighbors. Someone had planted it. The trail went back to the Duke of Cadiz or someone in his entourage, who did not want Diego Ponce de Leon's blood mixed with the conversos' as it would have meant forfeiting his future. When Maria learned of this concern from Diego himself, she became very sad. She had asked him to stay away from her. She did not want to harm him. He tried to come back several times, but she refused to see him. She explained to me how painful it had been to give him up. He finally ceased his attempt to continue his courtship. Diego was a strong man in battle and ambitious in his daily life. He had helped his uncle to capture the Grenadine King Boabdil at the Battle of Lucena in 1483. Although Maria's denouncer's identity was kept secret, gossipers mentioned the name of Ynes Marrufo, a Count's servant. It was also believed that she was the one who hid the evidence in the closet. Someone saw her coming out of the house on a Sunday morning when Maria was fulfilling her weekly religious duties: confession with Father Fernando Ochoa and attendance at Mass. Witnesses were afraid to come forward, for fear that they might be implicated and find themselves in the same situation as the detainee. Maria asked Gutierre Martines to be her defense counsel. The attorney had known her family for a long time. She sent me word through him not to come forward to testify on her behalf, because she did not want any harm to come upon me. She would offer her life to God for Jesus suffered on the cross more than she ever would."*

I could envision Maria standing before her interrogators: a big dark room with bare whitewashed walls, a big black wooden table where the imposing cross of the Inquisition sat, a golden Gospel to swear the accused, two big candles with their flickering flames casting their lights over the faces of the black-hooded judges, their eyes encircled by dark shadows as if belonging to beings from beyond the grave. Maria looked like a trembling little bird about to be ripped apart by vultures. Her eyes showed the fear and incredulity of the innocent who had been unfairly arraigned. The friars followed their manual to the letter. Do not provide the accused with the specific charges. Ask her whether she knows of what she has been accused. Make her believe that you have all the information to condemn her. Ask her if she knows who has denounced her but do not give any clues about their identities. Be soft spoken and suggest that she might not be responsible for her infraction, that someone else might have corrupted her. Try to get her to confess the names of other heretics. Cajole her into a prompt confession, stating that it would be rewarded with the expedited resolution of her cause. Use words to make her believe that she will be allowed to return home. Promise to vouchsafe grace on her without specifying the meaning. Let her think she will be pardoned. If she insists on her innocence, ask the same question over and over, for this will certainly cause her to contradict herself and allow you to put her to the question—this last word meant torture.

I was now in the last pages of the document,

"On April 27, 1488 her trial took place. I testified for Maria and vouched for her devotion to the Christian faith, her love for Jesus and Our Lady. My words fell on deaf ears. I encountered skepticism and the questions of the inquisitors brought to bear the danger about which Maria had forewarned me. I was even asked whether I had participated in the ceremonies to desecrate the crucifix. Maria had been imprisoned and tortured. I did not know what

kind of agony she had been put through, but I saw her in the procession on May 6, 1488, at the Act of Faith that preceded her death at the stake. Her face showed defiance and sadness. She looked gaunt, her eyes lusterless, and her hair had been cut short. Her smile was still prompt when she saw me among the crowd. She raised her eyes to Heaven to ask me for my prayers. Inside the cathedral, the charges for which she had been convicted were read and her punishment was proclaimed and cheered by the populace: death at the stake. Her last words were those of Christ to his executioners, 'Forgive them, Father, for they do not know what they do.'

A few days later, I learned the reason for her persistent expression of sadness from another inmate who had shared her cell for a few days. It did not have to do with the verdict, but rather with the lack of support from the man she gave up for love. Diego never testified in her favor or visited her in prison. She knew that their relationship had been behind her demise."

A thorough search in Cadiz for any document relating to the Inquisition yielded very little information. There was a book by Adolfo the Castro entitled *Little-known news about the history of Cadiz*, which briefly touched this subject. The historian related the existence of one hundred and eighty 'sambenitos.' Worn by the condemned, these penitential garments consisted of long yellow chasubles that displayed big red crosses or dragons and flames. They used to hang from the walls at San Juan de Dios Church in Cadiz, along with a painting depicting an Act of Faith. All these items had been removed from public view by order of the Cortes de Cadiz, which had abolished the Spanish Inquisition in 1813. I found nothing relating to Maria Spinola.

A week later I was on a Talgo train on my way to Madrid, to visit the Archivos Historicos Nacionales and find the inquisitorial documents that bore the footprints of her last days on earth. I had learned that all documents from the Dioceses of Seville were held in this library. My boss had granted me a three-day vacation. It was a rainy spring day and I had been so immersed in her tragedy that the noise of the train engine soothed my mind like a mantras. Through the faintly tinted windowpanes, I could see the waters of the bay and the ocean closing in on the narrow strait of land that connects Cadiz with the rest of the continent. Dark clouds clogged the horizon. The sea was restless. Over and over large waves broke and rushed toward the sandy shoreline with the same tenacity as my thoughts revisiting the painful images: the long and solemn procession heading for the cathedral, the front line of black robed Dominican priests who held the green cross of the Inquisition, the collaborators and members of the confraternities marching behind in their black cloaks stamped with a large white cross on the front, Maria and her fellow condemned heretics in dunce hats and infamous *sambenitos* trailing along under the custody of guards with lances and swords, and finally the white robed and black hooded inquisitors accompanied by members of the clergy. Once inside the church, the condemned sat on a raised platform for everyone to see. I did not want to conjure up more of these images. It was too taxing on me, but fire, screams, and the smell of burned flesh rose in my mind as uncontrolled as an unbridled horse.

Once the train arrived in Madrid, I wasted no time in starting my search. Home to the National Historical Archives, Serrano Street in Madrid looked stately, cozy, and was filled with beautiful buildings, which dated back to the early twentieth and late nineteenth centuries. Heavy traffic broke the enchantment of days of yore and brought back the not-so-romantic realities of today. The Archives were located in a three-story rusty pink structure. It boasted a façade with a large portico flanked with marbled columns and crowned with a rounded Roman arch. Inside flights of stairs led to several floors, where large rooms were occupied with long rows of wooden shelves packed with documents.

A librarian brought me the volumes for the cases sentenced in early 1484. My hands trembled when I leafed through those yellowish pages. They were filled with terrible sentences. One after another, the word *quemada* or *quemado*–burned—was repeated in a never-ending list. The inquisitors' organized and methodical minds were as noticeable on these papers as the evil that permeated the volumes of documents. I soon found her records. Seeing her name and the attached epithet sent a chill down my spine. *"Proçeso contra Maria Spinola quemada Con la sentençia."* After detailing the date of her detention on January 7, 1488 and her presence before the inquisitors, the chief prosecutor Alfonso Lopes outlined the accusations leveled against Maria. Witnesses said that they had never seen her having pork or bloody meat, or working on Saturdays; she had put on her best attires for Sabbath, eaten unleavened bread in the Jewish season, and failed to abstain from meat during Lent. The prosecutor elaborated on the presence of the mutilated crucifix in her home and considered it an act of hatred against Our Lord.

On February 25, 1488, Gutierre Martines, the defense counsel, refuted the charges and said that she had not eaten pork or bloody meat because she disliked them for nonreligious reasons. The rest of the prosecutor's statements had also been false, he added. He said she had not had any need to work on Saturday or any other day because of her financial situation. She had spent her days, including Saturdays helping the children in the neighborhood, teaching them and helping their needy mothers. Her client denied having any knowledge about the crucifix and asked the court to throw away such a charge. Someone with evil intentions must have planted the evidence. He asked the court to query the defense witnesses about how long they had known Maria and whether they had any knowledge, had seen, heard, or believed she had been guilty of committing the following transgressions ever since she became a Christian:

1. Being idle on Saturdays
2. Wearing her best clothes on Saturdays
3. Cooking her meals on Fridays to eat it on Saturdays
4. Lighting new candles on Friday evening
5. Eating meat during Lent
6. Indoctrinating children in Moses' Laws
7. Observing Jewish holidays such as Passover
8. Desecrating a crucifix

9. Going to confession, attending Mass, and receiving Communion on Sundays and festivities.

10. Displaying any images, pictures of saints, or crosses at home

He also urged the members to find out from the witnesses for the prosecution whether they had seen the desecrated crucifix at the defendant's home or her act of aggression against it.

The defense named three witnesses: Beatris Sanches de Santa Maria, the nun; Catalina Gascona, the shoemaker's wife; and Teresa Cheryno, the candle maker's wife. They all had known the accused for over ten years. Catalina and Teresa answered the questions in the defender's favor and abstained from the question of displaying Christian images as they had no knowledge. Beatris backed up their statements and said she had been inside the defendant's home numerous times, and seen the crosses and images of Our Lady hanging on the wall of Maria's bedroom. She said that Maria was a devoted Christian.

On February 28, 1488, the prosecution named three witnesses: Ynes Manruffo, Ana Bernal—both worked at the duke's castle—and Diego Ponce de Leon, his nephew. I was surprised to see his name. The man of her dreams, the person who had been responsible for her conversion into Christianity had turned on Maria and bitten her like a viper. I was glad that, while alive, Maria never learned that her former love had been behind her detention. The identities of the witnesses for the prosecution were always kept in absolute secrecy. He must have done it to prove his commitment to the statutes of "cleanliness of blood" that prevented the *conversos* from holding public offices. He probably wanted to bolster his claim to the duke's title and fortune. (Later I learned in a book—History of Cadiz—that Diego never succeeded. The duke bequeathed his fortune and the feudal title to a daughter who was born out of wedlock.)

Only the inquisitors, the prosecutor and their assigned interrogators knew who these witnesses were. Ynes Manruffo said she had seen Maria eating meat during Lent, and the defendant never consumed pork or bloody meat, and she cooked the

Saturday meals on Fridays. She said that she celebrated Passover, and enjoyed unleavened bread and the meat of a lamb that had been bled to death. On one occasion, she overheard Maria talking to some children and telling them that the Laws of Moses were holy, because they were God's words. Ana Bernal gave similar statements, but added that she had seen Maria hiding something under her mattress. It was almost certainly a crucifix, but she was not sure.

Her former love's testimony was the most damaging. He said that she had converted because she had wanted to marry him, but had never renounced her Jewish beliefs. He said that in front of him she pretended to be a Christian, but she was not. He went on to state that one day he walked into her house and surprised her lighting the seven candles of an expensive silver candelabrum. He recalled how her face reddened as she claimed that she wanted to show him the beauty of her parents' gift before selling it. But she never sold it. He stated that she had lied to him because she had been caught red-handed attending to her Jewish prayers. He had never seen her desecrating the crucifix, but he did not put it past her. She had experienced great anger when their engagement was broken.

On March 14, 1488 Gutierre Martines disclosed a list of people that his client thought were her enemies. Ynes Manrufo and Ana Bernal were among them as well as a couple of neighbors that Maria thought might have held a grudge against her. Her former love was not included. Of the two women, she stated that they had worked for her parents for two years, and during that time, they had given themselves to anyone who walked by the house. On several occasions she had admonished them because of their behavior. Their constant pilfering of food and other belongings had led her parents to dismiss them. Maria provided the name of witnesses who could vouch for the veracity of her statements.

On April 4, 1488 the judges deliberated and decided there was not enough evidence to condemn or free her. They asked to bring Maria before them. They asked her to tell the truth as to whether she practiced Judaism. She denied it and asserted her beliefs in the Christian religion. The judges voted unanimously to torture her to squeeze the truth out of Maria. The procedure was carried out the same day in the presence of Frey Juan Camacho. Anton Benites recorded the notes. They stripped her and placed her on a rack with her arms and legs outstretched and tied with cords. Her head was covered with a hood and tied around the forehead. The cords were further tightened and the defendant urged to be honest in her replies. She said she had already told the truth. The cords were tightened up. She did not scream or tell them anything.   Her arms were overstretched to the point of almost dislocating her joints, and the cords in her limbs cut into her flesh. She said nothing. A jar of water was then poured down her mouth and nose. She was again asked to confess the truth. She replied she had done so and, for God's sake, to release her.   At this point the inquisitor stopped her torture and she was returned to prison.

On April 27, 1488, her trial had taken place.   The prosecutor presented the testimony of two new witnesses: one guard, Rodrigo Garcia and one inmate, Marina Lopes. They both had alleged to hear Maria praying in Hebrew in the middle of the night. According to Rodrigo, she said in Castilian,

"Father, thank you for your blessings ... no, no, don't abandon me. I will follow the Laws of Moses."

On another occasion, Marina claimed the defendant said,

"Jesus, you don't mind, do you? You are a Jew; we are both Jews."

Maria did not remember saying those words, and said that she must have been dreaming. She asserted her Christian beliefs.

The document confirmed what the nun had written. The judges' verdict had been final. Maria was guilty of heresy and apostasy and condemned to die at the stake.

When I left the museum in the early evening, it was still sunny outside and a cool breeze from the Navacerrada Mountains refreshed my face like brisk cologne. It even bore the same minty aroma, which had been awakening my senses every morning. Groups of people rushed by and went into cafés to enjoy a cup of coffee and a cigarette. I walked into one of them to have a cup and gathered my thoughts. Inside, the clouds of smoke were reminiscent of the puffs of vapor expelled by the old locomotive engines. My senses were dulled by the drone of the customers' loud conversations, the casual laughter, and pungent smell of tobacco. In the midst of this crowded café, I felt lonelier than ever. I thought that no one cared that my hand held the copy of the horrendous court proceedings, which had taken the life of a young woman. Life had not changed. It had gone on without her as if nothing had happened. Yet, Maria meant the world to me. I knew that I was dealing with medieval justice. Back then torture and death at the stake were common practice everywhere. This fact did not alleviate my feeling of despair, the oppression of something squeezing my heart, the compulsion to scream at the top of my lungs. The man she loved was responsible for her death. Now I understood why Maria Spinola's spirit had not been able to rest in peace.

I arrived in Cadiz the next day and went to visit Father Pedro Arenzabal. The waiting room had a wooden bench and couple of small tables. Atop them were a few old copies of La Cruz, a Catholic magazine, and a few pamphlets about the various activities of the parish: novenas, taking care of the sick, collection of food and clothes for the poor. The room had a small window with a view of the ocean. The rippling surf shone with the sun, and a few seagulls soared above the waters, as a couple of idle fishermen sat chatting. I waited only for a few minutes and was ushered to the priest's office. Father Pedro Aranzabal sat with a calculator in his hand behind a desk full of papers.

"So ... did your ghost leave?" he said smiling.

"I don't know ... but I have to talk to you about her."

I updated him on every detail of what I had uncovered. He did not blink or frown. I showed him the parchment and the copy of Maria's court proceedings.

"This is really interesting. Do you want to donate the box and the parchment to the parish?"

"That's fine, but this is not the reason why I came to see you. I want you to initiate the necessary procedure to exonerate her. It was here in your church that she was wrongly convicted."

"That happened centuries ago. What do you want me to do?"

"Talk to the bishop and explain the situation ... I want Maria's sentence reversed. I want her name cleared of any wrongdoing. She was neither a heretic nor an apostate."

"You don't understand ... John Paul II already apologized for the Inquisition in a letter, *Tertio Millennio Adveniente*. It was written in 1993 or 1994. I remember some of his words, 'It is a painful chapter of history to which the sons and daughters of the Church must return with a spirit of repentance ....' The pope asked for forgiveness again on the Day of Forgiveness in the year 2000. I think it was March 12. You can check it in the library. The issue is settled."

"Not for Maria ... her spirit still dwells in my house."

"Okay, I will present the case to the bishop ... he might kick me out or think that I am crazy, but I will do it for you ... but in return I want you to get more involved in the parish."

I promised him. Back in my study, I felt the need of talking to Maria, but I found the idea absurd. My eyes and ears kept a constant watch for any sign of her. In the middle of the night, a strong scent of poppy flower woke me, but when I opened my eyes I did not see her. I turned the light on as if a ghost did not emanate enough glow to be seen in the darkness. It was not a dream, because I could still smell the fragrance in the morning. I checked for any sign or anything that she might have left for me. There was nothing that I could find. These nocturnal visits happened at least twice a month without any pattern, and she never left any trace except the scent. At times I stayed up all night, waiting for her. I figured that she would show herself to me if she wanted to communicate with me. Every now and then I walked up to the Santa Cruz Church and asked Father Arenzaba if he had any news for me. It had been six months since I handled him the documents, and so far nothing had come out of it. The last thing he told me was that the bishop had sent the information to Rome.

"To Rome?" I asked.

"Yes ... he doesn't have the power to do what you asked. It went to the Pope. John Paul II is a busy man ... you have to wait. But you know he is very much attuned with the subject. It takes time. The Vatican is afraid of propaganda and waking up sleeping dogs. I promised the Bishop that you'll stay away from the press ... that you will keep this matter to yourself."

Two months later, Father Arenzabal came to see me and let me know that the Holy See was going to make a decision. Before this was done, I was to hand over the original parchment and box, so that he could send them to the Vatican hierarchy. No pictures or copies were allowed in my possession. I accepted the conditions. Six months passed and the priest called me. He did not want to tell me anything on the phone. When I arrived he handed me an envelope from the bishop. Inside was a succinct note from the Vatican which read,

"In the matter of Maria Spinola, we find the defendant innocent on all counts."

It was dated September 24, 2004, and signed by Agostino Vallini, Prefect of the Supreme Tribunal of the Apostolic Signatura.

I was so happy and excited about the good news that I rushed home without thanking the priest. I sat in my bedroom at the little wooden table and placed the document on top of it. Somehow I expected Maria to come down and sit by my side. I reviewed all the events that had taken place since her first apparition, and reflected on how the experience had changed me. I had always been a believer in God and life beyond the grave, but now my strong conviction had become an absolute certainty. My notion of love had changed too. My former concept about my better half had been wrong. I had not given up on the idea that her passion in life should be to make me happy. But the most important lesson that I had learned was that she should excite in me such a passion that I should be the one ready to sacrifice everything, even my life, for her. True love lay in this commitment.

The terrible inquisitorial events that had occurred so long ago also made me see my Catholic faith in a different light. I looked upon the church as a maturing adult who had outgrown a terrible adolescence of terrible misdeeds. It had come out of the jail of errors and still had a long way to go before it reached the perfection that we all should be aiming for.

I had been so deep in thought that I felt asleep. I dreamed that Maria was sitting next to me. She was wearing a long dress with a light green lace bodice, high collar, and a long, dark green tulle skirt with a black satin sash at the waist. Her eyes seemed greener than ever. She smiled and watched me, floating and flying underneath the ceiling from corner to upper corner of the room like a sparrow that had inadvertently found itself trapped. I laughed and she laughed too. She held in her hand the poppy flower, which multiplied into forty, eighty, two hundred, a roomful of flowers.

I heard her say to me,

"Hold this poppy flower in your possession ... this is the gift I have kept for you all these years."

I heard the noise of a firecracker as little green and red lights formed crowns, crosses, and stars, in a glorious spectacle bigger than I had ever seen. I looked down at the table and she was gone. I woke up bewildered and happy. I looked to the table and saw a poppy flower on top of it. It was a beautiful red bud with six velvety petals and a long slender stem. I brought it to my nose and smelled the same scent that Maria's presence had left in my room. I did not want it to wither, so I hung it upside down inside a dark closet and let it dry for two weeks. Then I placed it in a long crystal container. I put it in my room and looked at it now and then. It reminded me of Maria. I knew she was gone. There was no sign of her, no visions, no smell of flowers, nothing. Her soul was finally resting in peace.

A year passed, and one day I went for a walk in Mina Plaza— an expansive old square that boasted a gazebo, arbors, gardens, large trees, romantic benches, and tables and chairs of coffee shops. It was sunny and the morning dew dabbed the foliage with emerald green. A young woman sat on a bench. She was a beautiful brunette with brown eyes and seemed to belong in the plaza as much as the palm trees, the flowers, or parakeets fleeting on the trees. She had a poppy flower pinned to her hair and a laptop open on her lap. I felt as if I had fallen in love with her at first sight. I approached her and said,

"I like your poppy flower."

"I put it on for you. Didn't we agree that I would wear it?"

"It can cause baldness ... do you know?"

"It is a superstition ... what harm could a poppy flower do? Where is yours?"

"At home."

"Weren't you going to wear it in your lapel?

I did not know what to answer.

"What are you waiting for? Go and get it."

ABOUT THE AUTHOR

Louis Villalba was born in Cadiz, Spain, in 1945. He graduated in Medicine and Surgery at the Medical Faculty of Cadiz in 1969 and finished the specialty of Neurology at the Chicago Medical School in 1974, where he has taught for thirty years. He has lectured extensively and is the author of seventy-three scientific papers. He studied creative writing at Northwestern University in Chicago, and has been writing fiction and nonfiction for the past ten years. *The Silver Teacup: Tales of Cadiz* is his first book for the general public.

CPSIA information can be obtained
at www.ICGtesting.com
Printed in the USA
BVHW052149110123
656148BV00012B/380